CTET

&

STETs

CHILD DEVELOPMENT

&

PEDAGOGY

WITH

PREVIOUS YEAR PAPERS (2012-26)

Himanshi Singh

(Creator of Let's LEARN)

Published By

Invincible Publication Pvt. Ltd.

Published by:

Invincible Publication Pvt.Ltd.

1103-A, 11th Floor, SAS Tower, Sector 38, Gurugram, Haryana – 122003

Email: sales@i-publish.in

Website : www.invinciblepublishers.com

Sales Office : - 4760-61/23, Basement, Pratap Street, Ansari Road,

Daryaganj, New Delhi - 110002

Phone: +91-11-40198405

Email: invinciblepublishers@gmail.com

ISBN : 978-93-88333-71-9

Book Name : CTET & STETs Child development & Pedagogy

Himanshi Singh

First Edition: 2019

Updated 6th edition 2026

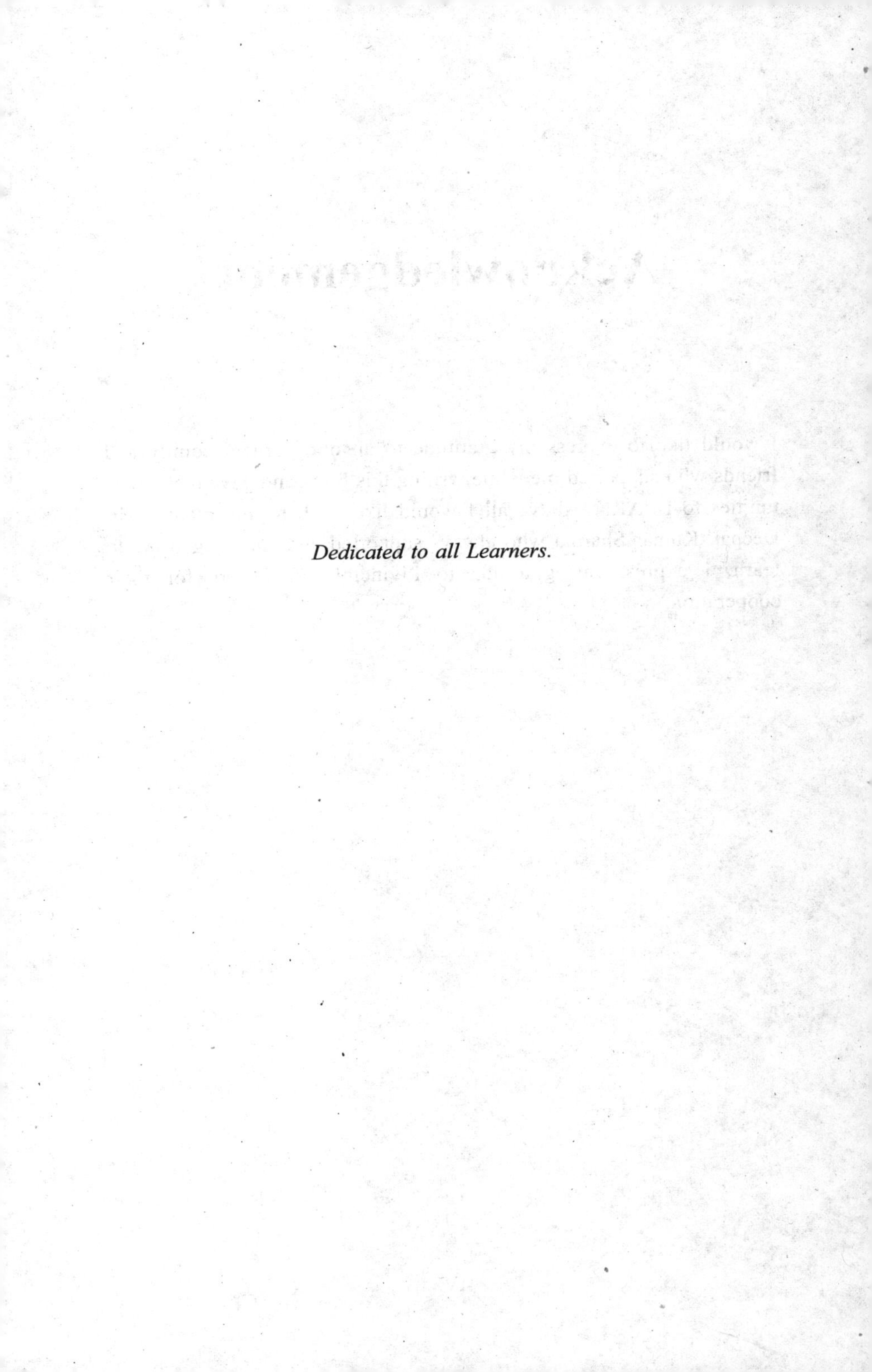

Dedicated to all Learners.

Acknowledgement

I would like to express my gratitude to all our learners, family and friends who supported me while writing this book and gave me opportunities to LEARN. Above all I would like to thank my mentor Mr. Deepak Kumar Sharma who always supported and encouraged me to learn. I express my gratitude to Invincible Publishers for their cooperation.

Disclaimer

The questions in this book has been collected from different sources, including different previous year examinations and other sources. The author and publisher have made good effort to make it error free, but make no accuracy and warranty of the questions. It is the responsibility of user to use this book. Neither the author nor Invincible shall have any liability to any party for any damages resulting from the use of information in this book.

Table of Content

Growth and Development 1
Socialisation Process 10
Cognitive Development 15
Child Centered & Progressive Education 27
Concept of Intelligence 32
Language and Thought 43
Gender as a social construct; gender roles, gender-bias and educational practice 46
Learning Theories 49
Pedagogical Issues 67
Supplementary Reading 84
CTET May 2012 Paper-1 91
CTET May 2012 Paper-2 99
CTET November 2012Paper-1 107
CTET November 2012 Paper-2 115
CTET July 2013 Paper-1 123
CTET July 2013 Paper-2 131
CTET February 2014 Paper–1 139
CTET February 2014 Paper–2 147
CTET September 2014 Paper–1 156
CTET September 2014 Paper–2 163
CTET February 2015 Paper–1 171
CTET February 2015 Paper–2 178
CTET February 2016 Paper–1 187
CTET February 2016 Paper–2 195
CTET September 2016 Paper-1 203
CTET September 2016 Paper-2 211

CTET December 2018 Paper-1 220
CTET December 2018 Paper-2 228
CTET July 2019 Paper-1 235
CTET July 2019 Paper-2 243
CTET Dec 2021 Paper-1 252
CTET Dec 2021 Paper-2 260
CTET December 2022 Paper-1 269
CTET December 2022 Paper-2 278
CTET August 2023 Paper-1 288
CTET August 2023 Paper-2 298
CTET July 2024 Paper-1 309
CTET July 2024 Paper-2 319
CTET December 2024 Paper-1 330
CTET December 2024 Paper-2 340
CTET 7th February 2026 Paper-1 351
CTET 7th February 2026 Paper-2 360
CTET 8th February 2026 Paper-1 370
CTET 8th February 2026 Paper-2 379

Chapter-01

Growth and Development

Human beings are not static entities, they keep on changing. Let's understand this change in terms of growth and development.

Growth

- Growth is change in quantitative aspects of our body;
- Changes that can be measured such as height, weight, size and shape of the body.
- Growth is not a lifelong process. It goes on till maturity.

Development

- Development refers to systematic changes which leads an individual from dependency to self-reliance throughout his lifetime i.e going from womb to tomb.
- It means development begins before birth i.e from prenatal period or from the time of conception and continues till an individual dies i.e his tomb.
- In this time period an individual grows in many ways such as physically, mentally, emotionally etc.
- Development includes progressive and relatively permanent changes and these changes can not be reversed; changes which occur due to some illness or tiredness does not get count in development.
- Development is a continuous process that includes growth, maturation and learning in itself.
- **Maturation:** Maturity is the ability to respond to the environment in an appropriate manner and is highly related to heredity (e.g. a child 2 years of age cannot perform tasks for whom he is not mature physically.)
- **Learning:** comes from efforts and practice or we can say a relatively desired permanent change in behaviour.

Differences between Growth and Development:

Growth	Development
• Growth is quantitative.	Development is both quantitative and qualitative in nature.
• Growth is restricted to physical aspects only.	Development includes all aspects such as physical, cognitive, emotional, social etc.
• Growth stops at a certain period of life.	Development continues till death.
• Growth can be measured.	Development can only be assessed.
• Includes structural changes.	Includes both structural and functional changes

Aspects/Types of Development:

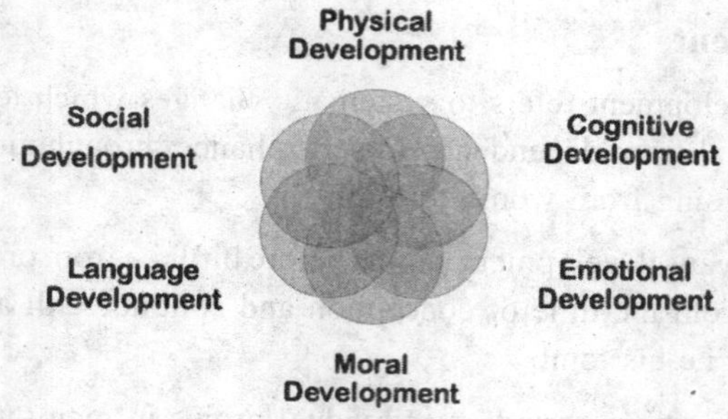

1. Physical Development:

- Physical development refers to the development of body structure including muscles, bones and organs.
- It includes motor development also which means to gain better control over our bones, muscles and other parts of our body which help us to manipulate the environment.
- Motor development is of two types:
  1. **Gross motor development:** which involves the development of the large muscles in the child's body. These muscles help us to sit, stand, walk and run, etc.
  2. **Fine motor development:** which involves the small muscles of the body, especially in the hand. These muscles helps us in activities like writing, drawing, throwing, grasping etc.

2. **Cognitive or Intellectual Development:**
   - It includes the development of our intellectual abilities such as thinking, reasoning, imagination, memory, problem-solving etc.
3. **Language Development:**
   - It is one of the important aspects of cognitive development. In language development we acquire the ability to learn, use, comprehend and manipulate skills of language.
4. **Emotional Development:**
   - Emotional development refers to the ability to recognize, express, and control over our emotions. It comes under social development too.
5. **Social Development:**
   - It is the ability to accommodate oneself according to the needs, values and norms of the society, such as cooperation, and leading healthy relations with people in our surroundings.
6. **Moral Development:**
   - Moral development is a part of social development which means the development of one's ability to take decision about right and wrong.

Factors influencing the Development:

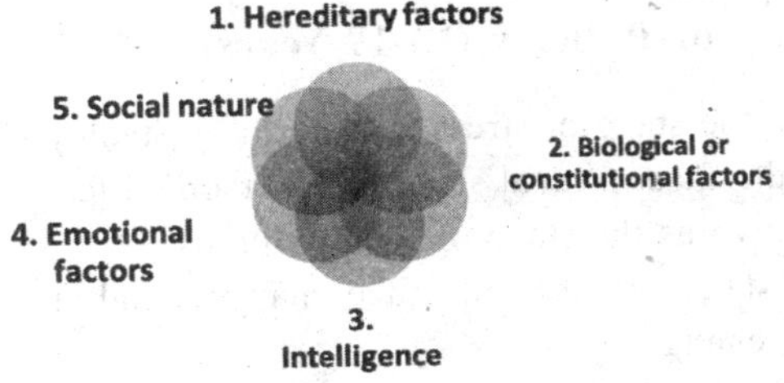

Stages of Development:

A child's development is generally classified in five stages:

1. *Prenatal Period:* 9 Months before Birth.
2. *Infancy (birth to 2 Years):* Senses are teachers.
3. *Early Childhood (2-6 Years):* Pre-school Age.
4. *Later Childhood (7-11 Years):* Gang Age.

5. *Adolescence (12-19 Years):* Identity Crisis.

1. Infancy (Birth to 2 Years):

- The development of language starts from this stage.
- During this stage, the child transitions from a dependent toddler to an active child.
- He or she is now able to crawl and walk.
- In terms of physical development, the stage of infancy records the most growth.

2. Early Childhood (2-6 Years):

- In this stage children spend a lot of time playing with toys.
- At this stage children do not attend the traditional system of education but they start going to pre-school or play school.
- Children are self-centric(egocentric) at this stage.
- It is a sensitive period for language development.

3. Later Childhood (7-11 years):

- Here, a child joins the traditional system of education that is why this stage is known as elementary school age.
- This stage is also known as troublesome age.
- Children devote more time with their peer group.
- Development of children's creative potential begins.
- Experiences of this period influence the child throughout his life.

4. Adolescence or Puberty (13-19 Years):

"Adolescence is the stage of stress and storm" - Stanley Hall.

- This is the most critical stage of a person's life.
- Also known as the stage of Identity crisis.
- At this stage, adolescents face many social, biological and personal change.
- This is the transitional stage; where a person transits from a child to an adult.
- Adolescents face adjustment problems.
- They become aggressive at times.
- In this stage thought becomes more abstract and logical.

Principles of the development of children:

The process of development is wide and complex; thus some principles need to be followed to understand it in a better way:

1. Principle of Continuity/Change:

Change is the law of nature.

- Development follows continuity. It goes from womb to tomb and never stops.
- An individual starts his life from a cell grows into a full fledged human being because of the constant change which goes from womb to tomb.
- The major changes include changes in size and proportions, acquisition of new mental, motor, and behavioural skills.

2. Principle of Proceeding from General to Specific:

- Individual exhibits general response at first and learn to show specific and goal directed responses later.
- For e.g when a newborn cries, he uses his whole body.

3. Principle of Individual Differences:

- Interaction between heredity and environment leads to individual differences in the developmental pattern.
- These differences are caused by the genes one inherits and the environmental conditions like food, medical facilities, psychological conditions and learning opportunities.
- Even twin-children have differences.

4. Principle of Uniform Pattern/Sequence:

- The process of development has uniformity and few individual differences.
- Uniformity shows up in aspects like development of body and language in children.
- The development starts from head. so the milk teeth fall first. Hence the development of particular species have a definite uniform pattern.
- At embryo stage, firstly head develops, then lower portion of the body. Similarly firstly spinal cord develops, then heart, chest etc.

5. Principle of Direction:

- The rate of development may vary in different children. However, the development of all human beings follows a similar pattern, similar sequence or direction.
- Sequential pattern of development can be seen in two directions:

- **Cephalo-caudal sequence:** Means that development spreads over the body from head to toe i.e. individual begins to grow from head region and then goes down wards.
- **Proxi-modistal sequence:** Development proceeds from central part of the body towards peripheries. In this sequence, the spinal cord of the individual develops first and then outward control is gained. e.g. babies cut their front teeth before they cut their side ones.

6. Principle of Integration:

- We know that development proceeds from general to specific or from whole to parts, it is also seen that specific responses are combined in the later process of development.
- It is the integration of whole and its parts as well as of the specific and general responses that makes a child develop properly in the different dimensions.

7. Principle of interrelation:

- The growth and development in various dimensions like physical, mental, social etc. are interrelated and interdependent.
- Each area of development is dependent on the other and thus influences other domains also.

8. Principle of Maturation and Learning:

- In the process of growth and development maturation and learning plays an important role.
- For instance if a child is keen to learn something and lacks maturity then he will not be able to learn it.
- We have discussed that maturation is unwinding of characteristics already present in the individual. For example, creeping, crawling, walking comes with maturation. These characteristics are highly influenced by heredity.

9. Principle of Heredity and Environment:

- Child's growth and development is the joint product of heredity and environment.
- Various examples have proved this fact. The effect of both of these cannot be separated.
- Heredity is the foundation of the personality of a child. Which sets the limit in the development.

10. Principle of Spiral vs. Linear Development:

- The child doesn't proceed on a straight line that means development goes back and forth.
- He makes advancement, during a particular period but takes rest in the next period to consolidate his development.
- Therefore, he turns back and makes forward again like a spiral.

11. Principle of Significance of Early Development:

- Early childhood experiences have more impact on the development of a child.
- Examples include nutritional, emotional, social and cultural experiences.
- So it is important to provide better quality care to a child in his/her initial years of life.

Influence of Heredity & Environment:

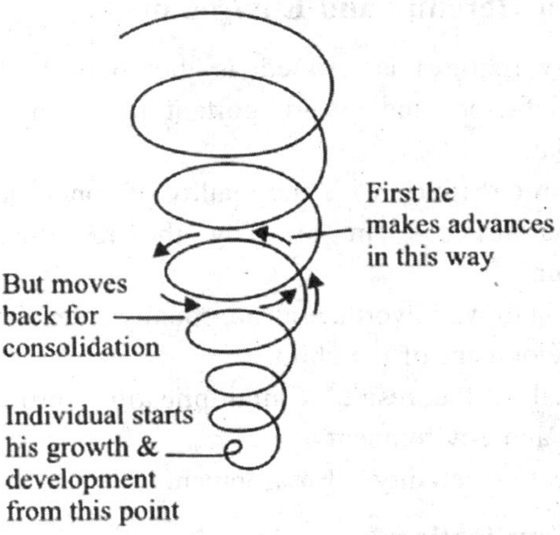

Fig. 5.1 Development is spiral.

Heredity: Heredity provides the basis for the development of human personality. Heredity is what a person is born with.

- *All the qualities that a child has inherited from the parents is called heredity.*
- At the time of Conception the union of male and female germ cells causes fertilization of the ovum. The fertilized egg is known as zygote.
- Zygote has 46 chromosomes; i.e 23 pairs of chromosomes are there in a zygote.

Environment: Environment includes all the aspects of our surroundings except one's genes.

- These factors influence the development of an individual.
- Environment consists of various types of forces like physical, social, moral, cultural emotional etc.
- Teachers should try to provide best environment, so that a child can flourish.

Identical and Fraternal Twins:

- Identical Twins: Identical twins develop from one ovum. Identical twins resemble each other and are always of the same sex while having almost same interests.
- Fraternal twins: Fraternal twins germinate from two separate ova. The fraternal twins are mostly of the same sex just brothers but they can be of different sex.

Significance of Heredity and Environment

- **Heredity** (nature) is defined as the totality of biologically acquired factors and is n important factor in the life of an individual.
- **Environment** (nurture) is the totality of conditions which play an important role in bringing the modification of our behaviour.
- According to Woodworth, both are equally essential in the growth and development of the child.
- Individual is the result of multiplication (product) between heredity and environment.

Development = Heredity x Environment

Educational Implication

- The knowledge of both the factors will help the teacher in finding out the individual differences among his students in learning different subjects.
- Hence teacher must provide a congenial atmosphere for the students and treat them equally.
- The children should be taught to adapt to the environment.

My Notes

Chapter-02

Socialisation Process

- Every society has its own codes of conduct, rules and regulations, norms and values.
- Every culture clearly demarcates the acceptable and unaccaptable behaviour in different social contexts.

What is socialisation?

- Socialization is the process of internalizing the norms and ideologies of the society.
- This process works at two different levels: one within the individual which is called internalization.
- And the other form includes the outside factors such as parents, other family members, peers etc.

Features of Socialisation

1. Inculcates basic discipline.
2. Helps to control human behaviour.
3. Socialisation takes place formally and informally.
4. Socialisation is continuous process which goes on throughout life.

Types of socialisation

1. Primary Socialisation:

- Primary socialisation takes place in the initial years of one's life, starting from childhood .
- In primary Socialisation, first the identity of a person is formed and then secondary socialisation supports it.

2. Secondary Socialization:

- It refers to the socialization that takes place throughout one's lifetime, and keeps on changing as one encounters new groups that require additional socialization.

Agents of Socialisation

- Family
- Religion
- Economic status
- Language
- Education
- Peer groups
- Laws of a society
- Media

Theories of Socialisation

1. Urie Bronfenbrenner's Ecological System Theory

- The Ecological system theory tells us about the changes happening between a child and his environment and how these changes influence him/her as he/she grows and develops into a full fledged human being.
- It demarcates the importance of environmental factors playing a major role in the development of a child.

There are five models in this theory:

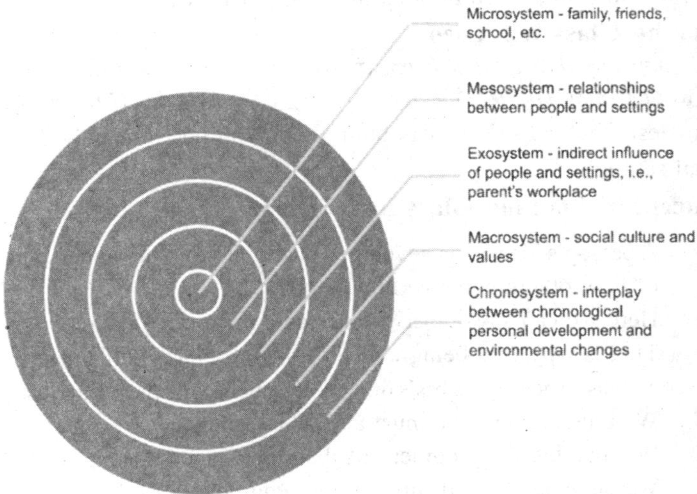

1. Microsystem:

- The immediate relationship of a child with his family, friends, siblings and teachers lies here.
- The better interaction with these agencies will bring the healthy development of a child.

2. Mesosystem

- Here, the interaction between two micro systems come such as relationship between one's family and teachers, relationship between the child's friends and family etc.

3. Exo-system

- In the exosystem children do not play active role but they are indirectly influenced by the consequences happening in their environment.
- *In this system comes the parent's workplace, relatives, mass media, etc.*

4. Macrosystem

- Cultural contexts comes at this level such as one's country, society, economic status, laws, etc.

5. Chronosystem

- The changes that happen over the period of one's lifetime lies at this level such as socio historic perspectives.

Looking Glass-self Theory

"I am not what I think I am, and I am not what you think I am. I am what I think you think I am." — ***Charles Horton Cooley***

It suggests that self-concept is built not in solitude, but rather within social settings.

Concept of Looking Glass Self Theory

- A person's identity is developed based on his or her understanding of how others perceive him or her.
- Here we can say society works as a mirror.
- That is why it is being called "Looking Glass Self theory".

Our self is constructed on the basis of our interactions with these three aspects:

1. We imagine how we must appear to others.
2. We imagine the judgment of that appearance.
3. We develop our self through the judgments of others.

Conclusion:

- The identity of ourselves is a constant relationship between society and ourselves.
- Basically, we form our identity on the basis of the perception of ourselves which we see in others. Here, society works as a mirror for ourself.

"I" and "Me" by G.H. Mead

The **"me"** is the socialized aspect of the person, and the **"I"** is the individualised aspect of the person.

- **"me"** or the self which focuses on how a person internalizes the attitude of others.
- **"I"** refers to the understanding or attitude we show towards others.

There are three stages of self- development that we pass through:

1. **Preparatory Stage (Birth to 2 years):** Children copy, or imitate, the behaviours of others around them without much understanding of what they are imitating.
2. **Play Stage (2-6 years):** Children start role-playing and taking on the role of significant people in their lives and they take on one role at a time.
3. **Game stage (7-up):** Children learn their roles in relation to others and how to take the role of everyone else in the game.

Forms of Symbolic Interaction:

1. Language,
2. Play, and
3. The game.

- These forms of "symbolic interaction takes place via these shared symbols such as words, definitions, roles, gestures, etc."

Conclusion

- Mead defines the **"me"** as "**a conventional, habitual individual,**" and the **"I"** as the "**reply**" of the individual to the generalized other.
- Both community and individual autonomy are necessary to identity

My Notes

Chapter-03

Cognitive Development

Jean Piaget

- Piaget was a Swiss psychologist.
- Piaget, emphasised the importance of the physical environment in our development;
- He also gave emphasis on the biological abilities we inherit from heredity and somewhere ignored the social aspect.
- He is also known as the father of Child Psychology.
- Piaget was a radical constructivist who believed in the independent construction of knowledge by a child himself.

Important Terms:

- Schema
- Assimilation
- Accommodation
- Reversibility
- Equilibrium
- Object permanence
- Egocentrism
- Animism
- Conservation
- Hypothetico-deductive reasoning
- Collective Monologue
- Transitivity

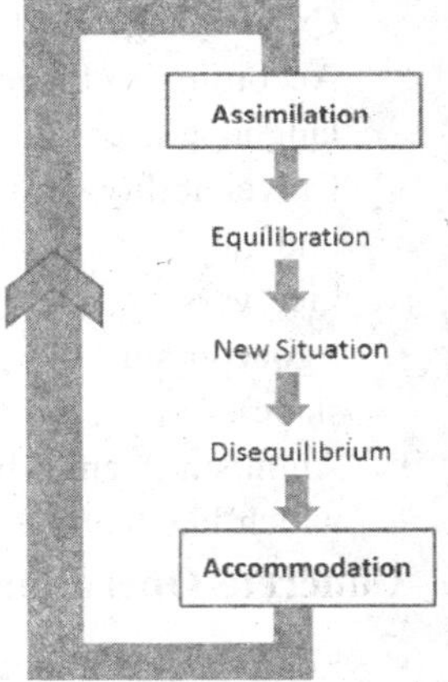

Schema: Schema is a set pattern or organized categories of information and relationship between these categories. E.g. Books, relationships, devices, monuments etc.

Assimilaiton: is the process of incorporating new information into the schemes.

Accommodation: is the process of adjusting or manipulating existing schemes due to disequilibrium in the existing schemes.

Assimilation and accommodation comes under the process of adaptation.

Equilibrium: the state of balance between the assimilated information and the information you encounter in the outside world.

Disequilibrium: the state of imbalance between the assimilated information and the information you encounter with the outside world.

Stages of Cognitive Development

1. Sensory Motor Stage (Birth to 2 years)

- Senses are teachers!
- Reflex actions.
- Imitative Behaviour.
- Object Permanence- (Out of sight, out of mind does not apply anymore)

2. Pre-Operational Stage (2-6 years)

- "Operation"means mental processes.
- Transductive Reasoning or somewhat we say not so logical reason comes.
- Crucial stage for Language Development.
- According to Piaget, child learns to think first and develops the language later.
- Irreversibility-Children believe that action cannot be reversed or undone. E.g. a 3 year old can't think of ice becoming water and vice versa.
- Egocentrism - "I" (Children can't take others perspective in this stage).
- Animism-A child believes of a non-living thing as living thing which has feelings in it.

3. Concrete Operational Stage (7-11 years)

- Logic begins about concrete objects.
- Reversibility develops.
- Transitivity develops: the ability to recognize relationships among various things.
- Classification comes.
- Seriation.
- *Conservation:* Ability to understand that the quantity, area or volume does not change with the change in form or shape and size.

- This stage is also known as later childhood or gang age.

Example of Transitivity:

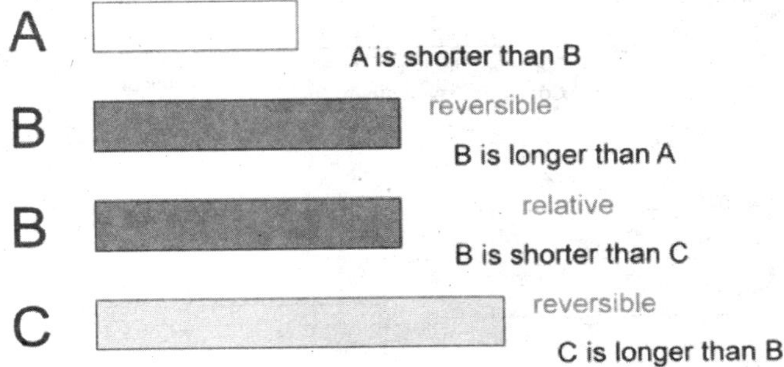

4. Formal operational Stage (12 year and up)

- In this stage child develops logic about abstract things.
- Deductive Reasoning comes- going from general to specific.
- **Hypothetico-Deductive Reasoning comes:** is the ability to think scientifically by generating predictions or hypotheses, about the solution of a problem.
- Age of Divergent/convergent/creative thinking.

Educational Implication

- This theory provides a broad development perspective to the teachers and policy makers to make a better curriculum for the children.
- Piaget's theory based curriculum requires that children should not skip any stage.
- Children learn faster if we provide concrete material to work with.
- A teacher should arouse the curiosity of the child through planned activities.
- Treat a child as a discoverer.

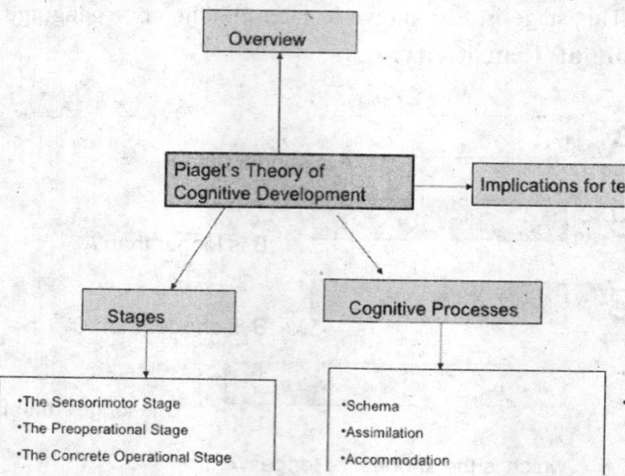

Vygotsky's Sociocultural Development

- Lev Vygotsky was a Russian Psychologist, died at the age of 38 years.
- A Social Constructivist.
- Focused on socio-cultural aspects i.e. he emphasised the role of the society and culture in the development of a child.

Three Important Aspects:

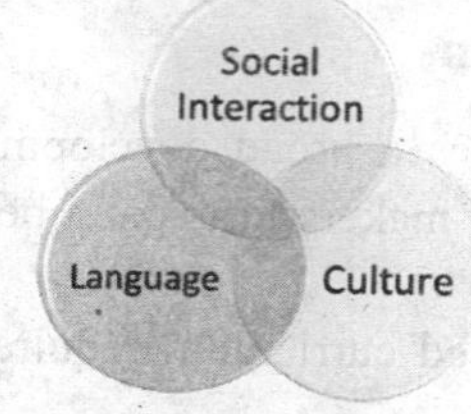

Some other important Terms:

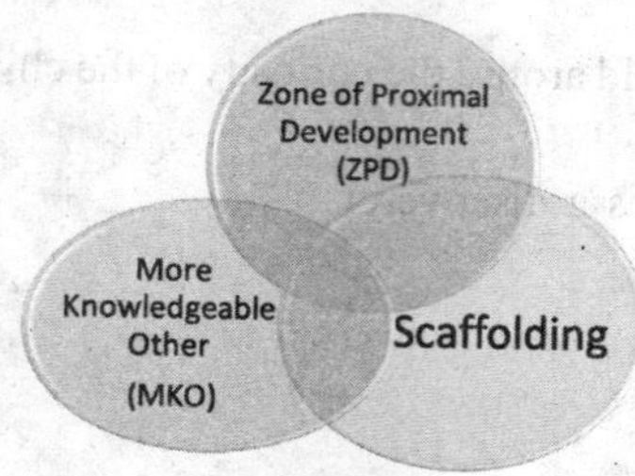

ZPD: zone of proximal development is the difference between what a learner can do by himself (or without help) and what he/she can do with help.

So, ZPD is the area of proximal development in which guidance should be given so that a child can reach the maximum potential.

Scaffolding:

- Scaffolding is a temporary structure of help; provided in the zone of proximal development.
- While providing scaffolding teachers, peers or any MKO breaks the problem in parts, can give clues or provide support according to
  the need.
- In scaffolding MKO need not to solve the entire problem but need to give hints, or can solve half problems, so that students can learn on their own.

MKO: More knowledgeable other is anyone who knows more than the learner in the ZPD, age does not matter here. Examples can be teachers, parents, peers, technology etc.

Here, in the following image, the father is providing scaffolding to the child by holding the bicycle from the back.

Here, in the second picture, scaffolding is stopped as the child learns to ride the bicycle independently; because scaffolding is temporary help given to the child in the image 1.

Some more terms related to the theory:

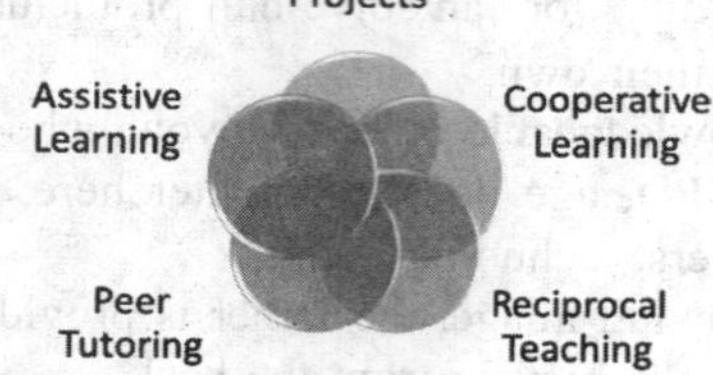

Note: Vyogtsky emphasised on assisted learning that means children learn better when they got assistance and cooperation.

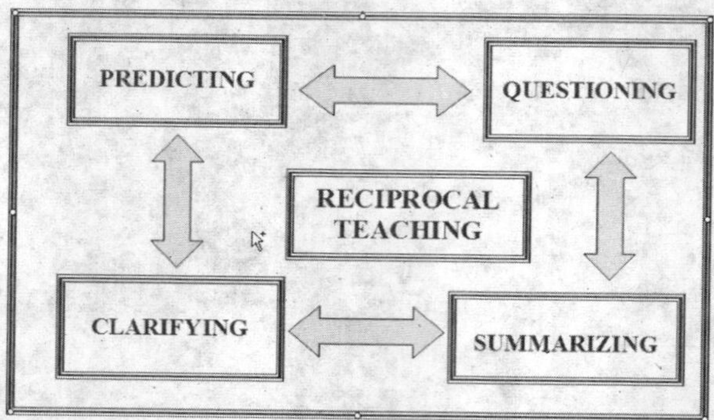

- Vygotsky strongly believed that society and culture plays a central role in the process of "*meaning-making*".
- According to him, Social learning tends to precede development.

Vygotsky's theory differs from that of Piaget in a number of ways:

1. Vygotsky places considerably more emphasis on social factors contributing to cognitive development.

2. Vygotsky places more emphasis on the role of language in cognitive development.
3. According to Vygotsky adults play an important source of cognitive development.
4. According to Vygotsky, social interaction involving cooperative or collaborative learning promotes cognitive development.

Vygotsky and Language

- Vygotsky believed that *language develop through social interactions.*
- Vygotsky viewed language as man's greatest tool, a means for communicating with the world.
- Thought and language are initially separate systems for intial years of life, merging at around three years of age.
- At this point speech and thought become interdependent.

Three forms of language:

1. **Social speech:** which is external communication used to talk to others (from the age of 2).
2. **Private speech:** (from the age of 3) which is directed to the self and serves a cognitive function.
3. **Silent inner speech:** finally private speech goes underground, and is transformed into silent inner speech (from the age of 7).

Educational Implication

- Vygotsky promotes the collaborative learning, heterogeneous groups are better way of learning.
- Social interactions are vital in the process of the development of a child.

Critical Evaluation

- The main criticism of Vygotsky's work is the assumption that it is relevant to all cultures.
- In some cases, observation and practice may be more effective ways of learning certain skills.

Jerome Bruner's Theory of Cognitive Learning:

- Jerome Seymour Bruner was an American psychologist who made significant contributions to human cognitive psychology and gave his cognitive learning theory in educational psychology.

- There are three stages of cognitive learning given by bruner:
  - Here in these stages, a child goes to the next stage without leaving or forgetting the previous one.
  - Learning should begin with the direct manipulation of objects.

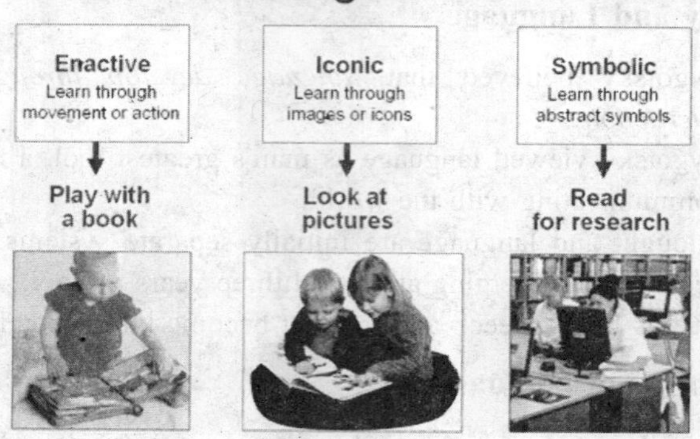

1. **Enactive Representation (birth to 3 years):** In this stage a child learns by doing physical actions that means this stage is action based stage.
2. **Iconic Representation (3-7 years):** In this stage a child learns by images or we can say here he/she better learns through visual representation.
3. **Symbolic Representation (8 years onwards):** In this stage, information is stored primarily as words, or in symbolic forms such as learning by words and symbols.

Kohlberg's Moral Development

Morality refers to the principles concerning the distinction between right and wrong; good and bad behaviour.

Moral Reasoning: Moral reasoning is a process of thinking by which a person determines whether an act,idea,intention is right or wrong. Moral reasoning is the process by which we take moral decisions.

Kohlberg, used to tell different stories to people, and used to pose dilemma's before them. One of the kohlberg's famous dilemma is of Heinz dilemma:

Heinz Dilemma

- Heinz's wife was dying from a particular type of disease.
- Doctors said a new medicine might save her.
- The medicine had been discovered by a local chemist and the Heinz tried desperately to buy some, but the chemist was charging ten times the money it cost to make the medicine and this was much more than the Heinz could afford.
- Heinz could only manage half the money, even after taking help from everyone may it be family, friends and relatives.
- He explained to the chemist that his wife was dying and asked if he could have the drug cheaper or pay the rest of the amount later.
- The chemist refused, he said, he had made the drug and will make money from selling it.
- Heinz couldn't leave his wife dying , so he broke into the chemist's shop and stole the drug.

Kohlberg would then ask the following questions:

1. Should Heinz have stolen the drug?
2. Would it change anything if Heinz did not love his wife?
3. What if the person dying was a stranger, would it make any difference?

On the basis of these, Kohlberg gave three levels (6 stages, each level includes 2 stages in it) of morality, these are:

Pre-conventional, Conventional, and Post-conventional.

Each level is associated with increasingly complex stage of moral development.

Level 1: Pre-Conventional (3-7 Years): Distributive Realism

Throughout the preconventional level, a child's sense of morality is externally controlled. Children accept and believe the rules of authorities around them, such as parents and teachers.

Stage 1: Obedience and Punishment Orientation

Focuses on the child's desire to obey rules and avoid being punished. For example, an action is perceived as morally wrong because the consequence of it is punishment; the amount punishment attached to the act will decide how bad an act is, more punishment, the more "bad" the act is perceived by the children.

Stage 2: Instrumental Orientation/Individualism & Exchange/ Personal Reward Orientation

This stage expresses the "***what's in it for me?***" intention. Here, children's reasoning shows a limited interest in the needs of others. So here, concern for others is not based on intrinsic respect, but rather a "***you scratch my back, and I'll scratch yours***" mentality.

An example would be when a child is asked by his parents to do a piece of work.

The child asks "***what's in it for me?***" and the parents offer the child an incentive by giving him a chocolate, pocket money or some toy.

Level 2: Conventional (Moral Realism)

At the conventional level, a child's sense of morality is related to personal and society's relationships. Children continue to accept the rules of authority figures, but this is now due to their belief that this is important to ensure positive relationships and societal order. Children consider rules rigid during this level.

Stage 3: Good Boy, Nice Girl Orientation

In this stage, children want the approval of others and act in ways to avoid disapproval. They are focused on showing good behaviour to people to gain appraisal.

Stage 4: Law-and-Order Orientation

In this stage, the child blindly accepts rules because of their importance in maintaining a functioning society. Rules are seen as being the same for everyone, and obeying rules by doing what one is "supposed" to do is seen as important. If one person violates a law, perhaps everyone would-so there is a duty to follow laws and rules.

Level 3: Postconventional (Morality of cooperation)

Throughout the postconventional level, a person's sense of morality is defined in terms of more abstract principles and values. People now believe that some laws are unjust and should be changed.

Stage 5: Social-Contract Orientation

In this stage, the world is viewed as holding different opinions, rights, and values. Such perspectives should be mutually respected. Laws are regarded as social contracts rather than rigid compulsions. Laws that do not promote the general welfare should be changed when necessary for the good of largest number of people.

Stage 6: Universal Ethical Principle Orientation

In this stage, moral reasoning is based on abstract reasoning using universal ethical principles.

Generally, the chosen principles are abstract rather than concrete and focus on ideas such as equality, dignity, or respect.

People choose the ethical principles they want to follow, very few people function at this level of morality. e.g. Mahatma Gandhi, Nelson Mandela.

Criticism

Carol Gilligan, criticized Kohlberg on the assertion that women are not deficient in their moral reasoning and instead proposed that males and females reason differently: **girls and women focus on maintaining interpersonal relationships**.

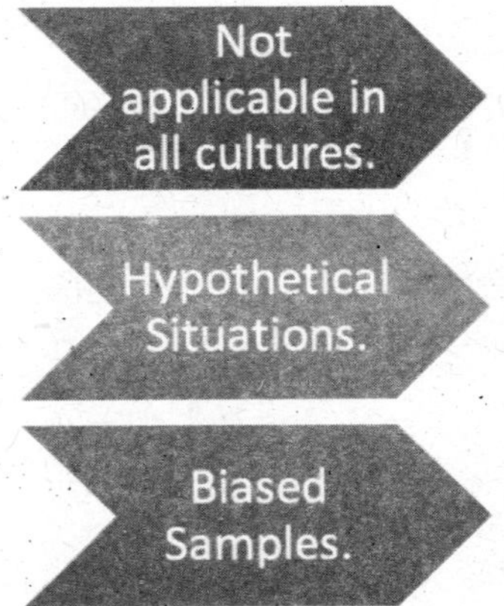

My Notes

Chapter-04

Child Centered & Progressive Education

- Children are curious, creative, and have an innate ability towards learning.
- We need to shift our attention from teacher centered classroom to child centered (i.e where children are the center of the classroom).

Teacher Centered

Teacher centered classrooms focuses on:

1. Here teacher is the center of knowledge and he leads the class totally.

2. In a teacher centered classrooms, students are viewed as empty vessels which need to be filled by the teacher's knowledge.

Teacher centered to Child centered

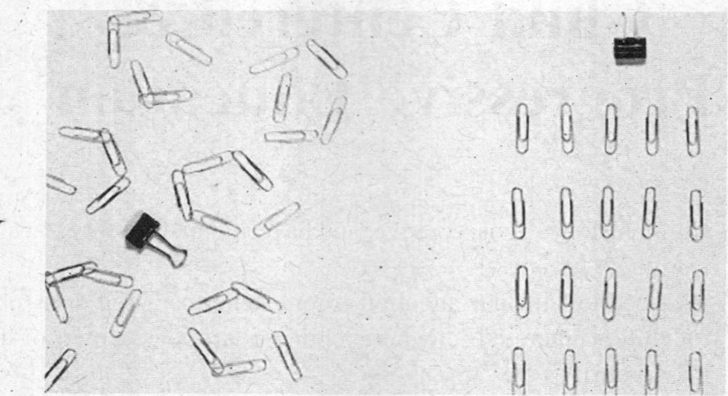

Child Centered Education focuses on:

- Focus on child's current life and experiences.
- Put children at the center of education.
- Provide opportunities to harness their skill.
- Support the choice of the child.
- The child has an individual identity-Go for differentiated instruction.

Qualities of a progressive school

Progressive education finds its roots in present experience:

- Learning by doing - hands-on experience.
- Problem-solving and critical thinking.
- Lifelong learning and social skills.
- Collaborative Group work and development of social skills.
- De-emphasis on textbooks.

1. John Dewey

- He is remembered as the "*father of Progressive education*".
- In 1894, John Dewey founded the lab school in Chicago, and promoted his principle 'learning by doing'.
- Dewey emphasized on the importance of democratic relationships in the classroom.
- A child's head and heart should be taken care of.
- A shift from teacher-centered to learner centered approach.

2. Rousseau

- Rousseau's principal contribution to education was his novel *Emile*, published in 1762.
- He attacked the idea of child being evil.
- Children are naturally good, they are innocent and pure.
- Things that are beyond the developmental capacity of students shouldn't be taught to them.

3. Friedrich Froebel

- Froebel established the Kindergarten in germany-a place for little ones to grow and blossom.
- He saw play as a means by which children externalized their inner nature. Also the propounder of play-way method.
- Kinder Garten teachers needed to be fully educated about the child's development stages.

4. The Montessori Method

- Maria Montessori was a physician, an educator and a humanitarian known for her philosophy of education.
- Dr. Maria Montessori believed that no human being is educated by another person.
- He must do it himself or it will never be done.
- Dr. Montessori felt, therefore, that the goal of early childhood education is to cultivate his own natural desire to learn.
- Dr. Montessori always emphasized that "*the hand is the chief teacher of the child.*"
- Montessori compared the young mind to a sponge. The mind absorbs information from the environment.

Bipolar and Tripolar Process Education

- Adams in his book '*Evolution of Education Theory*' stated education is a bipolar process in which one personality acts upon another to modify the development of the other.
- It considers the process of education in which two persons are involved.
- The one is the educator(teacher) and the other is the educand(student).
- It proposes that the teacher seeks the modification of the development not only through imparting knowledge and skills, but

also through his/ her direct influence on the child's personality.

Tripolar Process of Education by John Dewey

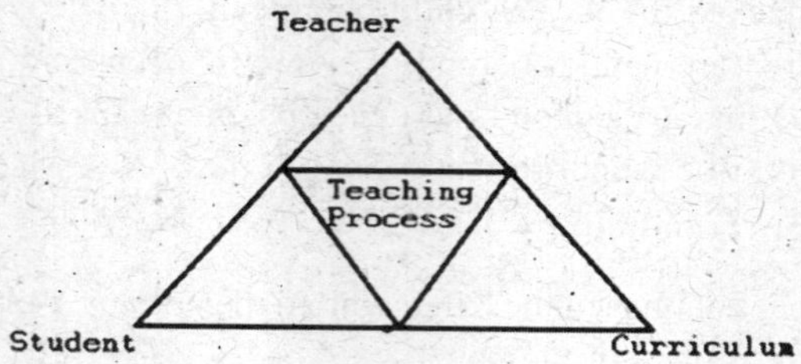

Here are three things involved

1. Teacher,
2. Student; and
3. Curriculum.

Types of Education:

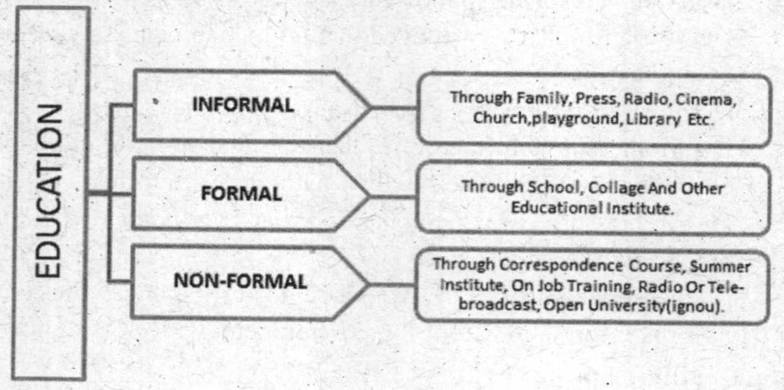

My Notes

Chapter-05

Concept of Intelligence

- The ability to acquire and apply knowledge and skills.
- Intelligence is derived from the word intelligere or intelligentsia which means to 'understand'.
- It is the ability to adjust with the environment, ability to learn and ability to carry out abstract reasoning.

Five Characteristics of Intelligence

1. The ability to adapt, Learn from life and Problem Solving.
2. The Capacity to Learn from Experiences.
3. Creativity and Interpersonal Skills are Included in Intelligence.
4. Intelligence Involves Ability of Judgement, Comprehension and Reasoning.
5. Intelligence Involves Ability to Understand People, Objects and Symbols Like Language.

Intelligence Quotient (IQ)

- Intelligence quotient (IQ) is a total score derived from several standardized tests designed to assess human intelligence.
- The abbreviation "IQ" was coined by the psychologist William Stern and the formula got revised by Terman.

$$IQ = \left(\frac{Mental\ Age}{Chronological\ Age}\right) \times 100$$

Where,

- IQ = Intelligence Quotient.
- MA = Mental Age
- CA = Chronological Age

Mental age is expressed as the age at which a child is performing intellectually.

IQ Table:

	Classification of Types	I.Q. (Intelligence Quotient)
1.	Near genius or genius	140 and above

	Classification of Types	I.Q. (Intelligence Quotient)
2.	very Superior	130-139
3.	Superior	120-129
4.	Above Average	110-119
5.	Normal or Average	90-109
6.	Bellow Average	80-89
7.	Dull or Borderline	70-79
8.	Feebleminded, Moron	50-69
9.	Imbecile	25-49
10.	Idiot	0-24

1. Single Factor/Unifactor Theory - Alfred Binet

- Alfred Binet developed the first intelligence test in France in 1904.
- He was the first one to introduce the concept of mental age.
- According to his uni-factor theory of intelligence we all have common sense or general factor of intelligence to apply in every task.

2. Two-factor Theory by -Charles Spearman

- He was famous as a pioneer of factor analysis, and for Spearman's rank correlation coefficient.
- He said intelligence is made up of two factors: the general or *g factor* and the specific or *s factor*.
- 'g' factor is acquired from heredity and cannot be increased from environment but on the contrary 's' factor is acquired from the enviornment and can be enhanced by practice and experience.
- Here, g factor refers to the general factor which is used in all the general tasks and s factor which helps you to excel in a specific field or task.

Here, Saina nehwal playing badminton is using her specific ability and on the other hand Virat Kohli who is a cricketer(specific factor) is playing football and using his general ability.

Difference between 'g' and 's' factor:

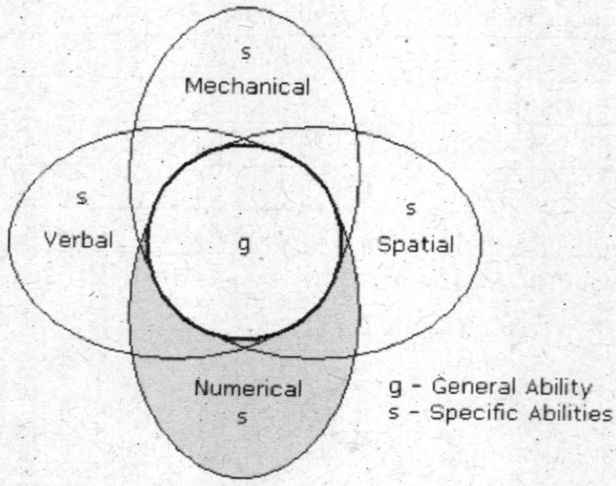

General Ability	Specific Ability
1. g-factor provides the base to perform any task; it is innate and received by heredity.	To perform a task effectively, one needs some specific abilities. This specific ability is called the s factor.
2. Training and education do not influence this factor.	The s factor is changeable in nature and is influenced by training and education.
3. He believed that g factor is more important than s factors.	S factor is applicable in some specific field.
4. If g factor is less in a person, s factor will not be developed to its best.	We need one type of s factor to do one task and another type for different skill sets may vary in the same person.
5. Spearman said that every task needed both a common g factor and a specific factor.	A person may have high s factor for music and low s factor for mathematics.

Theory of Multiple Intelligences - Howard Gardner

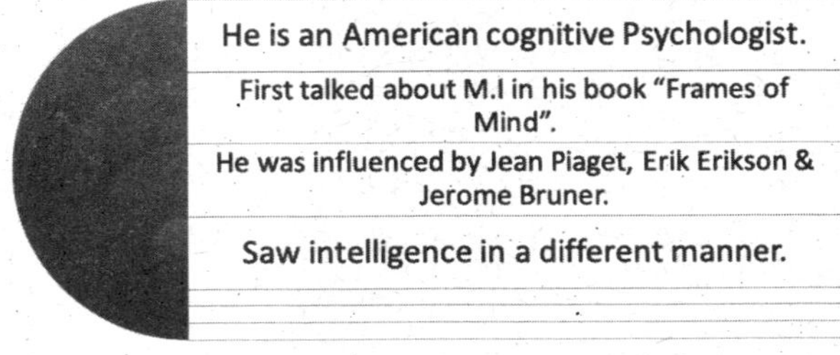

Multiple Intelligences

- Howard Gardner has suggested, everything can be taught in more than one way.
- According to this theory, people have many different ways of learning.
- *Gardner believed that people have different ways of thinking and learning.*

Eight Types of Intelligences

1. **Linguistic Intelligence**-Skills involved in the production and use of language.
2. **Logical Intelligence**-Mathematical skills in scientific thinking and problem solving.
3. **Spatial Intelligence**-Skills in forming visual images and patterns.
4. **Musical Intelligence**-Sensitivity to musical rhythms and patterns
5. **Bodily-Kinesthetic**-Using whole or portions of the body flexibly and creatively.

6. **Interpersonal Intelligence**-Sensitivity to subtle aspects of others' behaviours.
7. **Intrapersonal Intelligence**-Awareness of one's own feelings, motives, and desires.
8. **Naturalistic Intelligence**-Sensitivity to the features of the natural world.

- **Critique - It lacks empirical evidences.**

Group Factor Theory of Intelligence

Louis L. Thurstone

- Instead of viewing intelligence as a single, general ability, Thurstone's theory focused on seven different primary mental abilities.
- Thurstone extended Spearman's two-factor theory into multi-factor theory.
- Certain mental operations have in common a PRIMARY factor.

Sl no	*Factor*	*Ability*	*Description*
1	S	Spatial ability	Ability to perceive spatial relations
2	P	Perceptual ability	Ability to grasp visual held
3	N	Numerical ability	Ability to deal with numbers
4	V	Verbal comprehension	Ability to understand meaning of words
5	W	Word fluency	Ability to think and use words rapidly
6	M	Memory	Ability to remember
7	R	Reasoning	Ability to think logically

7. Primary Mental Abilities

1. Verbal comprehension
2. Reasoning
3. Perceptual speed
4. Numerical ability
5. Word fluency
6. Associative memory
7. Spatial visualization

Sternberg's Triarchic Theory

PCA- Practical, Creative, Analytical Intelligence

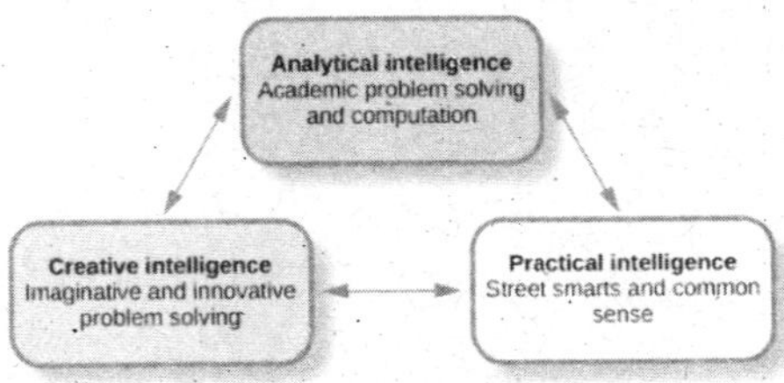

- His theory attempts to understand the human intelligence in terms of distinct components rather than a single ability.
- Practical Intelligence = Contextual Intelligence
- Creative Intelligence = Experiential Intelligence
- Analytical Intelligence = Componential Intelligence

Analytical	Creative	Practical
Analyze	Create	Apply
Critique	Invent	Use
Judge	Discover	Put into practice
Compare/contrast	Imagine if ...	Implement
Evaluate	Suppose that...	Employ
Assess	Predict	Render practical

Crystal & Fluid Intelligence - Raymond B. Cattell

- **Raymond Bernard Cattell** was a British and American Psychologist.
- Fluid intelligence refers to the ability to reason and think flexibly and it is gained from heredity i.e based on the neurological development.
- Crystallized intelligence refers to the accumulation of knowledge, facts, and skills that are acquired throughout life.

Fluid intelligence	Crystallized intelligence
• Identify complex relations • Peaks at mid 20's	• Learning • Cultural influence • Experience • Comprehension • Judgment • Wisdom • ↑ Until 70 y. o.

SOI - Structure of Intelligence or 3-D Model of Intelligence

- Joy Paul Guilford was an American psychologist.
- He gave distinction between convergent and divergent thinking.
- He proposed that three dimensions were necessary for accurate description of intelligence and these are operations, content, and products.

These 5 × 6 × 6 = 180 mental abilities are listed below :

1. **Content:** Five content dimensions
   (Broad areas of information to which the human intellect applies operations)
   - **Visual:** Information perceived through seeing.
   - **Auditory:** information perceived through hearing.
   - **Symbolic:** information perceived as symbols or signs that stand for something else (arabic numerals, letters of an alphabet, musical and scientific notations).
   - **Semantic:** concerned with verbal meaning and ideas.
   - Behavioural: information perceived as acts of people.

2. **Product:** (Six products, in increasing complexity)
   - **Units:** single items of knowledge.
   - **Classes:** sets of units sharing common attributes.
   - **Relations:** units linked as opposites or in associations, sequences, or analogies.

- **Systems:** multiple relations interrelated to comprise structures or networks.
- **Transformations:** changes, perspectives, conversions, or mutations to knowledge.
- **Implications:** predictions, inferences, consequences, or anticipations of knowledge.

3. **Operation:** Six operations (general intellectual processes)
   - **Cognition:** the ability to understand, comprehend, discover, and become aware of information
   - **Memory recording:** the ability to encode information
   - **Memory retention:** the ability to recall information
   - **Divergent production:** the ability to generate multiple solutions to a problem; creativity
   - **Convergent production:** the ability to deduce a single solution to a problem; rule-following or problem-solving
   - **Evaluation:** the ability to judge whether or not information is accurate, consistent, or valid.

Thorndike's multifactor theory

- Thorndike believed that there was nothing like General Ability.
- Each mental activity requires an aggregate of different set of abilities.
- Thorndike found that all factors in intelligence represent a specific mental ability which are different from each other but associated too like breaks in a wall.

He assumed that intelligence involves three mutually independent abilities.

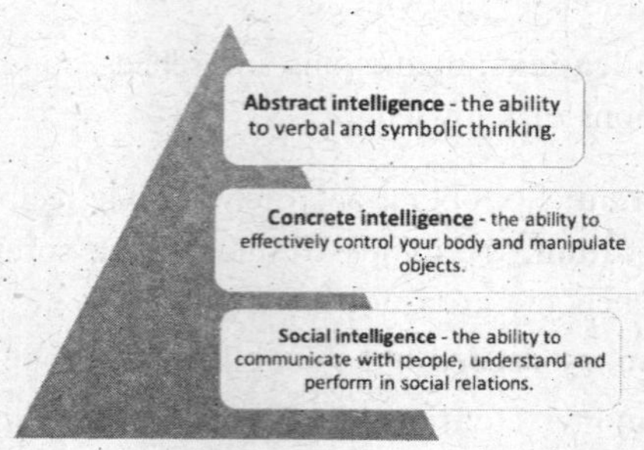

Social, Concrete, Abstract:

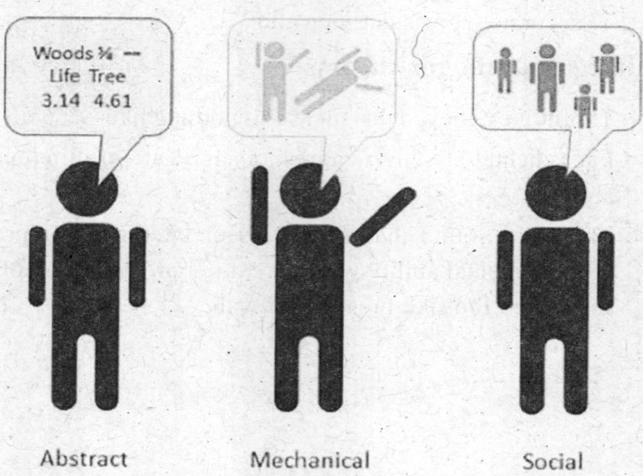

He distinguished the following four attributes of intelligence:

1. **Level** — refers to the level of difficulty of a task that can be solved.
2. **Range** — refers to a number of tasks at any given degree of difficulty.

3. **Area** — means the total number of situations at each level to which the individual is able to respond.
4. **Speed** — is the rapidity with which we can respond to the items.

My Notes

Chapter-06

Language and Thought

Factors Influencing Language Development:

1. Social Factors
2. Educational Factors
3. Biological Factors or Disorders

Stages of Language Acquisition

1. Cooing (six weeks)
2. Babbling (About 6 months)
3. One-word stage (Around 1 year)
4. Two-word stage (Around 18 months)
5. Longer utterances (2-4 years)

Piaget and Vygotsky on Language and Thought:

Piaget	Vygotsky
1. Thought precedes Language or determines it.	1. In the initial stage of life thought & language are independent.
2. Egocentric speech is of no use.	2. Whereas Private speech gives direction to children.
3. Cognitive development is independent of language.	3. Language is essential for cognitive development.

Skinner

- Skinner argued that children learn language based on behaviourist reinforcement principles by associating words with meanings.
- He described it in his book 'Verbal Behaviour'.

Noam Chomsky

- Children do not learn a new language but naturally acquire it through an innate language device.
- Neurological system in human brains that supports language acquisition. "Language Acquisition Device" or LAD.
- All humans have a universal grammar (UG).
- Children are exposed to unlimited data and by given data LAD produce a finite set of grammar rules.

Three schools of thought:

Behaviorist	Learned through operant conditioning (reinforcement) and imitation
Nativist	Language Acquisition Device (LAD) biologically prepares infants to learn rules of language through universal grammar
Interactionist	Inner capacities and environment work together; Social context is important

My Notes

Chapter-07

Gender as a social construct; gender roles, gender-bias and educational practice

"*One is not born, but rather becomes a woman*". - **Simone de Beauvoir**

Equality and gender roles

- Equality is a dominant concern of the modern time.
- It refers to same rights and same opportunities of learning and of working.
- It does not perceive any difference between two sets of individuals : males and females.
- The ideology of gender is based on an idea of assumed differences between two genders.
- Initial years in a child's life influence him/her throughout his life. so it is important that we raise our children in an equal way

Basis of Inequalities

- Differences in Terms of Sex
- Differences in Terms of Age
- Differences in Terms of Caste
- Differences in Terms of Socio-Economic Status

Gender Roles - Becoming Man or Woman

- Masculinity has been always appreciated over feminine qualities.
- A person's body language, the way a person walks, talks, works or even thinks is pre-determined by socially made gendered roles.
- *Gender roles have changed over time but we still need to realise this thing and need to brought up our upcoming generations with an equal mindset.*

Gender Stereotypes/Gender Discrimination/Gender Bias

- Stereotype refers to our pre-conceived notions about some persons or group.
- stereotypes are the norms that have to be followed by the members of a society and if one does not play the expected role, he or she has to face criticisms.
- Women are always perceived as vulnerable and weak, needing protection and not able to survive alone.

Gender Stereotypes in:

- Family
- Marriage
- Curriculum/Education
- Media

Educational Implications

- It is seen that some teachers in the school, while teaching, give examples and use teaching strategies which are biased against girl students.
- We, as teachers should make an attempt to recognize the individual differences between girls and boys and make use of these during the teaching-learning process.

My Notes

Chapter-08

Learning Theories

What is Learning?

"It is the modification of behaviour through experience and training."- **Gates**

So, learning brings out the desired changes our behaviour and these are relatively permanent changes.

Classical Conditioning - Ivan Pavlov

- Also known as Respondent Conditioning/ Conditioned Reflex or Conditioned Response or Pavlovian Conditioning.
- Given by Ivan Pavlov - A famous Russian Scientist. Got noble prize in 1904 for his work on digestion.

- Classical conditioning is all about associating the natural stimulus(food) with an artificial stimulus(bell).
- In this type of conditioning, the aim is to get the natural response from an organism by using a neutral or artificial stimulus.

Let's understand some important terms here:

1. Unconditioned Stimulus (UCS): The UCS is a stimulus which naturally brings about some particular response. e.g. food for the dog.
2. Unconditioned Response (UCR): The UCR is generated when some unconditioned stimulus i.e food is presented before the dog and the dog salivates; this salivation is UCR.
3. Conditioned Stimulus (CS): The conditioned stimulus is the neutral stimulus(bell) at the time of conditioning and after

conditioning it brings the natural response which was only triggered by UCS before conditioning.

4. Conditioned Response (CR): The conditioned response is learned response after the association of neutral stimulus to the natural or unconditioned stimulus.

Pavlov's Experiment on a dog:

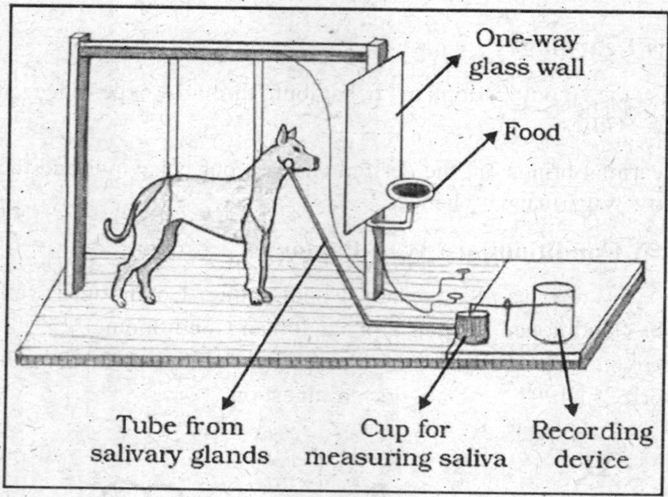

- During the 1890s, Russian physiologist, Ivan Pavlov was researching salivation in dogs in response to being fed.
- He inserted a small test tube into the cheek of the dog to measure saliva when the dogs were given food.
- Pavlov noticed that his dog would begin to salivate whenever heard the footsteps of his assistant who was bringing him the food.
- Then it was discovered by Pavlov that any object or event which the dog learned to associate with food(may it be a bell or his assistant's footsteps) would trigger the natural response which was salivation.

There are 3 levels to this conditioning:

1. Before Conditioning:

UCS = UCR
Here:
Neutral Stimulus does not equal to UCS.

2. At the time of Conditioning:

NS(Bell) + UCS(food) = UCR(Salivation)
Association and Repetition works here.

3. After Conditioning

Conditioned stimulus(Bell) = Conditioned Response(Salivation)
Note: here Artificial or neutral stimulus is generating the natural response.

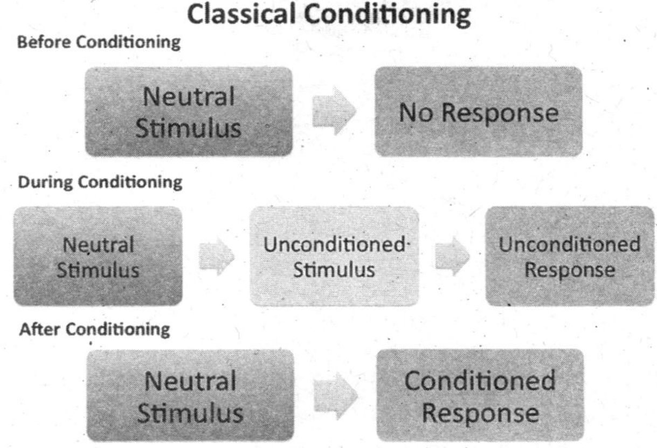

Operant Conditioning - B.F Skinner

- Also known as Instrumental conditioning.
- Most influential Psychologist of 20th century.
- In operant conditioning, there are association made between the response and the consequence of it.
- Behaviour which is reinforced tends to be repeated, on the other side, behaviour which is not reinforced goes down or becomes extinct.
- It is called the R-S type of conditioning, because response comes first and then the stimulus is presented.

One of the Skinner's experiment on a rat is here:

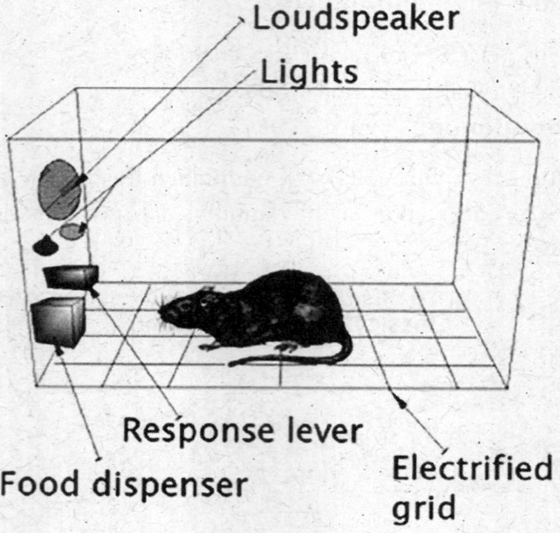

Skinner coined the term Operant Conditioning.

- Skinner placed a hungry rat in the box which he called the skinner box.
- There was a liver in that box when pressed would bring out the food pellet.
- The rat was giving some random responses but when the liver got pressed by him, he got the food pallet and that was the reward for his response.
- Everytime the rat pressed the liver, got food pallet for each right response he got rewarded.
- This was repeatedly done and the rat learnt the behaviour.
- Skinner gave schedules of reinforcement.

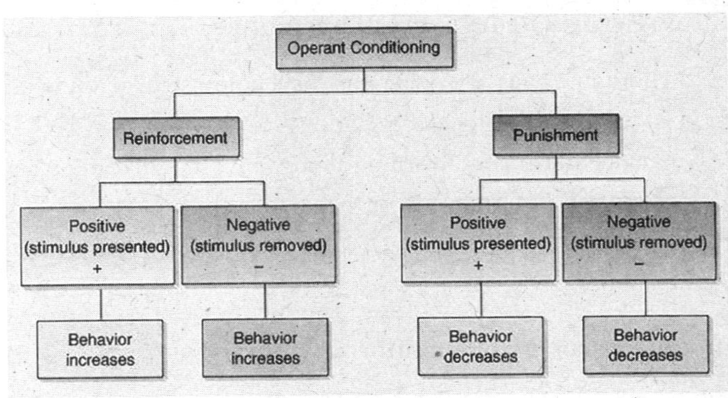

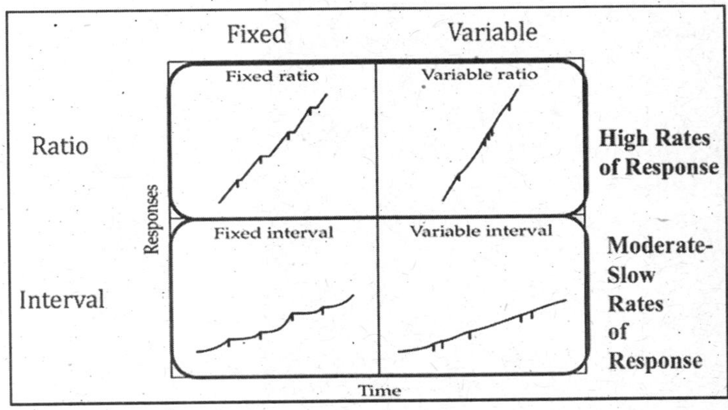

Classical conditioning	Operant conditioning
A signal is placed before a reflex	A reinforcing or punishing stimulus is given after a behavior
Developed in Russia	Developed in U.S.
Known as "Pavlovian"	Known as "Skinnerian"
Also called "respondent conditioning"	Also called "instrumental conditioning"
Works with involuntary behavior	Works with voluntary behavior
Behavior is said to be "elicited"	Behavior is said to be "emitted"
Typified by Pavlov's dog	Typified by Skinner Box

Trial & Error Theory - E.L Thorndike

- Thorndike was an American Psychologist also known as the father of Educational Psychology.
- Connectionism the learning theory of Thorndike represents the original S-R framework of behaviourism.
- Learning is the result of associations between stimuli and response.

Trial and Error experiment:

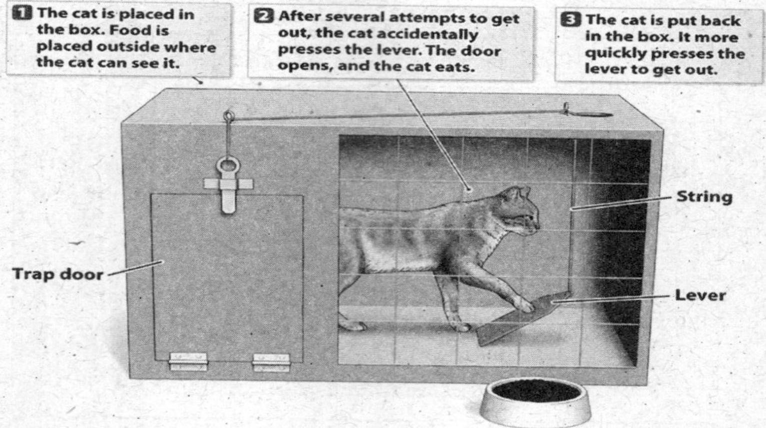

- In his experiment, he put a hungry cat in a puzzle box (cage) and kept a fish outside the box.
- The smell of the fish motivated the cat.
- Cat started giving random responses to come out of the box.
- By mistake she pushed the lever and came out.
- This experiment was repeated many times with that cat. So that associations can be made.
- Hence, the cat became conditioned.
- Finally, the cat was able to push the lever in less amount of time and used to come out fast.

Laws of Learning:

Thorndike classified two different categories of laws of learning:Primary Laws of Learning and Secondary Laws of Learning.

1. Primary Laws of Learning:

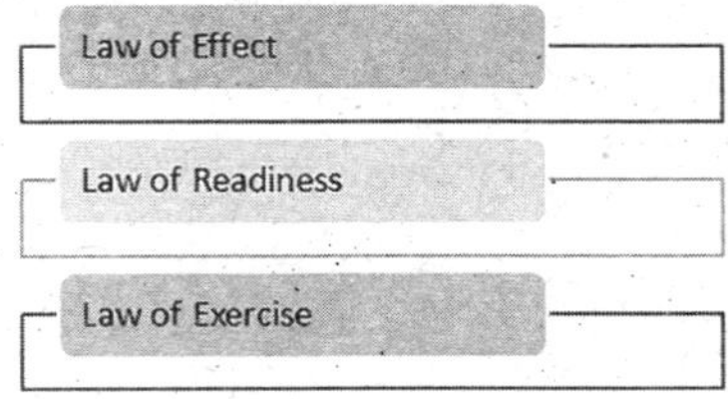

a. **Law of Readiness**

Mental preparedness, previous knowledge, maturity makes the child ready to learn which makes learning process easier. If the child is not ready to learn nobody can teach him anything so as teachers we need to provide an stimulating environment for learning.

b. **Law of Effect**

If the learning process has pleasant effect on the learner then the learner continues the learning process in future.

On the contrary, if learning process has negative effect on the learner then it won't go long.

c. **Law of Exercise/Practice**

- If learning process has a lot of practice or it is being used in daily life, learning becomes prominent.
- It is called the Law of Use: e.g. if a MBBS gets a job just after his degree, his competence and experience will be enhanced.
- Law of Disuse: On the other hand, if he doesn't get the job for a long period of time, his practice would be affected.

So, we can say practice directly influences the learning process and makes it better.

2. Secondary Laws of Learning:

1. **Law of Primacy**

Things which are learned first create a strong impression for a long time.

That's why we emphasise on the initial development of a child, these are the most influential years for him.

2. **Law of Recency**

Things learned recently are best remembered. E.g. students revising the chapters just before the examination.

3. **Law of Intensity and Stimulus**

Realistic and interesting experiences leave long lasting

impression on the mind. The intense stimulus will generate the strong response.

4. **Law of Multiple Response**
   When a learner is confronts a new situation, he responds in a different number of ways before arriving at a certain response.
5. **Law of Attitude**
   Learning is guided by the attitude of a learner. So, it is important that the attitude should be positive.
6. **Law of Analogy**
   The learner makes use of old experiences while learning in a new situation.
   For example, learning of typing will help an individual to work on a computer keyboard easily.
7. **Law of Associative Shifting**
   A learned behaviour (response) can be shifted from one stimulus to another.
8. **Law of Partial Activity**
   First learner collects small units of a task and then makes a whole concept from it.

Gagne's Hierarchy of Learning

- Robert Mills Gagne was an American educational psychologist known for his book Conditions of Learning.
- This hierarchy is based on simple to complex approach.
- Lower four levels are more associated with behavioural aspects and upper four levels are more devoted to cognitive aspects.

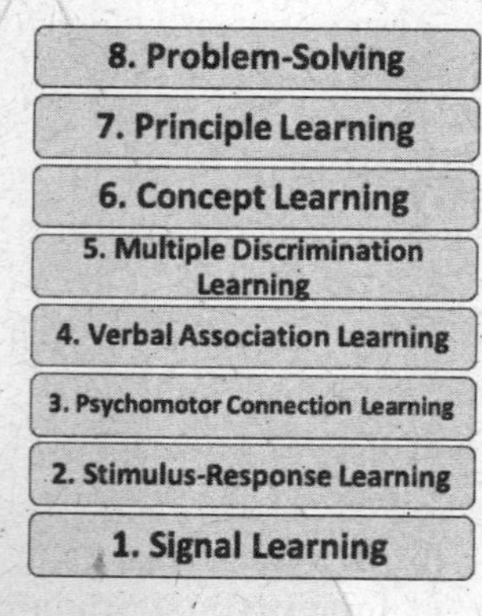

Kurt Lewin's Field Theory

Field theory is a psychological theory which examines patterns of interaction between the individual and the total field, or environment.

The concept first made its appearance in psychology with roots to the holistic perspective of Gestalt theories.

It was developed by Kurt Lewin, a Gestalt psychologist, in the 1940s. Lewin's field theory can be expressed by a formula: B = f (P, E), meaning that behaviour (B) is a function of the person (p) and their environment (e).

B = f (P. E)

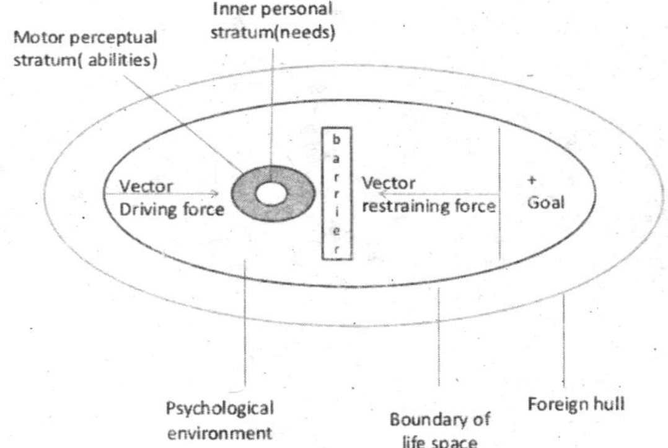

Bandura's social Learning theory

Society and Social learning:

A society is a group of individuals involved in persistent social interaction, follow certain set of rules. In our development, society plays a vital role.

Albert bandura's Observational Learning:

- Albert bandura gave the theory of social learning which is also known as Social Cognitive Theory.
- According to observational learning, people learn through observing others.
- He studied aggressive behaviour of children and did an experiment which is known as bobo doll.
- Those children who watched violent models, they learnt aggressive behaviour.

Bobo doll experiment!

During the 1960s, Albert Bandura conducted a series of experiments on observational learning, known as the Bobo doll experiment.

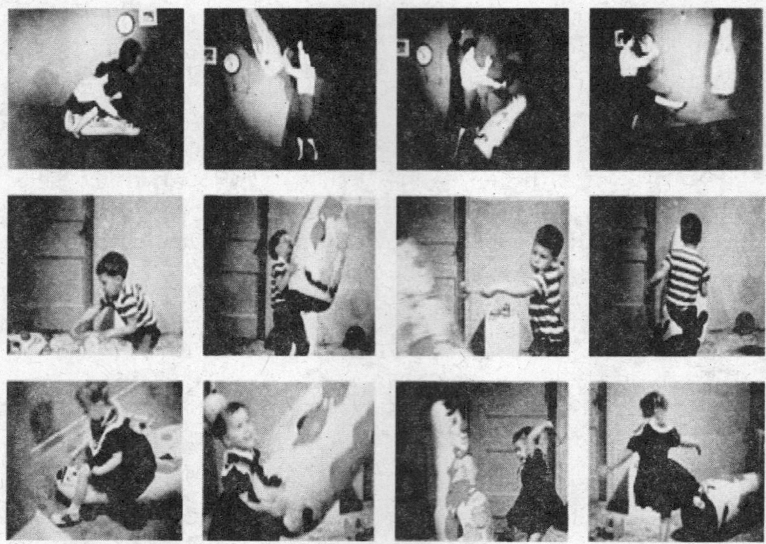

- He studied children's behaviour after they watched a human adult model act aggressively towards a Bobo doll.
- A doll-like toy with a rounded bottom and low center of mass that rocks back to an upright position after it has been knocked down.
- The social learning theory claims that people learn largely by observing, imitating, and modeling.
- It demonstrates that people learn not only by being rewarded or punished but they can also learn from watching somebody else being rewarded or punished.

4 steps of Modelling

1. Attention
2. Retention
3. Reproduction
4. Motivation

Reciprocal Determinism

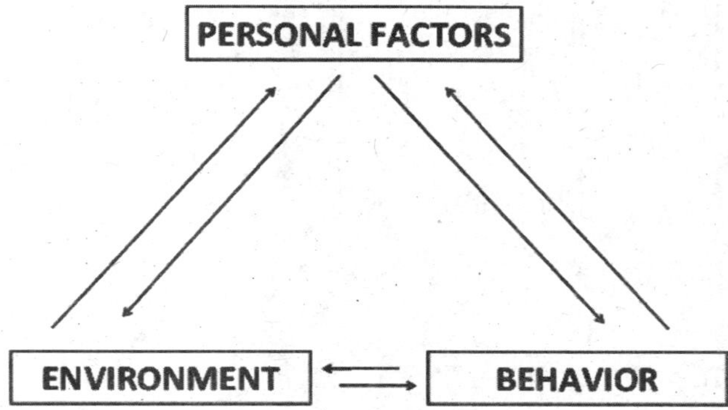

- Three things influence a person, his cognition i.e personal factors, his environment, in which he lives in, and his behaviour.
- These three reciprocate each other, and this is called reciprocal determinism.

1. **Vicarious Learning**: We not always learn things by direct experience but we learn a lot of things by observing others or there are many things which influence an individual indirectly, and this type of learning is called vicarious learning.
2. **Self Efficacy:** it is the belief in the ability of oneself.

Educational Implication

- The social learning theory claims that people learn through observing, imitating, and modeling.
- Children can be influenced by watching violent media. So it is important as adults to take care of what they spend time with.

Gestalt/Insight Theory

"The whole is greater than the some of its parts"-Aristotle.

- Also known as learning by insight.
- Max Wertheimer was the founder of gestalt psychology.
- Insight learning - the process by which the solution to a problem suddenly becomes clear.
- In insight learning, sudden solution is the rule.
- Gestalt psychology was primarily concerned with the nature of perception.
- According to it, an individual comprehends the wholes.

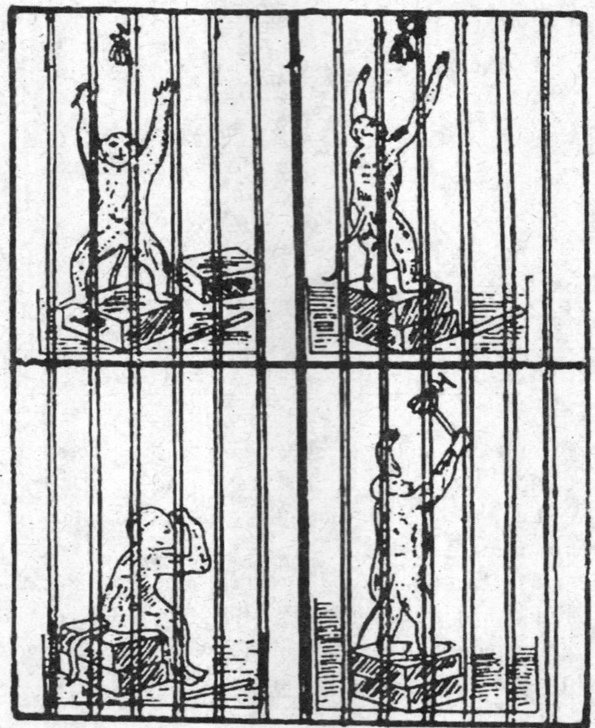

Fig. Kohler's experiment on chimpanzee.

Kohler's Experiment!

- Kohler experimented on a chimpanzee named Sultan.
- Sultan was kept in a cage where few bananas were hanged on the ceiling.
- Hungry sultan attempted to get the bananas several times but failed.
- First, Sultan sat on the floor and tried to think of a solution calmly.
- Sultan analyzed the situation in his mind.
- He found a solution with the help of two boxes kept inside the cage.
- Sultan thought, if those two boxes are kept on one another, he may get to the bananas.
- He applied this perception in his mind and found the solution. Kohler called it insightful learning.

David Ausubel's Modern Cognitive Theory-(RMRD)

Ausubel gave the "Modern Cognitive Theory". According to this theory there are four types of learning:

1. **Rote Learning** :Children learn counting, fables, alphabets etc. but it is not meaningful learning. It can be used in other operations in the following stages.
2. **Meaningful Learning :**
   Children incorporate knowledge by adding new information with previous knowledge.

E.g. a student learns basic mathematical functions like addition and subtraction, further solves the complex equations of multiplication and division.

3. **Receptive Learning**
   When a child receives written or oral learning material, child incorporates it either by rote or by meaningful learning. This kind of information is provided by someone and child receives it.
4. **Discovery Learning**
   When a child evolves knowledge or idea from the given information, it is called discovery learning.

Psycho-sexual Theory of Sigmund Freud

Psyche

- Freud compared the mind with an iceberg to describe the three levels of the mind:
- On the surface, it is consciousness, which consists of those thoughts that are the focus of our attention now, and this is seen as the tip of the iceberg. The sub-conscious consists of all which can be retrieved from memory.
- The most significant part is the unconscious: It plays an eminent role in deciding our behaviour.

Mind like an iceberg:

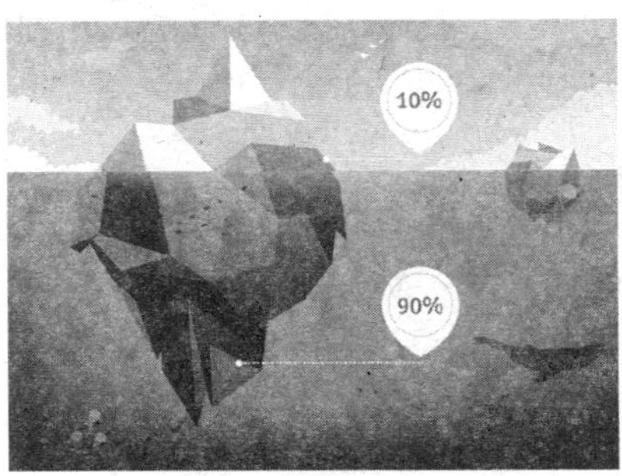

Personality is a three-tier system of Id, Ego and Superego:

Id

- The Id is the primary aspect of personality.
- Id is also known as the storehouse of unfulfilled desires.
- Id is amoral. It possesses no sense of values.

It cannot distinguish between good and evil. It is dominated by the pleasure principle.

- The Id is the part of unconscious.
- The id comprises two kinds of biological instincts (or drives) which Freud called Eros(life instinct) and Thanatos(death instinct).

Libido

- Libido is that part of the Id which seeks its gratification from sexual activities.
- Freud considered it as the total striving force of an organism.
- Libido is present even in the infants.

Fixation

- We need to spend an amount of energy at every level; fixation is when we spend more or less amount of energy at a particular level or stage.
- So we need not to spend more or less energy at a certain stage.

Libido can be stimulated through the following zones:

1. **Oral Stage** (Birth to 1 year): At this stage, the infant gets pleasure from sucking the mouth or from breastfeeding.
2. **Anal Stage** (1-3 years): The child derives much pleasure through anal manipulation or controlling the urination.
3. **Phallic Stage** (3-6 Years): the child derives gratification by touching his genitals. Oedipus and Electra complexes develop at this stage.

Oedipus & Electra

1. The Electra complex is a term used to describe a girl's sense of competition with her mother for the affections of her father.
2. Oedipus complex is a term used to describe a boy's sense of competition with her mother for the affections of his mother.
3. **Oedipus** and **Electra** complexes develop at Phallic stage (3-6 Years) of life.

4. **Latency Stage** (6-13 Years): this is the latency stage where the libido gets latent. The child gets busy in the school activities.
5. **Genital Stage** (Puberty to Death): During the final stage of psychosexual development, the individual develops a strong sexual interest in the opposite sex.

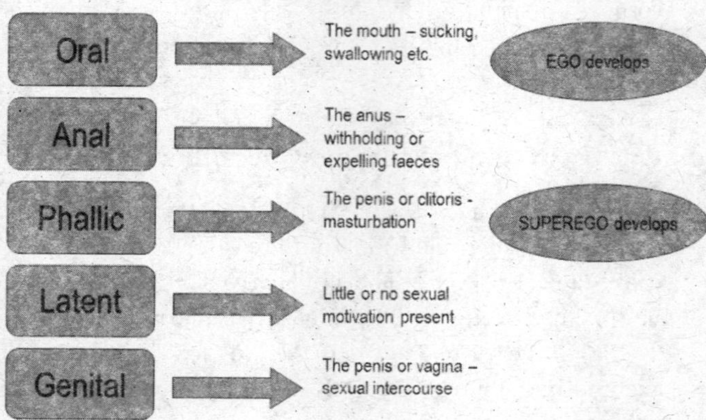

Criticism

- The sample was being collected from Freud's patients only.
- Too much importance on Sexuality.

Psychosocial Development (Erik Erikson)

Erikson focused on psychosocial development rather than psychosexual development.

Stages of Psychosocial Development

- **Erik Homburger Erikson** was a German-American developmental Psychologist.
- He is famous for coining the phrase identity crisis.
- Here are the eight stages, in each stage there are some crisis and virtues attached.
- If we successfully pass the stage then only the virtue comes for life otherwise the negative side goes along in the upcoming stages too.

Stage	Age(Years)	Psychosocial Crisis	Virtue	Task
1.	0 - 1½	Trust vs. Mistrust	Hope	Feeding, abandonment
2.	1½ - 3	Autonomy vs. Shame	Will	Toilet Training
3.	3 - 5	Initiative vs. Guilt	Purpose	Exploring(Play)
4.	5 - 12	Industry vs. Inferiority	Competency	School, Sports
5.	12 - 18	Identity vs. Role Confusion	Fidelity	Social Relationships
6.	18 - 40	Intimacy vs. Isolation	Love	Relationships
7.	40 - 65	Generativity vs. Stagnation	Care	Work and Parenthood
8.	65+	Ego Integrity vs. Despair	Wisdom	Reflection on Life

My Notes

Chapter-09

Pedagogical Issues

National Curriculum Framework, 2005 (NCF-2005)

"Connect yourself and the child to Life itself"

- The National Curriculum Framework 2005 is one of the four NCF published in 1975, 1988, 2000 and 2005 by the NCERT in India.
- The NCF 2005 document draws its policy basis from earlier government reports on education as Learning Without Burden and National Policy of Education 1986-1992 and focus group discussion.
- The recommendations of NCF-2005 are for the entire educational system to be implemented.
- NCF 2005 has been translated into 22 languages and has influenced the syllabi in 17 States.
- The NCERT gave a grant of Rs.10 lakh to each State to promote NCF in the language of the State and to compare its current syllabus with the syllabus proposed.

Common sources of physical discomfort:

1. Long walks to school.
2. Heavy school bags.
3. Lack of basic infrastructure, including support books for reading and writing.
4. Inadequate designs of furniture that gives children inadequate back support.

5. Rigid time-tables and no importance given to co-curricular activities.
6. The absence of toilets and sanitary requirements to girls.
7. Use of corporal punishment.postures.

Guiding Principles of NCF, 2005:

1. To shift learning from rote method.
2. Connecting knowledge to life outside the school.
3. To integrate examination into classroom learning and make it more flexible.
4. To enrich the curriculum so that it goes beyond textbooks.
5. Nurturing an overriding identity informed by caring concerns within the democratic polity of the country.

Learnings:

- The curriculum should focus on the holistic development of the learners.
- Constructive learning has to be the part of the curriculum.
- Don't misunderstand information as knowledge.

Subjects

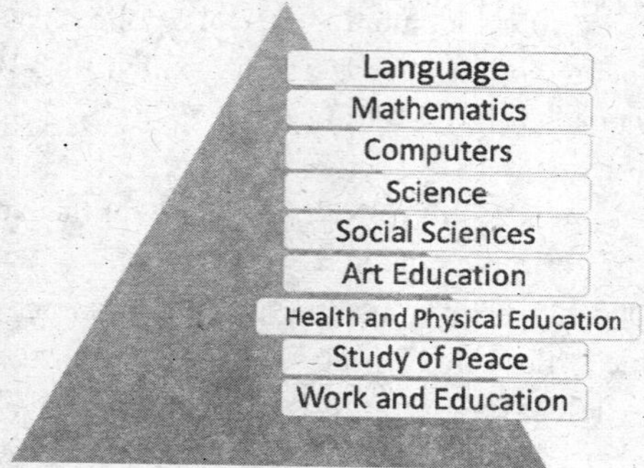

- **Mathematics**
  Teaching of Mathematics should bring mathematization of thought also and should focus on child's resources to think and reason so that he can solve problems with reason and knowledge.
- **Sciences**
  Teaching of science should focus on methods and processes that will nurture thinking process, logic curiosity and creativity.
- **Social Sciences**
  Integrated approach should be followed.

- **Art Education:** Covers music, dance, visual arts, street plays etc. so that children can develop aesthetic sense and self awareness in them.
- **Health and Physical Education:** Health depends upon nutrition and planned physical activities.
- **Education for Peace:** It is important that education should promote peace throughout the nation and beyond.
- **Work Education:** Necessary skills should be promoted through the education, education of head, heart and hand should be given.

- **Languages**
  - 3-language formula should be implemented.
  - Mother tongue should be the medium of instruction.
  - Focus on all skills of a language.

Three Language formula system to be followed:

1. **The First language**-to be studied must be the mother tongue or the regional language.
2. **The Second language** - In Hindi speaking States, the second language will be some other modern Indian language or English, and - In non-Hindi speaking States, the second language will be Hindi or English.
3. **The Third language** - In Hindi speaking States, the third language will be English or a modern Indian language not studied as the second language, and - In non-Hindi speaking States, the third language will be English or a modern Indian language not studied as the second language.

Let's Revise through some Points:

The process of development of NCF was initiated in November 2004 by setting up the **NATIONAL STEERING COMMITTEE** by Prof. Yashpal Singh.

1. Focus on Constructive thoughts of the child rather than instruction(because it's based on the Constructivist approach).
2. Discouragement of ROTE LEARNING.
3. It works on the Policy of Yashpal Committee- Learning without burden.
4. Content should be linked to life outside the school.
5. Primary Role of a teacher is that of a " Facilitator".
6. To integrate examinations with classroom learning and to make Examinations Flexible and not Rigid.

7. Pre-Service Training of Teachers.
8. NCF 2005 has been translated into 22 languages listed in 8th schedule of the constitution.
9. The NCERT gave **a grant of Rs.10 lakh to each State** to promote NCF in the language of the State.

Right To Education Act, 2009

- Every child has a right to full time elementary education, so he/she should not be deprived of that at any cost.
- **The Constitution's 86th Amendment Act, 2002 added Article 21-A** in the Constitution of India to provide free and compulsory education to all children.
- In the age group of 6-14 years as a Fundamental Right.
- The Article 21-A and the RTE Act came into effect on 1st April 2010.
- The title of the RTE Act includes the words 'free and compulsory'.
- It makes provisions for a non-admitted child to be admitted to an age appropriate class.

It Prohibits:

1. Physical punishment and mental harassment;
2. Interview or test procedures for admission of children;
3. fees.
4. Private tuition by teachers.
5. Running of schools without recognition.

Some other points to remember:

- 'Free education' means that any child admitted in the school will not be required to pay any kind of fee or expenses (tuition fee, uniform, books, etc.)
- In other words it implies an education which is free from anxiety, stress and fear.
- Schools should be within the defined area.
- This law came into effect in the whole of India except the state of Jammu and Kashmir from 1st April 2010.
- India became the 135th country to make education a fundamental right of every child.
- The Right to Education of persons with disabilities until 18 years of age is laid down under-**the Persons with Disabilities Act**.
- DUTY OF PARENTS- It is the duty of parents to admit the child in the elementary school .

1. No. of Teachers for class (1st - 5th)

1. Admitted Children (Up-to 60)- Number of teachers Required = 2
2. Children (Between 61-90)- Number of teachers Required= 3
3. Children between 91-120 = 4 Teachers
4. Above 150 Children= 5 Teacher + 1 Head Teacher

2. Building:

1. At least one classroom for every teacher and one head teacher's room.
2. Separate toilets for girls and boys.
3. A kitchen where mid-day meal is prepared.
4. Playground should be there.
5. Clean drinking water facility.

3. Minimum No. of Working Days:

1. 200 Working days for 1-5th Class.
2. 220 Working days for 6-8th Class.

4. Instructional Hours:

- 800 Instructional hours per academic year for 1st-5th Class and
- 1000 Instructional hours per academic year for 6-8th Class.

5. Minimum number of working hours per week for the teacher:

45 hours including preparation hours.

6. Library

There shall be a library in each school providing newspapers, magazines, books, and other such stuff.

7. Play Material, games and sports equipment:

It shall be provided to each class as per the requirement.

Revision

- Free & Compulsory Education.
- Pupil Teacher ratio: not more than 40:1
- No. of working days : 200, 220 days.
- Working hours a week: 45 hours.
- School should be around: 1 and 3 kms from home.
- No denial of admission and transfer, no corporal Punishment.
- Qualified Teachers and Recognized schools.
- School management committee should be there.

Micro-Teaching

1. The concept of micro-teaching was originated in Stanford University in 1963 by Dwight Allen.

2. In India micro teaching was introduced by D.D. Tiwari in 1967 at CPI, Allahbad.
3. Micro-teaching is an effective technique helps in the development of skills in teachers.
4. Also called scaled down teaching approach.

Reducing:

In micro-teaching we reduce:
Class size 5-10 pupils.
Time duration 5-10 minutes.
Topic Size.
Classroom complexities.

It helps in the modification of teacher behaviour.

Steps of Micro Teaching

The various steps involved in micro teaching are:
Step 1: Skill Defining
Step 2: Demonstration by Experts
Step 3: Preparing Micro Lesson Plan
Step 4: Teaching in small Groups
Step 5: Discussion
Step 6: Re-planning
Step 7: Re-teaching
Step 8: Re-evaluation

Various Skills to Practice:

1. Questioning
2. Explaining
3. Illustration
4. Stimulus variation
5. Blackboard Skill

Micro-teaching Cycle

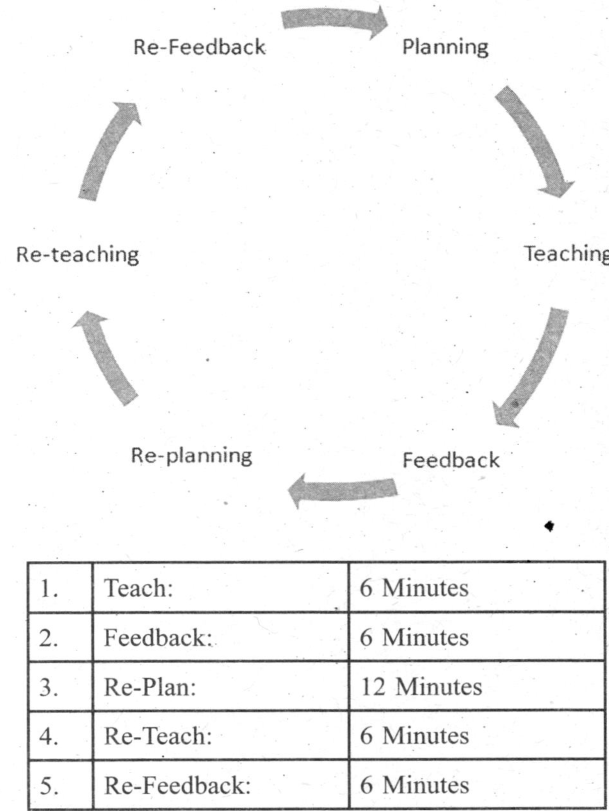

1.	Teach:	6 Minutes
2.	Feedback:	6 Minutes
3.	Re-Plan:	12 Minutes
4.	Re-Teach:	6 Minutes
5.	Re-Feedback:	6 Minutes

It starts from planning and goes to re-feedback; planning time is not included here.

(Total Minutes taken = 36 minutes)

Bloom's Taxonomy

Dr. Benjamin bloom classified educational objectives into three learning domains, these are:

1. Cognitive Domain (Mental skills)
2. Affective Domain (Attitude or self)
3. Psychomotor Domain (Motor skills)

1. Cognitive Domain:

- The **cognitive domain** involves the development of our mental skills and the acquisition of knowledge.

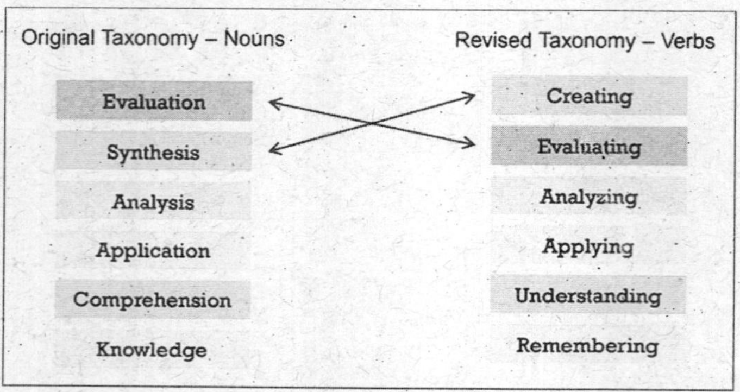

- There are six categories in the **cognitive domain**:
- He initially gave the taxonomy in 1956 and it was revised in 2001. All the noun forms of cognitive domains got replaced by verb forms.

1. **Knowledge:** the ability to recall information.
2. **Comprehension:** the ability to understand the meaning of what is known without necessarily relating it to anything else.
3. **Application:** the ability to use knowledge in a new situation.
4. **Analysis:** the ability to differentiate facts and opinions. Here, we kind of open up things and see minutely what the parts say about it.
5. **Synthesis:** the ability to integrate different elements or concepts in order to form a structure so a new meaning can be formed.
6. **Evaluation:** the ability to come up with judgments about the importance of concepts.

2. Affective Domain:

Affective domain is related with our emotions, feelings, values, motivations and attitudes.

- **Receiving:** awareness about the surrounding, willingness to hear. Key words: ask, choose, describe, follow, give, hold, identify, replies.
- **Responding:** Active participation on the part of the learners. Attends or reacts to a particular phenomenon.
  Key words: answers, assists, aids, complies, conforms, discusses, helps, tells, writes.
- **Valuing:** Valuing is based on the internalization of set of specific values.

Key Words: Completes, demonstrates, differentiates, joins, select, share, follows, initiates.

- **Organizing:** here values are prioritized, here one integrates a new value into one's general set of values.
  Key words: alter, combine, integrate, organize etc.
- **Internalizing values:** here one acts consistently with new values and adapts them for life.
  Key words: Acts, influences, qualifies, proposes, solves, verifies etc.

3. Psychomotor Domain:

The psychomotor domain refers to the use of motor skills, coordination, and physical movement.

1. **Reflex Movements:** Reflex action, is an involuntary response to a stimulus. E.g blinking of our eyes, functioning of our heart.
2. **Basic Movements:** Combination of reflex movements such as walking.
3. **Perceptual Abilities:** Perceptual learning, process by which the ability of sensory systems to respond to stimuli is improved through experience e.g jumping a certain height, catching a ball.
4. **Physical Abilities:** Basic movements pre required to higher skills such as lifting the weights.
5. **Skilled Movements:** Skilled movements are the result of the acquisition of a complex task effectively. Examples are: all skilled activities in sports, recreation, dance, etc.
6. **Non-discursive communication:** is communication through bodily movements such as body postures, gestures, and facial expressions in a skilled dance movement.

Inclusive Education

"Segregation is against the law of nature"

- We all are different in our looks, interests, abilities, aptitude, language etc. and that's the beauty of this world.
- Our differences should not be looked at negatively but we should celebrate this diversity in us.
- Inclusive Education is an approach to educate all children who are at stake of total involvement in the education system.
- It expects that all learners learn together through access to common educational provisions.
- the parents, community and teachers, all need to be cooperative towards the diverse needs of children.

Need of Inclusive Education

- It is the right of every child to get education.
- We should embrace the unity in diversity.
- Inclusive education becomes important to fulfill this.

Difference between Integrated and Inclusive Education

- The term 'Inclusive Education' has come to replace the term 'Integrated Education'.
- As the term inclusive education means much more than integrated education.

Integrated education	Inclusive education
1. Admission of children with disabilities in a regular school without modifying the existing system.	Admission of children with disabilities in a regular school with necessary provisions. That's why inclusion is a broad term.
2. Students are expected to suit the existing education system.	The education system will make suitable modifications to suit the needs of children.
3. For additional support the child is placed in a resource room.	All the required support will be made available to the students in the regular classroom.
4. The inadequacies of the students are highlighted.	Students are never made to feel inadequate as curricular and co curricular activities are modified to the requirement of the specific children.

Children With Disabilities

1. Children having cognitive and/or learning disabilities.
2. Children with social, emotional and behavioural disorders.
3. Problem with language and communication.
4. Children with visual, Hearing impairment.
5. Physical problems or orthopaedic disabilities.

Few other terms:

1. **Gifted Children:** Giftedness can be evident in one or more domains such as; intellectual, creative, artistic, leadership, or in a particular academic field such as language arts, mathematics or science.

Renzulli's Three-Ring Model of Giftedness: (ACC)

Renzulli considers three factors important for the development of gifted behaviour: Above average ability, creativity, and task commitment.

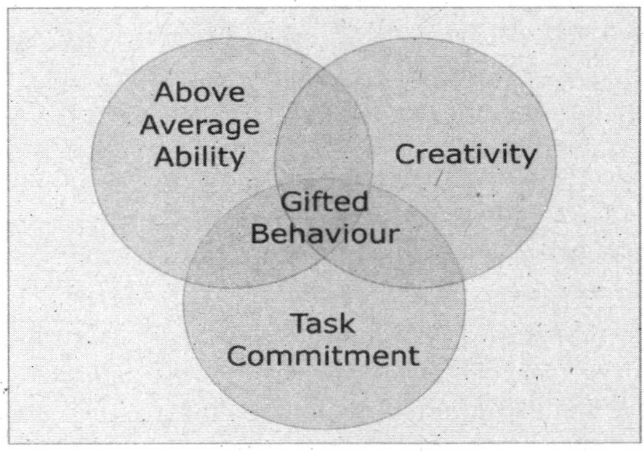

Common Characteristics of Gifted Individuals:

1. Unusual alertness, even in infancy.
2. Rapid learner; puts thoughts together quickly.
3. Excellent memory.
4. Large vocabulary and complex sentence structure for age.
5. Vivid sense of imagination.
6. Highly developed curiosity
7. Good sense of humor.
8. Asks probing questions.
9. Thinking is abstract,logical, and insightful.
10. Concern with social and political issues and injustices.
11. Longer attention span and great concentration power.

Creative Children:

Creative learners are those who use their imagination and critical thinking to create new and meaningful forms of ideas where they can take risks, be independent and be flexible in their ways of learning.

- Creative children are divergent thinkers.
- F. Osborn's brainstorming is also related to creativity.
- Edward de Bono's lateral thinking is too related with creativity.
- It's not necessary that all creative children have high IQ.

The Right Of Persons With Disabilities Act, 2016

- Comes under the **Ministry of Social Justice and Empowerment**.
- This act replaces the PWD Act, 1995.

- It came into force from 15th June 2017.
- This Law will be a game changer for the estimated 70-100 million disabled citizens of India.

Changes from PWD ACT, 1995

- This act will cover 21 Disabilities instead of 7 disabilities that were covered by PWD Act, 1995.
- This new Act lays complete emphasis on one's rights –

1. *Right to equality and opportunity,*
2. *Right to inherit and own property,*
3. *Right to home and family and reproductive rights among others.*
4. Every child with disability between the age group of ***6 and 18 years shall have the right to free education.***
5. **The New Act will bring our law in line with the *United National Convention on the Rights of Persons with Disabilities (UNCRPD).***

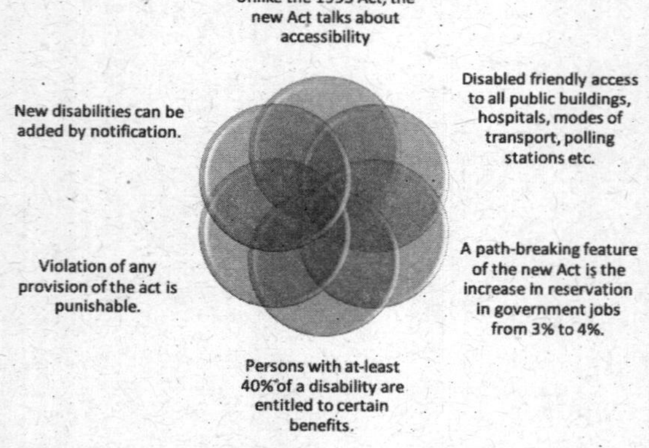

Definition of Person with Disability (PwDs)

➤ **Persons with Disabilities (Equal Opportunities, Protection of Rights and Full Participation) (PwD) Act, 1995, defines 'disability' as:-**

- **Blindness**
- **Low-Vision**
- **Leprosy-cured**
- **Hearing Impairment**
- **Locomotor Disability**
- **Mental Retardation**
- **Mental Illness**

There are the 21 disabilities stated in the RPWD act, 2016:

1. Blindness
2. Low-vision
3. Leprosy Cured persons
4. Hearing Impairment (deaf and hard of hearing)
5. Locomoter Disability
6. ***Dwarfism***
7. Intellectual Disability
8. Mental Illness
9. Autism Spectrum Disorder
10. ***Cerebral Palsy***
11. Muscular Dystrophy
12. Chronic Neurological conditions
13. ***Specific Learning Disabilities***
14. Multiple Sclerosis
15. ***Speech and Language disability***
16. ***Thalassemia***
17. ***Hemophilia***
18. Sickle Cell disease
19. Multiple disabilities- including deaf blindness
20. ***Acid Attack victim***
21. ***Parkinson's disease***

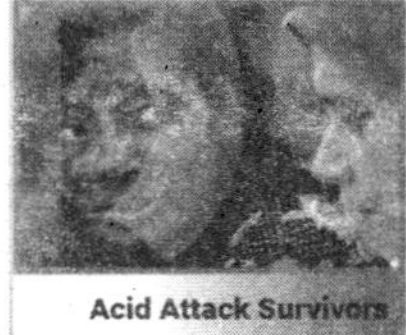
Acid Attack Survivors

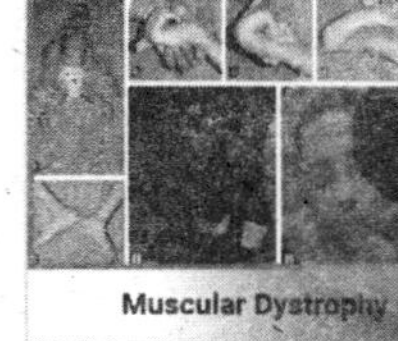
Muscular Dystrophy

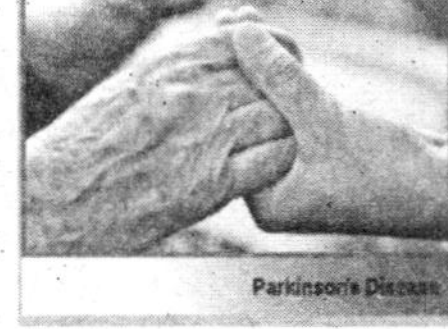
Parkinson's Disease

Specific Learning Disabilities

Speech and Language Disability

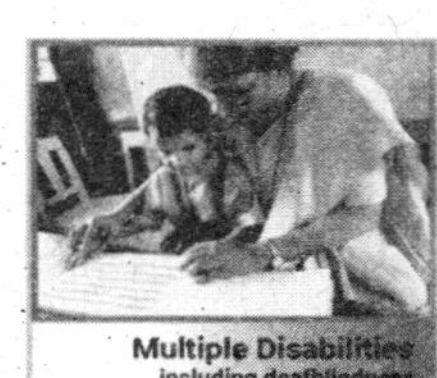
Multiple Disabilities including deafblindness

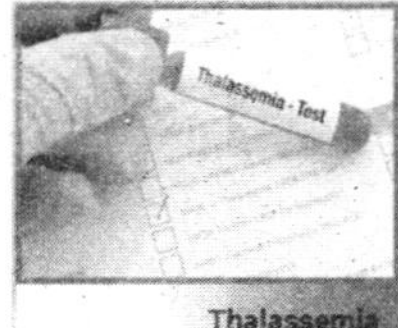

Thalassemia

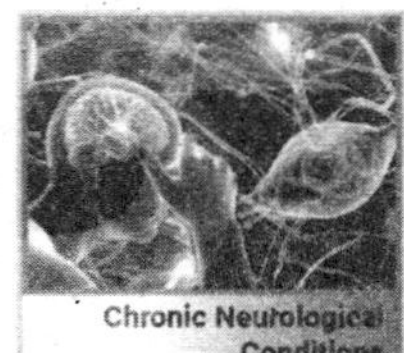
Chronic Neurological Conditions

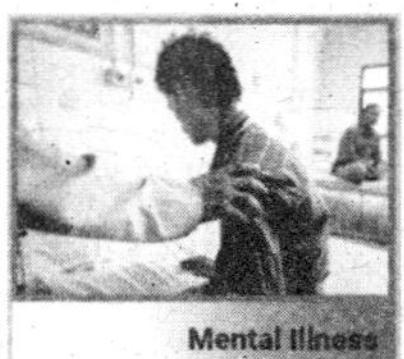
Mental Illness

Blindness

Leprosy Cured Persons

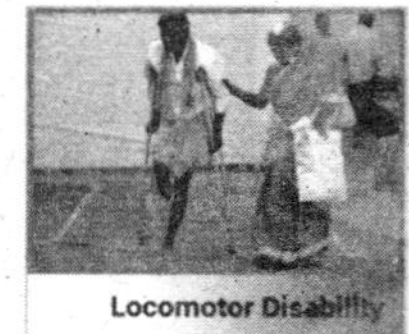
Locomotor Disability

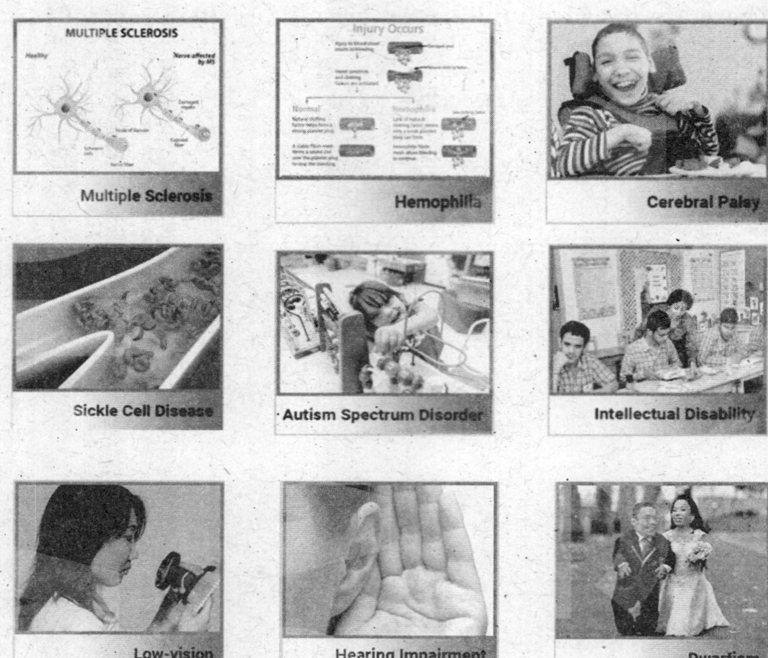

CCE: Assessment & Evaluation, SBA

Assessment is a process of collecting, reviewing and using data, for the purpose of improvement in the learning process.

- **Assessment for Learning** is often formative assessment because it takes place during the course of teaching learning process and provides information, so that teachers and students can use this information to make the teaching learning process better.
- **Assessment of Learning** is summative assessment which is used to know the student's competence after the instruction. E.g yearly exams.
- **Assessment as Learning** Through this process students are able to learn about themselves as learners and become aware of their own learning or we can say, here the learners reflect on their own learning.

An assessment will be called standard if it has the qualities such as validity, reliability.

- **Validity:** A test is said to be valid, if it tests what it is intended to measure.

- **Reliability:** If a test is consistent in its result than it is a reliable test
- **Evaluation** is described as an act of passing judgement on the basis of set of standards. Hence, It is a decision making process.

Evaluation includes in it:

1. Measurement
2. Assessment
3. Evaluation

What is a Standardised Test ?

A **standardized** test is any form of test that :

(1) requires all test takers to answer the same questions, or a selection of questions from common bunch of questions, in the same way, and

(2) that is scored in a "**standard**" or consistent manner, which makes it possible to compare the relative performance of individual students or groups of students.

For e.g: CBSE board exams, CTET, UPSC etc.

Norm Referenced Test and Criterion Referenced Test

Norm-referenced is a percentage ranking compared to an average population. For e.g DSSSB, SSC exams. On the other hand criterion-referenced means the test relates to some sort of established unit of measure. E.g 12th exams.

Difference between Assessment and Evaluation:

Assessment - (40% weightage)	Evaluation - (60% weightage)
1. Provides feedback on performance and areas of improvement.	Determines the extent to which objectives are achieved.
2. Diagnostic in nature.	Judgemental in nature.
3. Process Oriented and formative.	Product Oriented and summative.

School Based Assessment:

- School-based assessment (SBA) is an assessment which is embedded in the teaching and learning process in school itself.
- It is carried out in ordinary classrooms.
- It is conducted by the students' own teacher.
- It involves students more actively in the assessment process, especially if self and/or peer assessment is used in addition with teacher assessment

- Here in SBA, all aspects of evaluation are decided by the school such as teachers, learners and other participants of school.

Continuous and Comprehensive Evaluation

Continuous and Comprehensive Evaluation, commonly known as 'CCE' is introduced as school based system of evaluation by CBSE in 2009.

CCE has two terms in it which include all the aspect of a child and these are **continuous evaluation** which means assessment on a regular basis and the second one is **comprehensive** evaluation which takes care of the **scholastic** and **co-scholastic** aspects of evaluation.

Scholastic Aspect: Scholastic assessment is related with the curricular areas of the education such as the desirable behaviour related to the learner's knowledge, understanding, application, evaluation, analysis, and creating in subjects and the ability to apply it in an unfamiliar situation.

Co-scholastic Aspect:

The co-scholastic activities are co-curricular activities classified into five parts. These are:

1. **Life Skills**,
2. **Attitude and Values**,
3. **Wellness**,
4. **Service Activities** and
5. **Art and Work education**

Technique of Evaluation

1. Observation
2. Rating Scale
3. Sociometry
4. Cumulative Record
5. Interview
6. Anecdotal Record

My Notes

Chapter-10

Supplementary Reading

Motivation: Motivation is derived from the word "*motive*" in the English language which is defined as a need that requires satisfaction.

It has types:

1. **Intrinsic or internal Motivation**: Intrinsic motivation is the self-desire to achieve something, the locus of control is the inner self of a person not the external word.
2. **Extrinsic or External Motivation**: Extrinsic motivation is the self¬desire to achieve something, the locus of control is outside of a person thus, not internal.

Maslow's Hierarchy of Needs:

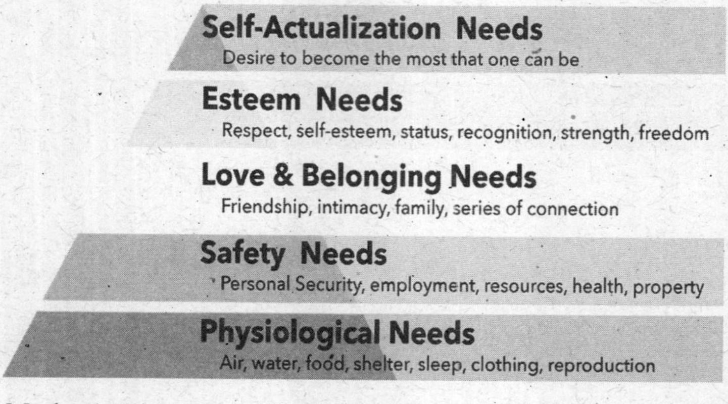

Self-Actualization Needs
Desire to become the most that one can be

Esteem Needs
Respect, self-esteem, status, recognition, strength, freedom

Love & Belonging Needs
Friendship, intimacy, family, series of connection

Safety Needs
Personal Security, employment, resources, health, property

Physiological Needs
Air, water, food, shelter, sleep, clothing, reproduction

Maslow's Hierarchy of Needs "A Theory of Human Motivation" in which he described our needs in an increasing order that goes on from Physiological needs to the self-actualization needs.**Motivation Cycle:**

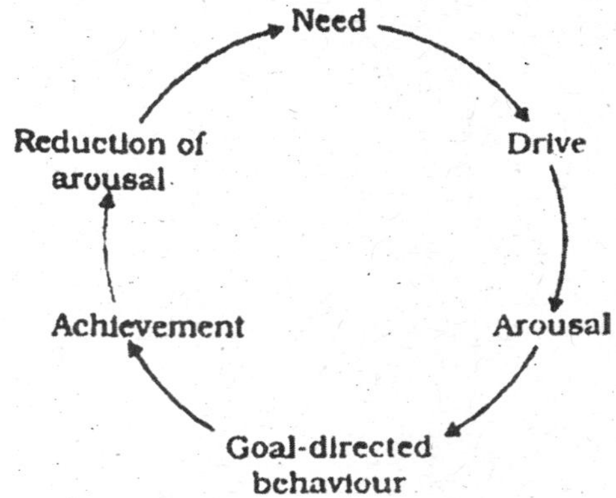

Learning and learning curve

- Learning is the relatively permanent change in behaviour due to experience and efforts/practice.
- This definition has three components:

1. The duration of the change is long-term rather than short-term;
2. The locus of the change is the content and structure of knowledge in memory or the behaviour of the learner;
3. The cause of the change is the learner's experience in the environment rather than fatigue, motivation, drugs, physical condition.

Transfer of learning

- Transfer of learning is the ability to take information learned in one situation and apply that to another:
- **Positive transfer** helps you. apply skills or knowledge to a new situation, whereas as negative transfer hampers the learning.
- **Zero transfer** means that old skills or knowledge have no effect on learning new skills or knowledge.
- **Negative transfer** refers to the interference of the previous knowledge with new learning.

Learning Curves

Learning process is not always similar. It progresses in curve lines, which psychologists have attempted to measure:

Learning curves refers to the graphical relationship between the amount of learning and the time it takes. The first person to describe the learning curve was **Herman Ebbinghaus** in 1885.

Stages of learning curves

Normally learning curve comprises of four stages.

- **Initial stage:** In this phase the learning is zero for first few attempts.
- **Steep up stage:** It is also called exponential phase. In this stage the learning suddenly increases.
- **Intermediate stage:** At this stage there is no progress in learning so, it is called as plateau in learning.

Reasons of plateau:

- faulty method of learning,
- physical and mental fatigue,
- complexity of a task,
- Lack of motivation and interest
- unfavorable environment,

- **Final stage** - this is the final stage. Here the learner has reached the maximum limit.

Types of curves

There are three types of learning curves:

Concave curve

This is also called positively accelerated curve.

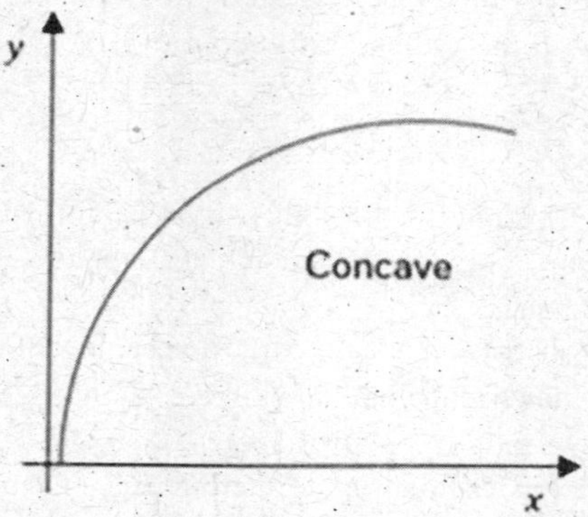

Convex curve

This learning curve is also called negatively accelerated curve.

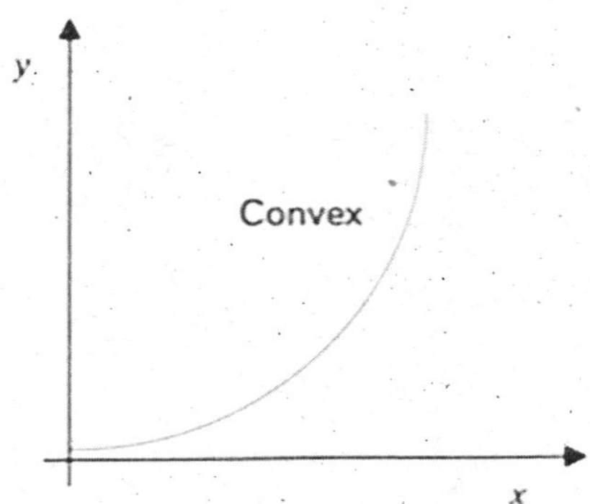

Concave and convex curve

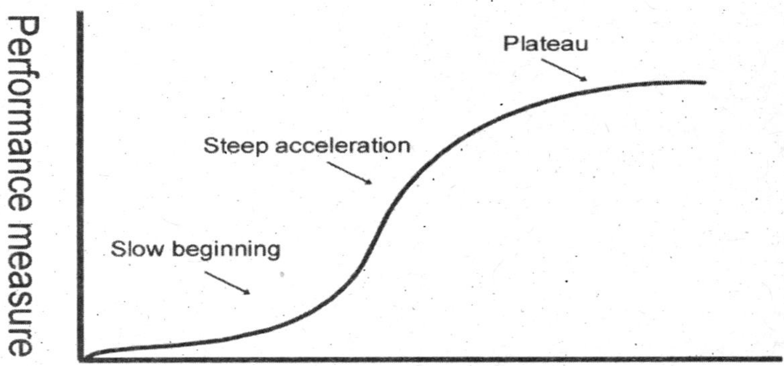

The third curve involves the combination of the first two that is why it is known as Concave-Convex Curve.

Also, called as ***S-shaped curve***.

Birth of Psychology

- Psychology was born at the time of two Greek Philosophers Plato and Aristotle.
- Etymologically Psychology has two Greek words - Psyche and Logos.
- Psyche means soul and Logos means study.
- John Locke described the, "*Mind of a child is Tabula Rasa*".

Woodworth, "**First Psychology lost its soul**, then it **lost its** mind, then **lost its** consciousness. It still has behaviour of a sort."

Schools of Psychology

1. Structuralism

Wilhelm Wundt (Father of Psychology).

- Established the first laboratory of Psychology at Leipzig, Germany in 1879.
- Initially used the Introspection Method.

2. Functionalism

- William James(Father of American Psychology).
- Known for his famous book "Principles of Psychology" (1890).
- Marry Whiton Calkins was his student and the first female President of American Psychological Association(APA).

3. Psychoanalysis

- Sigmund Freud was the father of Psychoanalysis.
- Three states of mind- Id, Ego, Super Ego.
- Analysed dreams in his "Analysis of Dreams".
- Talked about Oedipus and Electra, Eros and Thanatos.

Defense Mechanism

- Denial
- Regression
- Supression
- Repression
- Projection
- Sublimation
- Displacement
- Humor
- Rationalization
- Compensation

4. Behaviourism

"Give me a dozen healthy infants, well-formed, and my own specified world to bring them up in and I'll guarantee to take any one at random and train him to become any type of specialist I might select-doctor, lawyer, artist, merchant-chief and, yes, even beggar-man and thief, regardless of his talents, penchants, tendencies, abilities, vocations, and race of his ancestors."

- John Broadus Watson, Behaviourism

- J.B Watson- Father of Behaviourism.
- He admitted Psychology as a study of stimulus and response.

- He kind of neglected the human genes and only focussed on conditioning or observable behaviour.

5. Gestalt Psychology

- The assumption that whole is more than just sum of its parts is the basic principle of gestalt psychology.
- Father of Gestaltism is Wertheimer.
- People associated with it are Kohler, Koffka, Kurt Lewin.
- Insightful Learning

6. Cognitive Psychology

- In 1960, Miller and Jerome Bruner established cognitive school.
- Information Processing Theory is the product of cognitive psychology.

7. Humanism

- Spiritual father of humanism is Abraham Maslow.
- Carl Rogers- Theory of Self, non-directive counselling.
- Humanism is the third force of Psychology.

Carl Rogers

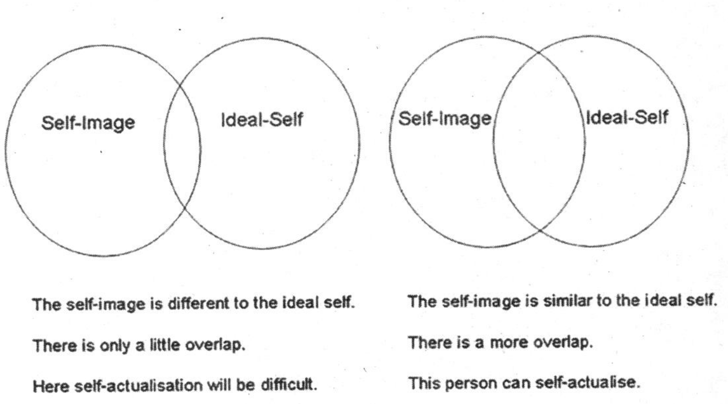

My Notes

CTET-2012

Held on: 5th May, 2012

Paper-1

1. **Human development is divided into domains such as**
   A. Psychological, cognitive, emotional and physical
   B. Physical, spiritual, cognitive and social
   C. Physical, cognitive, emotional and social
   D. Emotional, cognitive, spiritual, and socio-psychological

2. **Which of the following is a principle of development?**
   A. It is discontinuous process
   B. All processes of development are not inter-connected
   C. It does not proceed at the same pace for all
   D. Development is always linear

3. **Individual attention is important in the teaching-learning process because**
   A. It offer better opportunities to teachers to discipline each learner
   B. Learner always learn better in groups
   C. Children develop at different rates and learn differently
   D. Teacher training programs prescribe it

4. **Human personality is the result of**
   A. Only environment
   B. Only heredity
   C. Upbringing and education
   D. Interaction between heredity and environment

5. **In the context of education, socialization means**
   A. Adapting and adjusting to social environment
   B. Always following social norms
   C. Creating one's own social norms
   D. Respecting elders in society

6. **Young learners should be encouraged to interact with peers in the classroom so that**
   A. They learn social skills in the course of the study
   B. The teacher can control the classroom better
   C. They can learn answers to questions from each other
   D. The syllabus can be covered quickly

7. **According to Piaget's stage of cognitive development, the sensori¬motor stage is associated with**
   A. Ability to interpret and analyze options
   B. Concern about social issues
   C. Imitation, memory and mental representation
   D. Ability to solve problems in logical fashion

8. **According to Kohlberg, a teacher can instill moral values in**

children by

A. Involving them in discussions on moral issues
B. Giving strict instructions on 'how to behave'
C. Giving importance to religious techniques
D. Laying clear rule of behavior

9. Which of the following is a feature of progressive behavior?

A. Frequent tests and examination
B. Flexible time-table and seating arrangement
C. Instruction based solely on prescribed text-books
D. Emphasis on scoring good marks on examination

10. A teacher makes use of a variety of tasks to cater to the different learning styles of her learners. She is influenced by

A. Vygotsky's socio-cultural theory
B. Piaget's cognitive development theory
C. Kohlberg's moral development theory
D. Gardner's multiple intelligence theory

11. Vygotsky emphasized the significance of the role played by which of the following factors in the learning of children?

A. Physical B. Social
C. Heredity D. Moral

12. A school gives preferences to girls while preparing students for a state level solosong competition. This reflects

A. Progressive thinking B. Gender bias
C. Global trends D. Pragmatic approach

13. Learners display individual differences. So teacher should

A. Increase number of tests
B. Insist of uniform pace of learning
C. Provide a variety of learning experiences
D. Enforce strict discipline

14. School-based assessment is primarily based on the principle that

A. Schools are more efficient than external bodies of examination
B. Assessment should be very economical
C. Teachers know their learners' capabilities better than external examiners
D. Students should at all costs get high grades

15. Which of the following is an objective question?

A. True or false B. Essay type question
C. Short answer question D. Open ended question

16. Inclusive education
A. Includes indoctrination of facts
B. Includes teachers from marginalized groups
C. Celebrate diversity in the classroom
D. Encourages strict admission procedures

17. The emphasis from teaching to learning can be shifted by
A. Adopting frontal teaching
B. Focusing on examination results
C. Adopting child-centered pedagogy
D. Encouraging rote learning

18. When a child with a disability first comes to school, the teacher should
A. Discuss with the child's parents to evolve collaborative plans
B. Conduct an admission test
C. Refer the child to as special school according to the disability
D. Seclude him from other students

19. When a child 'fails', it means
A. The system has failed
B. The child is not fit for studies
C. The child has not memorized the answers properly
D. The child should have taken private tuition

20. The most effective method to teach the concept of germination of seeds is
A. To show pictures of seed growth
B. To give detailed explanations
C. To make the students plant seeds and observe stages of germination
D. To draw pictures on the black-board and give descriptions

21. When a child gets bored while doing a task, it is a sign that
A. The child is not capable of learning
B. The child needs to be disciplined
C. The task may have become mechanically repetitive
D. The child is not intelligent

22. Which of the following is a domain of learning?
A. Spiritual
B. Professional
C. Experiential
D. Affective

23. Which of the following is the first step in the scientific method of problem-solving?

A. Collection of relevant data
B. Formulation of hypotheses
C. Verification of hypotheses
D. Problem awareness

24. Errors of learners often indicate
A. Absence of learning
B. Socio-economic status of the learners
C. How they learn
D. The need for mechanical drill

25. A child starts to cry when his grandmother takes him from his mother's lap. The child cries due to
A. Stranger anxiety
B. Separation anxiety
C. Social anxiety
D. Emotional anxiety

26. A teacher uses a text and some pictures of fruits and vegetables and holds a discussion with her students. The students link the details with their previous knowledge and learn the concept of nutrition. This approach is based on
A. Operant conditioning of learning
B. Construction of knowledge
C. Classical conditioning of learning
D. Theory of reinforcement

27. Critical pedagogy firmly believes that
A. The experiences and perceptions of learners are important
B. The teacher should always lead the classroom instruction
C. The learners need not reason independently
D. What children learn out of school is irrelevant

28. A teacher after preparing a question paper, checks whether the question test specifies testing objectives. He is concerned primarily about the question paper's
A. Reliability
B. Validity
C. Content coverage
D. Typology of questions

29. Which of the following is a teacher-related factor affecting learning?
A. Nature of the content or learning experiences
B. Mastery over the subject matter

C. Proper seating arrangement
D. Availability of teaching-learning resources

30. A teacher never gives answers to questions herself. She encourages her students to suggest answers, have group discussions and adopt collaborative learning. This approach is based on the principle of

A. Readiness to learn
B. Active participation
C. Proper organization of instructional material
D. Setting a good example and being a role-model

My Notes

Answer Key

1.	(C)	11.	(B)	21.	(C)
2.	(C)	12.	(B)	22.	(D)
3.	(C)	13.	(C)	23.	(D)
4.	(D)	14.	(C)	24.	(C)
5.	(A)	15.	(A)	25.	(D)
6.	(A)	16.	(C)	26.	(B)
7.	(C)	17.	(C)	27.	(A)
8.	(A)	18.	(A)	28.	(B)
9.	(B)	19.	(A)	29.	(B)
10.	(D)	20.	(C)	30.	(B).

CTET-2012

Held on: 5th May, 2012

Paper-2

1. **"Socialization" means**
   A. Following the social norms strictly
   B. Adjusting in society
   C. Revolting against norms
   D. Understanding social diversity

2. **"Thought not only determines language, but also precedes it" was an idea put forward by**
   A. Jean Piaget   B. Kohlberg
   C. Vygotsky   D. Pavlov

3. **Which of the following statements is correct in relation to 'concept formation' by a child?**
   A. Concepts are emotionally ordered
   B. There is a set pattern of concepts development
   C. Concepts are not hierarchical in nature
   D. Concepts are not individual

4. **Which of the following statements is most appropriate in relation to adolescence?**
   A. Increase in the incidence of emotional upheavals
   B. Carefree nature towards studies
   C. Thinking starts reflecting in concrete actions
   D. Abrupt increase in the intelligence quotient

5. **Main characteristic of the 'emotionally motivated children' is their**
   A. Over reactive nature
   B. Introvert nature
   C. Balanced way of presenting their viewpoint
   D. Melancholic demeanor

6. **An important characteristic of 'formal operational stage of mental development' is**
   A. Abstract thinking   B. Concrete thinking
   C. Social thinking   D. Egocentric behavior

7. **Principle of reinforcement is related to ?**
   A. Thorndike   B. Kohlberg
   C. Skinner   D. Pavlov

8. **The most important factor in the effective teaching process is**
   A. Punctuality exhibited by teacher and students
   B. Mastery of the contents by the teacher & timely completion of the syllabus
   C. Teacher - student dialogue

D. Effective teaching process

9. The best way to inculcate moral values in children is

A. To give moral lectures in the morning assembly

B. Put across a situation and ask students to take a decision

C. Demonstration of moral values by teachers and elders

D. Teaching students to differentiate between moral and immoral

10. Which of the following factors is a basis for the 'child-centered education'?

A. Individual differences

B. Child rights

C. The Right of Children to Free and Compulsory Education Act, 2009

D. All children are equal in all respects

11. Which of the following is least important in the process of thinking?

A. Reasoning B. Problem

C. Generalizations D. Memory

12. The major responsibility of a teacher is to

A. Prepare lesson plans and teach accordingly

B. Organize as many activities as possible

C. Maintain strict discipline

D. Provide learning opportunities as per the different learning styles of students

13. Which of the following is most important in the process of learning?

A. Heredity of child

B. Style of learning

C. Examination-result of the children

D. Economic condition of the child

14. The most appropriate way of explaining the topic "Purification of water" is by

A. Demonstrating the process with the help of a chart

B. Asking the students to make a model of the purification plant

C. Taking students to the plant where the water is purified

D. Reading from the text-book

15. The appropriate logical predicate for the Continuous and Comprehensive Evaluation should be

A. Assessing more than one aspect of learning

B. Maximizing the assessment opportunities

C. Promoting the holistic nature of human personality
D. Increasing the burden on teachers

16. A teacher uses a dice labeled Describe, Predict, Explain, Summarize, Deconstruct and Evaluate. Each time after a topic is completed; the teacher throws the dice and asks students to answer a question based on the location of the dice. The teacher is
A. Conducting formative assessment
B. Provoking thoughts of students
C. Diversifying the thought process of the students
D. Finishing his/her lesson in a style

17. Which characteristic of a teacher is least important in inclusive education?
A. Sensitivity towards children
B. Patience and affection for students
C. Knowledge regarding disabilities of students
D. Socio-economic status of teacher

18. .... plays a significant role in the development of personality.
A. Heredity
B. Environment
C. A blend of heredity and environment
D. Number of examinations

19. Mohit likes to teach children and is preparing hard for the entrance examination for B. Ed. He is .... motivated.
A. Intrinsically
B. Extrinsically
C. Actively
D. Intellectually

20. "Logical-mathematical intelligence" is associated with
A. Two-factor theory
B. Group factor theory
C. Hierarchical theory
D. Multiple intelligence theory

21. 'Activity based teaching' emphasizes
A. Disciplined class
B. Completion of activity in due time
C. Active participation by all the students
D. Taking examination after completion of activity

22. A teacher took her class on an educational trip to

A. Provide a break from the routine teaching in school
B. Provide opportunity to children for direct observation
C. Do the activity specified in the school calendar
D. Provide entertainment to children

23. There are three polio-affected children in a class. During the games-period they should be
A. Seated in a corner so that these children can enjoy the game
B. Encouraged to take part in the games appropriate for them, with other children
C. Allowed to take part only in indoor games
D. Forced to play with all the students of the class

24. According to Kohlberg, 'children approach thinking about right and wrong'
A. Differently at different stages
B. In the same fashion at different stages
C. As per the context
D. As per the instructions given by the parents

25. 'Emotional catharsis' means
A. Suppression of emotions
B. Feeling highly depressed
C. Bringing out emotional repression
D. Increasing the ability to tolerate emotional repression

26. Presence of identical elements between already learnt skills and new skills results in
A. Negative transfer
B. Positive transfer
C. Generalized transfer
D. Zero transfer

27. A teacher normally assigns different tasks to the students. He/she believes that
A. Students do not like assigning same work to all the students
B. It promotes constructive competition among students
C. There are individual differences among students
D. The students will not be able to copy each other's work

28. .... are involved in thinking.
A. Image, language, imagination, proposition
B. Image, imagination, concept, proposition
C. Imagination, language, concept, proposition
D. Image, language, concept, proposition

29. Continuous and Comprehensive Evaluation is

A. Teacher-centered

B. Student-centered

C. Assessment-centered

D. Performance-centered

30. Which of the following is least important in an inclusive classroom?

A. Lesser stress on competition and grades

B. More co-operative and collaborative activity

C. More choice for students

D. More effort by teacher to "cover" course

My Notes

Answer Key

1.	*(B)*	*11.*	*(C)*	*21.*	*(C)*
2.	*(A)*	*12.*	*(D)*	*22.*	*(B)*
3.	*(B)*	*13.*	*(B)*	*23.*	*(B)*
4.	*(A)*	*14.*	*(C)*	*24.*	*(C)*
5.	*(C)*	*15.*	*(A)*	*25.*	*(C)*
6.	*(A)*	*16.*	*(A)*	*26.*	*(C)*
7.	*(C)*	*17.*	*(D)*	*27.*	*(C)*
8.	*(D)*	*18.*	*(C)*	*28.*	*(D)*
9.	*(C)*	*19.*	*(A)*	*29.*	*(B)*
10.	*(A)*	*20.*	*(D)*	*30.*	*(D).*

CTET-2012

Held on: 28th November, 2012

Paper-1

1. Learning disabilities are generally found

A. In specially those children whose parental relatives have such problems

B. In children with average to superior I.Q.

C. More often in boys as compared to girls

D. More often in children belonging to rural areas as compared to urban areas

2. A child cannot distinguish between 'saw' an 'was', 'nuclear' and 'unclear'. He/she is suffering from

A. Dysmorphemia B. Dyslexia

C. Word jumbling disorder D. Dyslexemia

3. In the Information Processing Model of thinking, the following steps are said to take place:

1. Response execution 2. Response selection
3. Pre-processing 4. Categorization

The correct sequence of these steps is

A. 4, 3, 2, 1 B. 3, 4, 2, 1

C. 2, 4, 3, 1 D. 3, 1, 4, 2

4. Gifted students are

A. Independent in their judgments

B. Independent of teachers

C. Introvert in nature

D. Non-assertive of their needs

5. Partial reinforcement

A. Is more effective than continuous reinforcement

B. Is less effective than continuous reinforcemen

C. Cannot be applied in actual classrooms

D. Works best in training animals

6. Orthopedically impaired children are likely to have

A. Dysgraphia B. Dysthymia

C. Dyscalculia D. Dyslexia

7. Adolescents may experience

A. Feeling of sanitation about life

B. Anxiety and concern about themselves

C. Feeling of fear about sins committed in childhood

D. Feeling of self-actualization

8. Which of the following is an example of a fine motor skill?

A. Hopping B. Running

C. Writing D. Climbing

9. Vygotsky theory implies

A. Collaborative problem solving

B. Individual assignment to each student

C. After initial explanation, do not support a child in solving difficult questions

D. Child will learn best in the company of children having IQ lesser than his/her

10. Smallest unit of meaning in a language is

A. Syntax B. Morpheme

C. Phoneme D. Pragmatics

11. A child of 16 years scores 75 in an IQ test; his mental age will be .... years.

A. 8 B. 14

C. 15 D. 12

12. IQ scores are generally .... correlated with academic performance.

A. Perfectly B. Highly

C. Moderately D. Least

13. Which of the following optimizes motivation to learn?

A. Extrinsic factor

B. Motivation to avoid failure

C. Tendency to choose very easy or difficult

D. Personal satisfaction in meeting targets

14. Theory of multiple intelligences implies the following except

A. Disciplines should be presented in numbers of ways

B. Learning could be accessed through a variety of means

C. Emotional intelligence is not related to IQ

D. Intelligence is a distinct set of processing operations used by an individual to solve problems

15. One of the identical twin brothers is adopted by a socio-economically rich family and the other by a poor family. After one year, which one of the following may be most likely observed about their IQ scores?

A. The boy with rich socio-economic family will score greater than the boy with poor family

B. Both of them will score equally

C. The boy with poor family will score greater than the boy with rich socio-economic family

D. Socio-economic level does not affect the IQ score

16. Assessment for learning takes into account the following except

A. Learning styles of students B. Strength of students
C. Needs of students D. Mistakes of students

17. An empowering school will promote which of the following qualities the most in its teacher?

A. Memory B. Disciplined nature
C. Competitive attitude D. Tendency to experiment

18. Monika, a math teacher, asks Radhika a question. On not getting any answer from Radhika, she quickly moves on and asks Mohan another question. She rewards her question after realizing that Mohan is struggling to find the answer. This tendency of Monika reflects that she is

A. Trying to put Radhika in an embarrassing situation
B. Well aware of the fact that Radhika is not capable of answering questions
C. Slightly moves about her question
D. Supporting gender stereotype of roles by favoring Mohan

19. The best way to avoid gender discrimination in a school may be

A. Metacognition of their gender-biased behavior by teachers
B. Selection of more boys than girls for a music competition
C. Formation of a rule to shun gender discrimination in the school and enforce it strictly
D. Recruitment of equal number of male and female teachers

20. Which of the following would be most suitable for encouraging deprived children of a regular presence in school?

A. Paying Rs. 5 per day to attract children
B. Opening residential schools
C. Not allowing children to attend school may be made a legally punishable offence
D. A child collector employed by the school, must bring children from homes everyday

21. Successful inclusion requires the following except

A. Capacity building B. Sensitization
C. Segregation D. Involvement of parents

22. The up-scaling of performance in the scholastic areas on the basis of performance on co-scholastic areas can be justified as

A. It ensures universal retention

B. It develop respect for manual labor
C. It caters to individual differences
D. It follows the policy of compensatory discrimination for the marginalized students

23. While selecting material for the portfolio of student's .... of .... should be there.

A. Exclusion; students
B. Inclusion; other teachers
C. Inclusion; students
D. Inclusion; parents

24. Of the following, the greatest advantage of interdisciplinary instruction is that

A. Students are less likely to develop a dislike for particular topics of different subjects areas
B. Teachers are permitted greater flexibility in planning lessons and activities
C. Students are given opportunities to generalize and apply newly learned knowledge in multiple contexts
D. Teachers are less likely to feel overwhelmed by the multiplicity of topics needed to be addressed in a traditional curriculum

25. A teacher can make problem-solving fun for students by doing all the following except

A. Giving time for free play
B. Providing endless opportunities for creative thinking
C. Expecting perfection from the students while they are trying to do things by themselves
D. Providing open ended material

26. Learners who demonstrate an earnest desire for increased knowledge and academic competence are said to have a

A. Mastery orientation
B. Performance- approach orientation
C. Performance- avoidance orientation
D. Work- avoidance orientation

27. In order to instill a positive environment in a primary class, a teacher should

A. Wish each child in the morning
B. Not discriminate and set the same goal for every child C. Allow them to make groups on their own on the basis of sociometry during group activities
D. Narrate stories with positive endings

28. Which would be the first theme to start with a nursery class?

A. Neighborhood
B. School

C. Family D. Best friend

29. Which of the following is true in relation to errors made by children?

A. Errors can be corrected by children themselves, therefore a teacher should not immediately correct them

B. If a teacher is not able to correct all errors in the classroom it indicates that the system of teacher education has failed

C. A teacher should not notice every error otherwise syllabus will not be covered

D. Correcting every error would take too much time and be tiresome for a teacher

30. Which of the following characteristic is the hallmark of the problem-solving approach?

A. There is an implicit hint given in the problem statement

B. The problem is original

C. There is usually one approach for getting the right answer

D. The problem is based on only one principle/topic

My Notes

Answer Key

1.	*(A)*	*11.*	*(D)*	*21.*	*(C)*
2.	*(B)*	*12.*	*(B)*	*22.*	*(C)*
3.	*(B)*	*13.*	*(D)*	*23.*	*(C)*
4.	*(A)*	*14.*	*(C)*	*24.*	*(C)*
5.	*(A)*	*15.*	*(D)*	*25.*	*(C)*
6.	*(A)*	*16.*	*(D)*	*26.*	*(A)*
7.	*(B)*	*17.*	*(D)*	*27.*	*(B)*
8.	*(C)*	*18.*	*(D)*	*28.*	*(C)*
9.	*(A)*	*19.*	*(A)*	*29.*	*(A)*
10.	*(B)*	*20.*	*(B)*	*30.*	*(A).*

CTET-2012

Held on: 28th November, 2012

Paper-2

1. **Child-centered education was advocated by which of the following thinkers?**
   A. B. F. Skinner　　B. John dewey
   C. Eric Erikson　　D. Charles Darwin
2. **While teaching a single parent-child, a teacher should**
   A. Treat such a child differently
   B. Assign lesser home assignments to such a child
   C. Providc stable and consistent environment
   D. Overlook this fact and treat such a child at per with other children
3. **Acceleration with reference to gifted children means**
   A. Accelerating the transaction of scholastic activities
   B. Speeding up the transaction of co-scholastic activities
   C. Promoting such students to next higher grade by skipping the present grade
   D. Accelerating the process of assessment
4. **Which of the following is the most appropriate activity for gifted students?**
   A. Solve exercise given at the end of five chapters at one go
   B. Teach their class on teachers day
   C. Write a report on a school match recently held
   D. Write a original play on given concepts
5. **Which one of the following could be an end stage of a child possessing bodily-kinesthetic intelligence?**
   A. Orator　　B. Political leader
   C. Surgeon　　D. Poet
6. **Gifted students**
   A. Are generally physically weak and not good at social interactions
   B. Generally do not like their teachers
   C. Realize their full potential without any help
   D. Perform exceptionally well in any field important to human beings
7. **Knowledge of .... will be most significant for a teacher dealing with a class comprising students of mixed age groups**
   A. Cultural background
   B. Developmental stages
   C. Occupation of their parents
   D. Socio-economic background
8. **Classroom after the implementation of RTE Act 2009 are**
   A. Age-wise more homogeneous
   B. Age-wise more heterogeneous

C. Unaffected, as RTE does not affect the average age of a class in a school
D. Gender-wise more homogeneous

9. Systematic presentation of concepts may be related with which of the following principles of development?
A. Students develop at different rates
B. Development is relatively ordered
C. Development leads to growth
D. Development proceeds from heteronomy to autonomy

10. Scaffolding in the context of learning theories refers to
A. Simulation teaching
B. Recapitulation of previous learning
C. Temporary support in learning by adults
D. Ascertaining the cause of mistakes done by students

11. The sentence 'Madam drives a bicycle' is
A. Correct syntactically but semantically incorrect
B. Correct semantically but syntactically incorrect
C. Semantically as well as syntactically correct
D. Semantically as well as syntactically incorrect

12. Classification of students in different groups on the basis of their IQ tends to .... their self-esteem and .... academic performance.
A. Increase; decrease B. Increase; increase
C. Decrease; decrease D. Decrease; has no effect on

13. Raven's progressive matrices are examples of .... test.
A. Verbal IQ B. Culture free IQ
C. Non-Group IQ D. Personality

14. The news of 'a woman selling her child to obtain food'may be understood best on the basis of
A. Psychoanalytical theory B. Theory of hierarchical needs
C. Psychosocial theory
D. Theory of reinforced contingencies

15. The word 'Comprehensive' in the scheme of CCE is supported by following, except
A. Theory of multiple intelligence
B. Theory of information processing
C. J. P Guilford theory of structure of intellect
D. L. L. Thurstone's theory of primary mental abilities

16. Assessment ....learning influences learning by reinforcing

the between assessment and instruction.

A. For; connections B. For; difference

C. Of; difference D. Of; variance

17. In science practical, boy generally takes control of apparatus and asks girls to record data or wash utensils. This tendency reflects that

A. Girls being delicate prefer such less energy consuming tasks

B. Girls are excellent observers and record data

C. Stereotyping of masculine and feminine roles takes place in schools also

D. Boys can handle equipments more efficiently as they are naturally endowed for doing such things

18. How teachers and students .... gender in the classroom, it .... the learning environment.

A. Interpret; does not affect B. Construct; impacts

C. Adapt; perturbs D. Define; vitiates

19. The word 'Compulsory' in the 'Right to Free and Compulsory Education 2009' means

A. Parents are compulsory forced to send their children to school to avoid punitive action

B. Compulsory education will be imparted through continuous testing

C. Central Government will ensure admission, attendance and completion of elementary education

D. Appropriate governments will ensure admission, attendance and completion of elementary education

20. Which of the following principles is not involved in lesson planning?

A. Clarity of objectives B. Knowledge of teaching

C. Rigidity of planning D. Knowledge of pupils

21. What does self-regulation of learners mean?

A. Self-discipline and control

B. Ability to monitor their own learning

C. Rules and regulations made by the student body

D. Creating regulations for students behavior

22. The 'Lab schools' advocated by John Dewey were examples of

A. Factory schools B. Progressive schools

C. Public schools D. Common schools

23. Group project activity as prescribed by CBSE is a powerful means

A. Of facilitating social participation

B. Of alleviating the burden of teachers

C. Of relieving the stress caused due to routine teaching

D. To promote the concept of unity I diversity

24. For intrinsically motivated students

A. Rewards are not at all required

B. External rewards are not enough to keep him/her motivated

C. The level of motivation is lower than an extrinsically motivated student

D. There is no need for formal education

25. Achievement motivation is

A. The tendency to persist at challenging tasks

B. The tendency to avoid failure

C. Willingness to accept success and failure equally

D. Tendency to act impulsively

26. Ideal 'Waiting time' for getting response from students should be proportional to

A. Time allotted to specific topic in the curriculum

B. Difficulty level of the question

C. Time taken by the students for answering questions from previous lessons

D. Relevance of the question in the real life

27. Suppose you are the chairperson of a Board of School Education, how would you plan to improve the overall quality of education in the schools under your jurisdiction? This type of question is an example of

A. Higher order convergent B. Higher order divergent

C. Lower order convergent D. Lower order divergent

28. Which one of the following is the best technique of teaching at the primary stage?

A. Game teaching B. Practical training

C. Self-learning D. Black board and chalk training

29. Children in primary schools follow which of the following stages as proposed by Lawrence Kohlberg?

a. Obedience and punishment orientation

b. Individualism and exchange

c. Good interpersonal relations

d. Social contract and individual rights

A. a and d B. a and c

C. b and a D. b and d

30. the following are features of anecdotal record, except

A. it is an accurate description of events

B. it describes personal development or social interactions of a child

C. it is a factual report with enough detail

D. it is subjective evidence of behavior and therefore does not provide feedback for scholastic area

My Notes

Answer Key

1.	*(B)*	*11.*	*(B)*	*21.*	*(A)*
2.	*(D)*	*12.*	*(C)*	*22.*	*(B)*
3.	*(C)*	*13.*	*(B)*	*23.*	*(A)*
4.	*(D)*	*14.*	*(B)*	*24.*	*(B)*
5.	*(C)*	*15.*	*(B)*	*25.*	*(A)*
6.	*(D)*	*16.*	*(A)*	*26.*	*(B)*
7.	*(B)*	*17.*	*(C)*	*27.*	*(B)*
8.	*(C)*	*18.*	*(D)*	*28.*	*(B)*
9.	*(D)*	*19.*	*(D)*	*29.*	*(B)*
10.	*(C)*	*20.*	*(C)*	*30.*	*(D)*

CTET-2013

Held on: 28th July, 2013

Paper-1

1. The following three aspects of intelligence are dealt by Sternberg's triarchic theory except

A. Componential B. Social
C. Experimental D. Contextual

2. Howard Gardner's theory of multiple intelligences emphasizes

A. General intelligence
B. Common abilities required in school
C. The unique abilities of each individual
D. Conditioning skills in students

3. The sound th, ph, ch are

A. Morpheme B. Grapheme
C. Lexeme D. Phoneme

4. In order to avoid gender stereotyping in class, a teacher should

A. Try to put both boys and girls in nontraditional roles
B. Appreciate student's good work by saying 'good girl' or 'good boy'
C. Discouraging girl from taking part in wrestling
D. Encourage boys to take risk and be bold

5. School should cater to individual differences to

A. Narrow the gap between individual students
B. Even out abilities and performance of students
C. Make individual students feel exclusive
D. Understand why students are able or unable to learn

6. What kind of support can a school provide to address the individual differences in students?

A. Follow a child-centered curriculum and provide multiple learning opportunities
B. Apply every possible measure to remove the individual differences in students
C. Refer slow learners to special schools
D. Follow same level of curriculum for all students

7. CCE emphasizes

A. Continuous testing on a comprehensive scale to ensure learning
B. How learning can be observed, recorded and improved upon
C. Fine-tuning of tests with the teaching
D. Redundancy of the board examination

8. School Based Assessment

A. Dilute the accountability of Boards of Education
B. Hinders achieving Universal National Standards
C. Help all students learn more through diagnosis

D. Makes students and teachers non serious and usual

9. "Reading of Learning" refers to

A. General ability level of students

B. Present cognitive level of students in the learningcontinuum

C. Satisfying nature of the act of learning

D. Thorndike's law of readiness

10. A teacher has some physically challenged children in her class. Which of the following would be appropriate for her to say?

A. Wheel-chaired bound children may take help of their peers in going to hall

B. Physically inconvenienced children may do an alternate activity in the classroom

C. Mohan why don't you use your crutches to go to the playground

D. Polio affected children will now present ass song

11. Learning disabilities may occur due to all of the following except

A. Cerebral dysfunction B. Emotional disturbance

C. Behavioral disturbance D. Cultural factors

12. An inclusive school

A. Committed to improve the learning outcomes of all students irrespective of their capabilities

B. Differentiate between students and sets less challenging achievement targets for specially abled students

C. Committed particularly to improve the learning outcomes of specially abled students

D. Decides learning needs of the students according to their disability

13. Gifted students

A. Need support not ordinarily provided by the school

B. Can manage their studies without a teacher

C. Can be good models for other students

D. Cannot be learning disabled

14. Giftedness is due to

A. Genetic makeup B. Environmental motivation

C. Combination of A and B D. Psychosocial factors

15. Which of the following is appropriate for the environmental conducive to thinking and learning in children?

A. Passive listening for long periods of time

B. Home assignments given frequently

C. Individual tasks done by the learners

D. Allowing students to take some decisions about what to learn and how to learn

16. Learning disability in motor skills is called

A. Dyspraxia B. Dyscalculia

C. Dyslexia D. Dysphasia

17. Learning disability

A. Is a stable state B. Is a variable state

C. Need not impair functioning

D. Does not improve with appropriate input

18. The following are the steps in the process of problem solving except

A. Identification of a problem

B. Breaking down the problem into smaller parts

C. Explore possible strategies

D. Anticipate outcomes

19. A teacher should

A. Treat errors committed by students as blunders and take serious note of each error

B. Measure success as the number of times students avoid making mistakes

C. Not correct students while they are trying to communicate ideas

D. Focus more on lecturing and provide a foundation for knowledge

20. Seema is desperate to score A+ grade in an examination. As she enters the examination hall and the examination begins, she becomes extremely nervous. Her feet go cold, her heart starts pounding and she is unable to answer properly. The primary reason for this is that

A. She may not be very confident about her preparation

B. She may be thinking excessively about the result of the examination

C. Invigilator teacher on duty may be her class teacher and she is of very strict nature

D. She may not be able to deal with sudden emotional outburst

21. Which of the following cognitive verbs are used to analyze the information given?

A. Identity B. Differentiate

C. Classify D. Describe

22. Rajesh is a voracious reader. Apart from studying his course books, he often goes to library and read diverse topics. Rajesh does his project even in the lunch break. He does not need prompting by his teachers or parents to study for tests and

seems to truly enjoy learning. He can be best described as an

A. Fact-centered learner
B. Teacher-centered learner
C. Assessment-centered learner
D. Intrinsically motivated learner

23. Children in pre-primary get satisfaction from being allowed to discover. They become distressed, when they are discouraged. They do so due to their motivation to

A. Reduce their ignorance B. Affiliate with the class
C. Create disorder in the class D. Exercise their power

24. Understanding human growth and development enables a teacher to

A. Gain control of learners' emotions while teaching
B. Be clear about teaching diverse learners
C. Tell students how they can improve their lives
D. Practice her teaching in an unbiased way

25. Which one of the following is true?

A. Development and learning are unaffected by socio-cultural contexts
B. Students learn only in a certain way
C. Play is significant for cognition and social competence
D. Questioning by teacher constrains cognitive development

26. Which one of the following is true about the role of heredity and environment in the development of a child?

A. The relative contributions of peers and genes are not additive
B. Heredity and environment do not operate together
C. Propensity is related to environment while actual development requires heredity
D. Both heredity and environment contribute 50% each in the development of a child

27. Socialization is

A. Rapport between teacher and taught
B. Process of modernization of society
C. Adaptation of social norms
D. Change in social norms

28. A PT teacher wants her students to improve fielding in the game of cricket. Which one of the following strategies will best help his students achieve that goal?

A. Tell students how important it is for them to learn to field

B. Explain the logic behind good fielding and rate of success
C. Demonstrate fielding while students observe
D. Give students a lot of practice in fielding

29. A teacher wishes to help her students to appreciate multiple views of a situation. She provides her students multiple opportunities to debate in this situation in different groups. According to Vygotsky's perspective, her students will ___ various view and develop multiple perspectives of the situation on their own

A. Internalize B. Construct
C. Operationlize D. Rationalize

30. Sita has learned to eat rice and dal with her hand. When she is given dal and rice, she mixes rice and dal and starts eating. She has .... eating rice and dal into her scheme for doing things.

A. Accommodated B. Assimilated
C. Appropriated D. Initiated

My Notes

Answer Key

1.	*(B)*	*11.*	*(D)*	*21.*	*(B)*
2.	*(C)*	*12.*	*(A)*	*22.*	*(D)*
3.	*(D)*	*13.*	*(A)*	*23.*	*(A)*
4.	*(A)*	*14.*	*(C)*	*24.*	*(B)*
5.	*(D)*	*15.*	*(D)*	*25.*	*(C)*
6.	*(A)*	*16.*	*(A)*	*26.*	*(A)*
7.	*(B)*	*17.*	*(B)*	*27.*	*(C)*
8.	*(C)*	*18.*	*(B)*	*28.*	*(D)*
9.	*(B)*	*19.*	*(C)*	*29.*	*(A)*
10.	*(C)*	*20.*	*(D)*	*30.*	*(B)*

CTET-2013

Held on: 28th July, 2013

Paper-2

1. **Which one of the following is a critique of theory of multiple intelligences?**
   A. Multiple intelligence are only the 'talents' present in intelligence as a whole
   B. Multiple intelligence provides students to discover their opportunities
   C. It over emphasizes practical intelligence
   D. It cannot be supported by empirical evidence at all

2. **Which one of the following pair is least likely to be a correct match**
   A. Children enter in - Chomsky the world with certain knowledge about language
   B. Language and - Vygotsky thought are initially two different activities
   C. Language is - Piaget contingent on thought
   D. Language is a - B. F. Skinner stimuli in environment

3. **Feature assigned due to social roles and not due to biological endowment are called**
   A. Gender role attitudes B. Gender role strain
   C. Gender-role stereotype D. Gender-role diagnosticity

4. **Which of the following will be most appropriate to maximize learning?**
   A. Teacher should identify her cognitive style as well as her student's cognitive style
   B. Individual differences in students should be smoothened by pairing similar students
   C. Teacher should focus on only one learning style to bring optimum result
   D. Students of similar cultural background should be kept in the same class to avoid difference in opinion

5. **All of the following promote assessment as learning except**
   A. Telling students to take internal feedback
   B. Generating a safe environment for students to take chances
   C. Tell students to reflect in the topic taught
   D. Testing students as frequently as possible

6. **When a cook taste a food during cooking it may be a kin to**
   A. Assessment of learning B. Assessment for learning
   C. Assessment as learning D. Assessment and learning

7. **Differentiated instruction is**

A. Using a variety of groupings to meet students needs
B. Doing something different for every students in the class
C. Disorderly or undisciplined student activity
D. Using groups that never change

8. In a culturally and linguistically diverse classroom, before deciding whether a student comes under special education category, a teacher should

A. Not involve parents as parents have their own work
B. Evaluate students on her/his mother language to establish disability
C. Segregate the child to neutralize environmental factors
D. Use specified psychologists

9. Learning disabilities may occur due to all of the following except

A. Teacher way of teaching
B. Prenatal use of alcohol
C. Mental retardation
D. Meningitis during infancy

10. An inclusive school reflects on all the following questions except

A. Do we believe that all students can learn
B. Do, we work in teams to plan and deliver learning enabling environment
C. Do we properly segregate special children from normal to provide better care
D. Do we adopt strategies catering for the diverse needs of students

11. Gifted students are

A. Convergent thinkers
B. Divergent thinkers
C. Extrovert
D. Very difficult working

12. The shaded area represents students in a normal distribution who fall

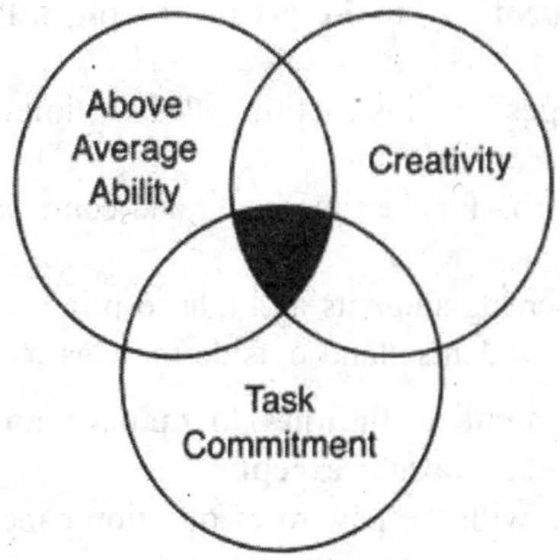

A. At $\sigma = 0$
B. Between $2\sigma - 3\sigma$

C. After 3 σ D. Between a – 2 σ

13. Which one of the following pair would be most appropriate choice to compute the following sentence? Children .... faster when they are involved in the activities that seems to be

A. Forget; useful in a classroom

B. Recall; linked with their class work only

C. Memorize; culturally neutral

D. Learn; useful in real life

14. CBSE prescribed group activities for students in place of activities for individual students. The idea behind doing so could be

A. To overcome the negative emotional response to individual competition which may generalize across learning

B. To make it easy for teachers to observe groups instead of individual students

C. To rationalize the time available with schools most of which do not have enough time for individual activities

D. To reduce the infrastructural cost of the activity

15. The conclusion that 'Children can learn violent behavior depicted in movies' may be derived on the basis of the following psychologist?

A. Edward L. Thorndike B. J. B. Watson

C. Albert Bandura D. Jean Piaget

16. Students observe fashion and try to imitate models. This kind of imitation may be called

A. Primary simulation B. Secondary simulation

C. Social learning D. Generalization

17. If students repeatedly make errors during a lesson, a teacher should

A. Make changes in instruction, tasks, timetable or seating arrangements

B. Leave the lesson for the time being and come back to after some times

C. Identify the erring students and talk to principal about them

D. Make erring students stand outside the classroom

18. Following are some techniques to manage anxiety due to an approaching examination, except

A. Familiarizing with the pattern of question paper

B. Thinking too much about the result

C. Seeking support
D. Emphasizing strengths

19. Bloom's taxonomy is a hierarchical organization of .

A. Achievement goals
B. Curricular declarations
C. Reading skills
D. Cognitive objectives

20. A, B and C, are three students studying English. 'A' finds it interesting and thinks it will be helpful for her in future. 'B' studies English as she wants to secure first rank in the class. 'C' studies it as she is primarily concerned to secure passing grades. The goals of A, B and C respectively are

A. Mastery, performance, performance avoidance
B. Performance, performance avoidance, mastery
C. Performance avoidance, mastery, performance
D. Mastery, performance avoidance, performance

21. Even though this was clearly in violation of his safety needs, Captain Vikarm Batra died fighting in the Kargilwar while protecting his country. He might have

A. Sought novel experience
B. Achieved self-actualization
C. Ignored his belongingness need
D. Wanted to earn a good name to his family

22. Extinction of a response is more difficult following

A. Partial reinforcement
B. Continuous reinforcement
C. Punishment
D. Verbal reproach

23. Mastery orientation can be encouraged by

A. Focusing on students' individual effort
B. Comparing students' successes with each other
C. Assigning lot of practice material as home assignments
D. Taking unexpected tests

24. Which one of the following is correctly matched?

A. Physical - environment development
B. Cognitive - maturation development
C. Social - environment development
D. Moral - maturation development

25. All the following facts indicate that a child is emotionally and socially fit in a class, except

A. Develop good relationships with peers
B. Concentrate on and persist with challenging tasks
C. Manage both anger and joy effectively

D. Concentrate persistently on competition with peers

26. Which of the following statements support role of environment in the development of a child?

A. Some students quickly process information while others in the same class do not

B. There has been a steady increase in students' average performance on IQ tests in last few decades

C. Correlation between IQs of identical twins raised in different homes is as high as 0.75

D. Physically fit children are often found to be morally good

27. Socialization includes cultural transmission and

A. Discourages rebellion

B. Development of individual personality

C. Fits children into labels

D. Provide emotional support

28. A teacher shows two identical glasses filled with equal amount of juice in them. She empties them in two different glasses one of which is taller and the other one is wider. She asks her class to identify which glass would have more juice in it. Students reply that the taller glass has more juice. Her students have difficulty in dealing with

A. Accommodation

B. Egocentrism

C. Decentring

D. Reversibility

29. Karnail Singh does not pay income tax despite legal procedures and expenses. He thinks that he cannot support a corrupt government which expends million of rupees in building unnecessary dams. He is probably in which state of Kohlberg's stages of moral development

A. Conventional

B. Post conventional

C. Pre conventional

D. Para conventional

30. Intelligence theory incorporates the mental processes involved in intelligence (i.e. metacomponents) and the varied forms of that intelligence can take (i.e. creative intelligence)

A. Spearman's 'g' factor

B. Sternberg's triarchic theory of intelligence

C. Savant theory of intelligence

D. Savant theory of motivation

My Notes

Answer Key

1.	*(A)*	*11.*	*(B)*	*21.*	*(B)*
2.	*(D)*	*12.*	*(C)*	*22.*	*(A)*
3.	*(C)*	*13.*	*(D)*	*23.*	*(A)*
4.	*(A)*	*14.*	*(A)*	*24.*	*(C)*
5.	*(D)*	*15.*	*(C)*	*25.*	*(D)*
6.	*(B)*	*16.*	*(C)*	*26.*	*(B)*
7.	*(A)*	*17.*	*(A)*	*27.*	*(B)*
8.	*(B)*	*18.*	*(B)*	*28.*	*(C)*
9.	*(A)*	*19.*	*(D)*	*29.*	*(B)*
10.	*(C)*	*20.*	*(A)*	*30.*	*(B)*

CTET-2014

Held on: 16th February, 2014

Paper-1

1. In the perspective model of education as implemented by CBSE, socialization of children is done in such a way so as to expect them to

A. Give up time- consuming social habits and learn how to score good grades

B. Be an active participant in the group work and learn social skills

C. Prepare themselves to conform to the rules and regulations of society without questioning

D. Accept what they are offered by the school irrespective of their social background

2. Which one of the following is based in Vygotsy's socio-cultural theory?

A. Operant conditioning

B. Reciprocal teaching

C. Culture-neutral cognitive development

D. Insight learning

3. A teacher says to her class, "As individual assignment is designed to help individual students more effectively, all students should complete assignment prescribed without any assistance. She is referring to which of the following stages of Kohlberg's moral development?

A. Conventional stage 4- law and order

B. Post-conventional stage 5- social contract

C. Pre-conventional stage 1- punishment avoidance

D. Pre-conventional stage 2- individualism and exchange

4. Fourteen year old Devika is attempting to develop a sense of herself as a separate, selfgoverning individual. She is developing

A. Hatred for rule B. Autonomy

C. Teenage arrogance D. Maturity

5. In context of progressive education which of the following statement is true according to John Dewey?

A. There should not be a place for democracy in a classroom

B. Student should be able to solve social problem themselves

C. Curiosity does, not belong to the inherent nature of students rather it is to be cultivated

D. Students should be observed and not heard in the classroom

6. A disorder to language comprehension is

A. Apraxia B. Dyslexia

C. Aspeechxia D. Aphasia

7. **Following are the critical views about the 'Theory of Multiple Intelligence', except**
   A. It is not research based
   B. Different intelligences demand different methods for different students
   C. Gifted students usually excel in a single domain
   D. It lack of empirical support

8. **'Theory of Multiple Intelligence' cannot be legitimized as it**
   A. Is not possible to measure different intelligences as there are no specific tests
   B. Does not place equal importance on all seven intelligences
   C. Is based only on sound empirical studies done by Abraham Maslow throughout his life
   D. Is not compatible with general intelligence 'g', which is most important

9. **The individual differences of students in a classroom are**
   A. Disadvantaged as teacher need to control a diverse classroom
   B. Detriment as they lead to students- student
   C. Inexpedient as they reduce the speed of the curriculum transaction to the level of the slowest student
   D. Advantageous as they lead teacher to explore a wider pool of cognitive structures

10. **School- based assessment was introduced to**
   A. Decentralize the power of Boards of school
   B. Ensure the holistic development of all the students
   C. Motivate teachers to punctiliously record all the activities of the students for better interpretation of their Progress
   D. Encouraging schools to excel by co-meeting with the other schools in their area

11. **Which one of the following is not related to other options?**
   A. Organizing question-answer sessions
   B. Taking feedback from students on a topic
   C. Conducting quiz
   D. Modeling the skills of self- assessment

12. **Which of the following questions is correctly matched with its specified domain?**
   A. Could you group your students on the basis of their achievement in Mathematics? : Evaluating
   B. What was the turning point in the cricket match telecasted last night: creativity

C. Write down a new recipe to cook chicken by using herbs: application

D. Determine which of the given, measure would most likely lead to achieve best results: analyzing

13. Which one of the following is the most effective way toconvey students from disadvantaged sections that youexpect them to participate and succeed?

A. Articulate your confidence in their ability to succeed

B. Develop your own interest in the topics to be taught

C. Compare them with other children as frequently as possible to make them realize' their goal

D. Emphasize the point that you have high expectation of them

14. Following are the examples of developmental disorder except

A. Autism B. Cerebral palsy

C. Post-traumatic stress

D. Attention deficit hyperactivity disorder

15. Multiple pedagogical techniques assorted learning material, multiple assessment techniques and varying the complexity and nature of the context are associated with which of the following?

A. Universal design for learning B. Remedial teaching

C. Differentiated instruction D. Reciprocal teaching

16. Which of the following is true about gifted learners?

A. They make everyone else smarter and are essential for collaborative learning

B. They always lead others and assume extra responsibility in the classroom

C. They may achieve lower grades due to their heightened sensitivity

D. Their importance is primarily due to their brainpower

17. Inclusion in schools primarily focuses on

A. Making subtle provisions for special category children

B. Fulfilling the needs of children with disabilities

C. Meeting the need of the disabled child at the expense of entire class

D. Including the educational needs of illustrate parents in schools

18. The cause of learned helplessness in children is their

A. Acquired behavior that they will not succeed

B. Callous attitude towards classroom activities

C. Non-compliance with expectations of their parents

D. Moral decision for not taking up studies seriously

19. If a student is consistently getting lower grades in school, her parents can be advised to help her by

A. Working in close association with teacher

B. With holding mobile phones, movies, comics and extra time for play

C. Narrating her the hardships of life for those who do not possess proper education

D. Forcing her to work harder at home

20. Which of the following does not determine problem solving?

A. Insight
B. Mental set
C. Entrenchment
D. Fixation

21. A teacher is connecting a text to the previously learnt text and showing children how to summarize it. She is

A. Helping children to develop their own strategy to comprehend it

B. Insinuating that there is no need to go through the entire text

C. Reinforcing the importance of text from the assessment point of view

D. Encouraging children to mug it up as effectively as possible

22. What kind of error is common between a learner who is learning his mother tongue and the learner who learns the same language as a second language?

A. Overgeneralization
B. Simplification
C. Development
D. Hypercorrection

23. The stress affects performance in examinations. This fact reflects which of the following relationships?

A. Cognition - emotion
B. Stress - omission
C. Performance - anxiety
D. Cognition - completion

24. A teacher is trying to counsel a child who is not performing well following is most appropriate about counseling in schools?

A. It is about palliative measure for making people comfortable

B. It build self- confidence of people by letting them explore their own thoughts

C. It is about giving the best possible advice to students about their future career options

D. It can be done only by the professional experts

25. Which of the following would encourage the least a student who wants to become a highly creative theater artist?

A. Try to win state level competition that will ensure you scholarship

B. Develop empathetic, amicable and supportive relationships with your peer theater artists

C. Devote your time to those theatrical skills that you find most enjoyable

D. Read about the performance of the world's best theater artists and try to learn

26. Which of the following theorists would be the opinion that students study hard for their personal growth and development?

A. Bandura B. Maslow

C. Skinner D. Piaget

27. Which of the following factors supports learning in a classroom?

A. Increasing the number of tests to motivate children to learn

B. Supporting the autonomy of children by the teachers

C. Sticking to one particular method of instruction to maintain uniformity

D. Increasing the time interval of period from 40 minute to 50 minutes

28. Mature students

A. Believe that emotion has no place in their studies

B. Resolve easily all their conflicts with their intellect

C. Sometimes need emotional support in their studies

D. Do not get upset by studies in difficult situations

29. A child coming to pre-school for the first time cries profusely. After two years when the same child goes to the primary school for the first time, he does not express his tension by crying rather his shoulder and neck muscle become tense. This change in his behavior can be explained on the basis of the following principles?

A. Development proceeds in a sequential manner

B. Development is gradual

C. Development is different in different people

D. Development is characterized by differentiation and integration

30. Which of the following statement is true?

A. Genetic makeup impacts responsiveness of an individual to qualities of the environment

B. Adoptive children possess same IQ as their adoptive Siblings

C. Experience does not influence brain development

D. Intelligence remains unaffected by the schooling

My Notes

Answer Key

1.	*(B)*	*11.*	*(D)*	*21.*	*(A)*
2.	*(B)*	*12.*	*(D)*	*22.*	*(C)*
3.	*(A)*	*13.*	*(A)*	*23.*	*(A)*
4.	*(B)*	*14.*	*(C)*	*24.*	*(B)*
5.	*(B)*	*15.*	*(C)*	*25.*	*(A)*
6.	*(D)*	*16.*	*(C)*	*26.*	*(B)*
7.	*(C)*	*17.*	*(A)*	*27.*	*(B)*
8.	*(A)*	*18.*	*(A)*	*28.*	*(C)*
9.	*(D)*	*19.*	*(A)*	*29.*	*(D)*
10.	*(B)*	*20.*	*(A)*	*30.*	*(A)*

CTET-2014

Held on: 16th February, 2014

Paper-2

1. Which of the following figures correctly represents the development according to Piaget's developmental Theory

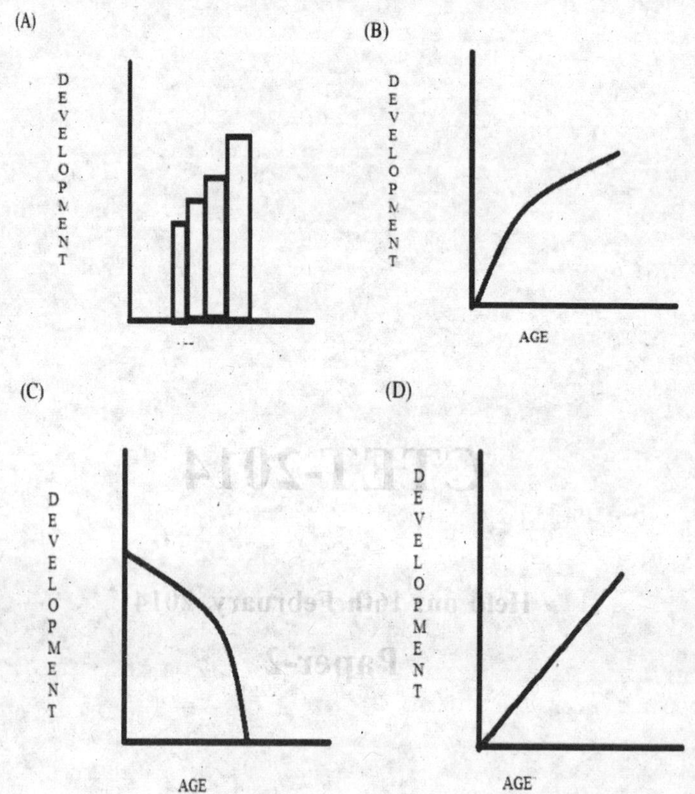

2. A teacher found that a student is facing difficulty in drawing a square. He/she assumes that this student would also find it difficult to draw a diamond. He/she applies which of the following principles to arrive at his/her assumption?

A. Development tends to follow an orderly sequence

B. Development is salutatory

C. Development is gradual

D. Development is different for different people

3. Which of the following statements is true regarding the role of heredity and environment in human development?

A. The role of environment is almost fixed, whereas the impact heredity can be altered

B. The theories based on the behaviorism are largely based on the role of nature in human development
C. The relative effects of heredity and environment vary indifferent areas of development
D. The policy of compensatory discrimination of the Government of India is based on the role of nature in human development

4. In the context of socialization, school often have a hidden curriculum which consists of
A. Forcible learning, thinking and behaving in particular ways by imitating peers and teachers
B. The informal cues about social roles presented in schools through interaction and materials
C. Negotiating and resisting socialization of students through their families
D. Teaching and assessment of values and attitudes

5. Which of the following implications cannot be derived from Piaget's theory of cognitive development?
A. Sensitivity to children's readiness to learn
B. Acceptance of individual differences
C. Discovery learning
D. Need of verbal teaching

6. Which of the following is a characteristic of Kohlberg's stages of moral development?
A. Variable sequence of stages
B. Stages are isolates response and not general pattern
C. Universal sequences of stages across all cultures
D. Stages proceed in a non-hierarchic manner

7. Teachers and students draw on one another's expertise while working on complex projects related to real-world problems in classroom.
A. Traditional B. Constructivist
C. Teacher-centric D. Social-constructivist

8. In the context of progressive education, the term 'equal educational opportunity' implies that all students should
A. Receive equal education irrespective of their caste, creed, color, religion and region
B. Be allowed to prove their capability after receiving an equal education
C. Be provided an education by using the same methods and materials without any distinction

D. Be provided an education which is most appropriate to them and their future life at work

9. In the context of language development, which of the following areas was underestimated by Piaget?

A. Heredity

B. Social interaction

C. Egocentric speech

D. Active construction by the child

10. The students of class V make too much of noise in Math class. The probable reason for this could be

A. That the teaching methodology of the teacher is not well

B. That the student of that class do not like the subject

C. That the student of that class do not pay attention

D. That the student of that class do not like that teacher

11. Which of the following observations supports Howard Gardner's theory of multiple intelligences?

A. Damage to one part of the brain affects only a particular ability sparing students

B. Intelligence is an interaction of analytical, creative and practical intelligences

C. Different intelligences are hierarchical in nature

D. Teacher should follow one specific theory of educational innovation at the time of designing instruction

12. Which of the following statements is true about ability and ability grouping?

A. Students learn better in homogeneous groups

B. For smooth and effective teaching class should be homogeneous

C. Children are intolerant and do not accept differences

D. Teacher may use multilevel teaching to cater to different ability groups

13. Which of the following statement is true?

A. The formative assessment can sometimes be, summative assessment and vice versa

B. The summative assessment implies that assessment is a continuous and integral part of learning

C. The major objective of the formative assessment is to grade the achievement of the students

D. The formative assessment summarizes the development of learners during a time interval

14. A teacher asks his/her students to draw a concept map to reflect their comprehension of a topic. He/she is

A. Jogging the memory of the students
B. Conducting formative assessment
C. Testing the ability of the students to summarize themain points
D. Typing to develop rubrics to evaluate the achievementof the students

15. Which of the following represents the domain's 'evaluating' in the Bloom's revised taxonomy?

A. Creating a graph or chart using the data
B. Judging the logical consistency of a solution
C. Evaluating the pertinence of the data provided
D. Formulating a new way for categorizing objects

16. Teachers must believe in which of the following values in the context of dealing with disadvantaged learners

A. Personal accountability for student's success
B. High expectations of appropriate behavior
C. For immediate compliance of students, use of being shocked and angry
D. No demands of any sort on the student

17. Stuttering problems in students can be dealt by applying which of the following methods?

A. Dictated speech
B. Prolonged speech
C. Pragmatic speech
D. Protracted speech

18. In the context of learning-disabled children, providing immediate connections, stressing collaboration and leveraging non-learning technologies such as instant messaging, intelligent search and content management are associated with which of the following design?

A. Embedded learning
B. Interventional learning
C. Reply to remediation
D. Universal design for learning

19. An inclusive classroom is that where

A. Assessments are repeated till the time every learner achieves minimum grades
B. Teachers teach from only prescribed books to lessen the burden of the students
C. There is an active involvement of children in solving as many problems as possible
D. Teachers create diverse and meaningful learning experiences for every learner

20. Which of the following is an appropriate assignment for a gifted student?

A. Many more exercises of the same type in comparison to other students

B. Asking him/her to tutor the peers to channelize the energy and keep him/her busy

C. Create a prototype of a new science book based on different scheme

D. Letting him/her finish the textbook on him/her own before the entire class

21. Many measures have been taken at institutional level to check the dropout cases in the schools run by government agencies. Which of the following is an institutional reason for children dropping out of these school?

A. There is a lack of infrastructure, such as blackboard

B. Teachers are not having appropriate qualifications and are paid lesser salaries

C. Teachers haven't seen sensitized about the need of treating children well

D. There is no alternative curriculum for children who rejects the compulsory curriculum offered

22. Learning disabilities are

A. Objective facts and culture has no role in determiningthem

B. Synonymous to Dyslexia

C. Also present in children with average or above average IQ

D. Not immutable irrespective of time and nature of interventions

23. Problem solving is more likely to succeed in schools where

A. A flexible curriculum is in place

B. Homogeneous groups of students are present in the classes

C. The emphasis is only on higher order academic achievement

D. Teacher-centric pedagogy is in effect

24. Cognitive apprenticeships and instructional conversations

A. Conceive learning as a social activity

B. Are based on application of inductive reasoning

C. Emphasize on systematic organization of textual material

D. Highlight the need of practice training to achieve efficiency

25. Which of the following should be a right way for a teacher who intends to correct errors of his/her students?

A. He/she must correct every error of his/her students even if it require late sitting in the school

B. He/she should correct less frequent errors more oftenthan high-frequent and generality errors
C. He/she should correct errors that interfere with the general meaning and understand ability
D. He/she should not correct errors if it irritates children

26. The following skills are involved in emotional intelligence, except
A. Awareness of emotions
B. Management of emotions
C. Criticism of emotions
D. Amicable relation with class fellows

27. While appearing in an assessment, Devika finds her arousal as energizing, whereas Rajesh finds his arousal as discouraging. Their emotional experiences are most likely to differ with respect to
A. The duration of time
B. The extremity of emotion
C. The level of adaptation
D. The intensity of thought

28. The Government of India has started Midday Meal Scheme for the elementary schools. Which of the following theories of motivation supports this scheme?
A. Behaviorist B. Socio-cultural
C. Cognitive D. Humanistic

29. Attaching importance to the home setting of students for understanding children's behavior and using this information for building effective pedagogy is related to which of the following theories of learning?
A. Behaviorist B. Ecological
C. Constructivist D. Social constructivist

30. Which of the following may be the best way to deal with an inattentive child in the classroom?
A. Nag the child as frequently in front of the class to make him/her realize
B. Make the child sit in the most distractionreduced area
C. Allow the child to stand while working so as to enable the child to focus attention
D. Provide the child frequent breaks to refresh his/her attention

My Notes

Answer Key

1.	*(A)*	*11.*	*(A)*	*21.*	*(A)*
2.	*(A)*	*12.*	*(D)*	*22.*	*(A)*
3.	*(C)*	*13.*	*(D)*	*23.*	*(D)*
4.	*(B)*	*14.*	*(B)*	*24.*	*(A)*
5.	*(B)*	*15.*	*(B)*	*25.*	*(C)*
6.	*(C)*	*16.*	*(A)*	*26.*	*(C)*
7.	*(D)*	*17.*	*(B)*	*27.*	*(B)*
8.	*(D)*	*18.*	*(B)*	*28.*	*(D)*
9.	*(B)*	*19.*	*(D)*	*29.*	*(C)*
10.	*(A)*	*20.*	*(C)*	*30.*	*(B)*

CTET-2014

Held on: 21st September, 2014

Paper-1

1. **Cognitive development is supported by**
   A. Conducting relevant and well- designed tests as frequently as possible
   B. Presenting activities that reinforce traditional methods
   C. Providing a rich and varied environment
   D. Focusing more on individual activities in comparison to collaboration

2. **Human development is**
   A. Quantitative
   B. Qualitative
   C. Immeasurable to a certain extent
   D. Both quantitative and qualitative

3. **The nature- nurture debate refers to**
   A. Genetics and environment B. Behavior and environment
   C. Environment and biology D. Environment and upbringing

4. **Which of the following is a positive agency of socialization?**
   A. Health club B. Family
   C. Eco club D. Public library

5. **In Vygotsky's theory, which aspect of development gets neglected?**
   A. Social B. Cultural
   C. Biological D. Linguistic

6. **Which of the following stages are involved when infants "THINK' with their eyes, ears and hands?**
   A. Concrete operational stage B. Pre-operational stage
   C. Sensory motor stage D. Formal operational stage

7. **Ria does not agree with Rishabh about setting up a class picnic. She thinks that the rules can be revised to suit the majority. This kind of peer disagreement according to Piaget refers to**
   A. Heteronomous normality B. Cognitive immaturity
   C. Reaction D. Morality of cooperation

8. **Which one of the following is a form of Sternberg's Triarchic Theory of Intelligence?**
   A. Practical intelligence B. Experimental intelligence
   C. Resourceful intelligence D. Mathematical intelligence

9. **Who developed the first intelligence test?**
   A. David Wechsler B. Alfred Binet
   C. Charles Edward Spearman D. Robert Sternberg

10. Phonological awareness refers to the ability to

A. Reflect and manipulate the sound structure

B. Speak fluently and accurately

C. Know, understand and write

D. Masters the rules of the grammar

11. Gender discrimination in a classroom

A. Does not affect the performance of the students

B. May lead to diminished effort or performance of the students

C. May lead to enhanced effort or performance of the male students

D. Is done more by the male teachers than their female counterpart

12. Which one of the following is an example of learning style?

A. Visual B. Accrual

C. Factual D. Tactual

13. A teacher collects and reads the work of the class, then plans and adjusts the next lesson to meet student needs. He/she is doing

A. Assessment of learning B. Assessment for learning

C. Assessment as learning D. Assessment at learning

14. Teachers who work under school based assessment

A. Are over burdened as they need to take frequent tests in addition to

Monday tests

B. Need to assign project work in each subject to individual students

C. Observe students minutely on a daily basis to assess their values and attitudes

D. Feel a sense of ownership for the system

15. "How do grades differ from marks?" this question belongs to which of the following classes of questions?

A. Divergent B. Analytic

C. Open- ended D. Problem solving

16. Girls students

A. Learn questioning on Mathematics will but face difficulty only when they are asked to reason them out

B. Are as good in Mathematics as boys of their age

C. Perform less competently in spatial concepts than boys of their age

D. Possess more linguistic and musical abilities

17. Difficulty in recalling sequence of letters in words and frequent loss of visual memory is associated with

A. Dyslexia B. Dyscalculia
C. Dysgraphia D. Dyspraxia

18. 'Education-of-all in schools-for-all' could be a tagline for which of the following?

A. Cohesive education B. Inclusive education
C. Cooperative education D. Exclusive education

19. Fluency, elaboration, originality and flexibility are the factors associated with

A. Giftedness B. Talent
C. Divergent thinking D. Acceleration

20. Gifted students may be asked to spend more time on questions dealing with

A. Remembering B. Understanding
C. Creating D. Analysis

21. Learning disabilities in Mathematics can be assessed most appropriately by which of the following tests?

A. Aptitude test B. Diagnostic test
C. Screening test D. Achievement test

22. Concept maps are most likely to increase understanding of new concepts by

A. Transferring knowledge between content areas
B. Focusing attention on specific detail
C. Prioritizing academic content for study
D. Increasing ability to organize information logically

23. According to the theory of social learning of Albert Bandura which one of the following is true?

A. Play is essential and should be given priority in school
B. Modeling is a principle way for children to learn
C. An unresolved crisis can harm a child
D. Cognitive development is independent of

24. Deductive reasoning involves

A. Reasoning from general to particular
B. Reasoning from particular to general
C. Active construction and reconstruction of knowledge
D. Methods including inquiry learning and heuristics

25. When children learn a concept and use it, practice helps in reducing the errors committed by them. This idea is given by

A. E. L. Thorndike B. Jean Piaget

C. J. B. Watson D. Lev Vygotsky

26. Which of the following skill is associated with emotional intelligence?

A. Memorizing B. Motor processing

C. Envisaging D. Empathizing

27. The inner force that stimulates and compels a behavioral response and provides specific direction tom that response is

A. Motive B. Perseverance

C. Emotion D. Commitment

28. Which term is often interchangeably used with the term motivation?

A. Incentive B. Emotion

C. Need D. Inspiration

29. .... motives deal with the need to reach satisfying feeling states and to obtain personal goals.

A. Effective B. Affective

C. Preservation- oriented D. Safety- oriented

30. Which one of the following is a factor that affects learning positively?

A. Fear of failure B. Competition with peers

C. Meaningful association D. Pressure from parents

My Notes

Answer Key

1.	*(C)*	*11.*	*(B)*	*21.*	*(B)*
2.	*(D)*	*12.*	*(A)*	*22.*	*(D)*
3.	*(A)*	*13.*	*(B)*	*23.*	*(B)*
4.	*(D)*	*14.*	*(D)*	*24.*	*(A)*
5.	*(C)*	*15.*	*(B)*	*25.*	*(A)*
6.	*(C)*	*16.*	*(B)*	*26.*	*(D)*
7.	*(D)*	*17.*	*(A)*	*27.*	*(A)*
8.	*(A)*	*18.*	*(B)*	*28.*	*(C)*
9.	*(B)*	*19.*	*(A)*	*29.*	*(B)*
10.	*(A)*	*20.*	*(C)*	*30.*	*(C)*

CTET-2014

Held on: 21st September, 2014

Paper-2

1. Development of teaching demands teachers to

A. Be strict disciplinary as children experiment quite frequently

B. Adapt instructional strategies based on the knowledge of developmental factors

C. Treat children in different developmental stages in an equitable manner

D. Provide learning that results in the development of only the cognitive domain

2. Learners cannot learn unless

A. They are taught according to the needs of social aims of education

B. They know that the material being taught will be tasted in the near future

C. They are prepared to learn

D. They are asked about their learning in schools by their parents at home on a daily basis

3. Theory of social learning emphasis on which of the following factors?

A. Nature B. Nurture

C. Adaptation D. Emendation

4. Psychosocial theory emphasizes on which of the following?

A. Stimuli and response

B. Phallic and latency stages

C. Industry Vs. inferiority stage

D. Operant conditioning

5. The fact that children require culturally relevant knowledge and skills is attributed to

A. Charles Darwin B. B. F. Skinner

C. Urie Bronfenbrenner D. Lev Vygotsky

6. As a teacher you firmly believe in saying no to ragging and bullying and put up posters and form committees in schools. The young adolescents who join you with strong beliefs, are at which of the following stage?

A. The conventional stage

B. The pre-conventional stage

C. The post- conventional stage

D. Social order maintaining leve

7. Progressive education is associated with which of the following statement?

A. Teachers are the originators of information and authority

B. Knowledge is generated through direct experience and collaboration

C. Learning proceeds in a straight way with factual gathering and skill mastery

D. Examination is non-referenced and external

8. Inc context of "theory of multiple intelligence", which one of the following intelligence is required for an air force pilot?

A. Interpersonal B. Linguistic

C. Kinesthetic D. Intrapersonal

9. The factor 'g' in the Spearman definition of intelligence stands for

A. Genetic intelligence B. Generative intelligence

C. General intelligence D. Global intelligence

10. Retrieving hidden objects is evidence that infants have begun to master which of the following cognitive functions?

A. International behavior B. Object- permanence

C. Problem- solving D. Experimentation

11. Which one of the following may be the criteria of gender in a society?

A. Comparison of number of male and female teachers in school

B. Equal number of distinctions achieved by boys and girls in class 12

C. Comparison of number of boys and girls who survive up to class 12

D. Whether the girl students are allowed to participate in competitions organized outside the school

12. He knowledge of individual differences help teachers in

A. Understanding the futility of working hard with backwards students as they can never b par with the class

B. Accepting and attributing the failure of students to their individual differences

C. Making their presentation style uniform to benefit all students equally

D. Assessing the individual needs of all students and teaching them accordingly

13. Assessment for learning

A. Fosters motivation

B. Is done for the purpose of segregation and ranking

C. Emphasis the overall importance of grades

D. Is an exclusive and a per se assessment activity

14. School based assessment

A. Focus on exam techniques rather than outcomes
B. Offer less control to the students over what will be assessed
C. Improve learning by providing a constructive feedback
D. Encourage teaching to the test as they involve frequent teaching

15. Students in a class are asked to assemble various arte facts of their works in a notebook, to demonstrate what they can do for their society. What kind of activity is this?

A. Essay type assessment B. Anecdotal records
C. Problem solving assessment D. Portfolio assessment

16. By placing students in the least restricted school environment, the school

A. Equalizes the educational opportunities for girls and disadvantaged group
B. Normalizes the lives of children from deprived group who were increasing the linkage of school with theparents and communities of these children
C. Gets disadvantaged children's involvement in activities such as science fair and quizzes
D. Sensitize other children not to bully or to put the disadvantaged children down

17. Reducing the time allotted to complete an assignment to make it coincide with time of attention and increasing this time in a phased manner will be best suited to deal with which of the following disorders?

A. Disruptive behavior disorder B. Dysphasia
C. Sensory integration disorder
D. Attention deficit hyperactivity disorder

18. Which one of the following approaches suggests integration of the child with the people around him with social institutions to deal with disruptive behavior disorder?

A. Psychodynamic B. Ecological
C. Biological D. Behavioral

19. Renzulli is known for his .... definition of giftedness.

A. Four-tiered B. Four level
C. Three circle D. Three sided

20. For gifted students

A. It is safe to consider aptitude as a skill
B. There is no need to monitor progress

C. The teacher should adapt as the student changes
D. The teacher should initiate and lead problem solving

21. Which one of the following is the most appropriate method to monitor the progress of children with learning disabilities?
A. Case study
B. Anecdotal records
C. Behavior rating scale
D. Structured behavioral observation

22. The best way to increase the chances of learning disabled students to lead to a full and productive life, is by
A. Focusing on weakness of such students
B. Maintaining a high expectation from such students
C. Teaching a variety of skills and strategies that can be applied across a range of contexts
D. Encouraging these children to define their own goals

23. According to soci- cultural theory of Vygotsky
A. Culture and language play a crucial role in development
B. The child thinks in different domains and does not take a complete perspective
C. Children think in abstract terms if presented abstract material at a lower stage
D. Self directed speech is the lowest stage of the scaffolding

24. To explain, predict, and/or control phenomena are the goals of
A. Traditional reasoning B. Inductive reasoning
C. Deductive reasoning D. The scientific method

25. A class VII student makes error in mathematics. As a teacher you should
A. Provide the student the correct answer
B. Allow the student to use calculator
C. Ask the students to use alternative method or redo it to find out errors on his/her own
D. Show the student where the errors were made and ask the student to redo it

26. Emotional intelligence may be associated with which domain of theory of multiple intelligence/
A. Interpersonal and intrapersonal intelligence
B. Naturalistic intelligence
C. Visual- spatial intelligence D. Existential intelligence

27. Which of the following facts has been least discussed in the psychology of emotion?

A. Emotion is a subjective feeling and varies from person to person
B. Emotions may not only occur within individual students, but also within the entire class
C. Emotions are a complex pattern of arousal and cognitive interpretation
D. Emotional process involves psychological as well as psychological reactions

28. Which of the following facts has been least discussed in the psychology of emotion?

A. Motive
B. Personality trait
C. Emotion
D. Perception

29. Which one of the following is properly sequenced in the context of motivation cycle?

A. Arousal, drive, need, achievement, goal-directed behavior, reduction of arousal
B. Drive, need, arousal, goal-directed behavior,achievement, reduction of arousal
C. Need, goal- directed behavior, drive, arousal, achievement, reduction of arousal
D. Need, drive, arousal, goal- directed behavior, achievement, reduction of arousal

30. Which one of the following is a process in the social observational learning theory of Bandura?

A. Reflection
B. Retention
C. Repetition
D. Recapitulation

My Notes

Answer Key

1.	*(B)*	*11.*	*(C)*	*21.*	*(D)*
2.	*(C)*	*12.*	*(D)*	*22.*	*(C)*
3.	*(B)*	*13.*	*(A)*	*23.*	*(A)*
4.	*(C)*	*14.*	*(C)*	*24.*	*(D)*
5.	*(D)*	*15.*	*(D)*	*25.*	*(C)*
6.	*(C)*	*16.*	*(D)*	*26.*	*(A)*
7.	*(B)*	*17.*	*(D)*	*27.*	*(B)*
8.	*(C)*	*18.*	*(B)*	*28.*	*(B)*
9.	*(C)*	*19.*	*(C)*	*29.*	*(D)*
10.	*(B)*	*20.*	*(C)*	*30.*	*(B)*

CTET-2015

Held on: 22nd February, 2015

Paper-1

1. Teachers, in order to help learners construct knowledge, need focus on

A. Scores/marks obtained by the learner
B. Involving the learner for active participation
C. Mastering learning of concepts by the learner
D. Making sure the learner memorizes everything

2. Giftedness from teacher's point of view is a

A. High Motivation- High Commitment- high Talent
B. High Ability- High Talent- High Commitment
C. High Talent- High Creativity- High Memory
D. High Ability- High Creativity- High Commitment

3. According to NCF-2005, errors are important because they

A. Provide a way to teachers to scold the children
B. Provide an insight into the child's thinking and help to identify solutions
C. Provide space for removing some children from the class
D. Are an important tool in classifying students into groups of 'passed' and 'failed'

4. A child's notebook shows error in writing like reverse images, mirror imaging etc. such a child is showing sign of

A. Learning disability B. Learning difficulty
C. Learning problem D. Learning disadvantage

5. Which one of the following is best suited for emotional development of children?

A. No involvement of the teachers as it is the task of the parents
B. Controlled classroom environment
C. Authoritarian classroom environment
D. Democratic classroom environment

6. Teachers need to create a good classroom environment to facilitate children's learning. To create such a learning environment, which one of the given statement is not true?

A. Compliance with teachers B. Acceptance of the child
C. Positive tone of the teacher D. Approval of the child's effort

7. Given below are statements about boys and girls. According to you, which one of these is true?

A. Boys should help in household chores
B. All boys should be taught since and girls, home science
C. Girls should help in household chores
D. Boys should help in activities outside the home

8. To be an effective teacher it is important to

A. Focus on individuals learning rather than group activity

B. Avoid disruption caused due to questioning by students

C. Be in touch with each and every child

D. Emphasize dictating answers from the textbook

9. Which one of the following is not a suitable formative assessment?

A. Project B. Observation

C. Ranking the students D. Open ended questions

10. Deficiency in the ability to write, associated with impaired handwriting, is a symptom of

A. Dyspraxia B. Dyscalculia

C. Dyslexia D. Dysgraphia

11. According to Piaget theory, which one out of the following will not influence one's cognitive development?

A. Social experience B. Maturation

C. Activity D. Language

12. Which of these does not imply practical intelligence in the Triarchic theory?

A. Thinking practically about oneself only

B. Choosing an environment in which you can succeed

C. Adapting to the environment

D. Reshaping the environment

13. "Anyone can become angry - that is easy, but to be angry with the right person, to the right degree, at right time, for the right purpose, at the right- way-that is not easy". This is related to

A. Social development B. Cognitive development

C. Physical development D. Emotional development

14. In learning, assessment is essential for

A. Screening test B. Motivation

C. Fostering of the purpose of segregation and ranking

D. Grades and marks

15. Fitting new knowledge into existing schemas is known as

A. Equilibrium B. Assimilation

C. Organization D. Accommodation

16. We all differ in terms of our intelligence, motivation, interest etc. this principle refers to

A. Theory of intelligence B. Heredity

C. Environment D. Individual difference

17. Students of disadvantaged groups should be taught along with the normal students. It implies

A. Special education B. Integrated education
C. Exclusive education D. Inclusive education

18. 'Out of the box' thinking is related to

A. Memory based thinking B. Divergent thinking
C. Convergent thinking D. Consistent thinking

19. The assessment of students can be used by teachers in teaching to develop insight into

A. Not promoting those students who do not meet school standards
B. Changing the teaching approach according to the learner's need
C. Identifying the students who need to be prompted to the higher class
D. Creating groups of bright and weak students in the class

20. Learning experiences should be planned in a manner so as to make learning meaningful. Which of the given learning experiences does not facilitate meaningful learning for the children

A. Formulating questions on content
B. Discussion and debate on the topic
C. Presentation on the topic
D. Repetition based on mere recall of content

21. Giving punishment, verbal or non- verbal to the children results in

A. Protecting the child's image B. Improving their scores
C. Damaging their self- concept D. Motivating them to work

22. A teacher labeled the head of a committee, as 'chairperson' instead of 'chairman'. It indicates that the teacher

A. Has a good command of language
B. Is using a gender free language
C. Has gender bias
D. Follows a more acceptable term

23. Continuous Comprehensive Evaluation is essential for

A. Diluting the accountability of the board of education
B. Correcting less- frequent errors more than more- frequent- errors
C. Understanding how learning can be observed, recorded and improved upon
D. Fine tuning of test with the teaching

24. In Lawrence Kohlberg's theory, which level signifies the absence of morality in true sense?

A. Level IV B. Level I
C. Level II D. Level III

25. Which one of the following is not correct for the progressive model of socialization of children?

A. Children accept what they are offered by the school irrespective of their social backgrounds
B. There should be a place for democracy in the classroom
C. Socialization is an adaptation of social norms
D. Active participation in the group work and learning social skills

26. The teacher noticed that Pushpa cannot solve a problem on her own. However she does so in the presence of adult or peer guidance. This guidance is called

A. Pre-operational thinking B. ZPD
C. Scaffolding D. Lateralization

27. Which one out of the following provides information about the roles and behaviors which are acceptable in a group, during early childhood period?

A. Teacher and peers B. Peers and parents
C. Parents and siblings D. Siblings and teachers

28. Which one of the following age group falls under later childhood category/

A. 18 to 24 years B. Birth to 6 years
C. 6 to 11 years D. 11 to 18 years

29. Aarnav says that language development is influenced by one's innate predisposition while Sonali feels that it is because of the environment. This discussion between Aarnav and Sonali is about

A. Stability and instability argument
B. Continuous and discontinuous learning
C. Nature and nurture debate
D. Critical and sensitive feeling

30. Making students members of a cleanliness community to motivate them for the same, reflects

A. Behaviorist approach to motivation
B. Humanistic approach to motivation
C. Cognitive approach to motivation
D. Socio-cultural approach to motivation

My Notes

Answer Key

1.	*(B)*	*11.*	*(A)*	*21.*	*(C)*
2.	*(D)*	*12.*	*(A)*	*22.*	*(B)*
3.	*(B)*	*13.*	*(D)*	*23.*	*(C)*
4.	*(A)*	*14.*	*(B)*	*24.*	*(B)*
5.	*(D)*	*15.*	*(B)*	*25.*	*(A)*
6.	*(A)*	*16.*	*(D)*	*26.*	*(C)*
7.	*(A)*	*17.*	*(D)*	*27.*	*(C)*
8.	*(C)*	*18.*	*(B)*	*28.*	*(C)*
9.	*(C)*	*19.*	*(B)*	*29.*	*(C)*
10.	*(D)*	*20.*	*(D)*	*30.*	*(D)*

CTET-2015

Held on: 22nd February, 2015

Paper-2

1. **Which one of the following statements best summarizes the relationship between development and learning as proposed by Vygotsky?**
   A. Development is independent of learning
   B. Development process lags behind the learning process
   C. Development is synonymous with learning
   D. Learning and development are parallel processes

2. **What is a major criticism of Kohlberg's theory?**
   A. Kohlberg proposed a theory without any empirical basis
   B. Kohlberg proposed that moral reasoning is developmental
   C. Kohlberg did not account for cultural differences in moral reasoning of man and women
   D. Kohlberg did not give clear cut stages of moral development

3. **In a learner- centered classroom, the teacher would**
   A. Encourage children to compete with each other for marks to facilitate learning
   B. Demonstrate what she expects her students to do and then give them guidelines to do the same
   C. Employ such method in which the learners are encouraged to take initiative for their own learning
   D. Use lecture method to explain key facts and then access the learners for their attentiveness

4. **According to Gardner's theory of multiple intelligence, the factor that would contribute most for being a 'self-aware' individual would be**
   A. Musical
   B. Spiritual
   C. Linguistic
   D. Intrapersonal

5. **A major difference between the perspectives of Vygotsky and Piaget pertains to be**
   A. Their critique of behaviorist principles
   B. The role of providing a nurturing environment to children
   C. Their views about language and thought
   D. Their conception of children a s active constructor of knowledge

6. **A lot of debate surrounds whether girls and boys have specific sets of abilities due to their genetic materials. Which one of the following are you most likely to agree with this context?**
   A. Girls are socialized to be caring while boys are discouraged to show emotions such as caring
   B. After puberty boys and girls cannot play with each other since their interests are complete opposite

C. All girls have inherent talent for arts while boys are genetically programmed to be better at aggressive sports

D. Boys cannot be caring since they are born in that way

7. A teacher wants to ensure that her students are motivated intrinsically. She would

A. Specify uniform standards of achievement for all children

B. Focus on the processes of learning of individual children rather than on the final outcomes

C. Offer tangible rewards

D. Plan learning activities which encourages convergent thinking

8. Failure of a child to perform well in class tests leads to believe that

A. Assessment is objective and can be used to clearly identical failure

B. There is a need to reflect upon the syllabus, pedagogy \ and assessment process

C. Some children are deemed to fail irrespective of how hard the system tries

D. Children are born with certain capabilities and deficits

9. There are few children in your class who make errors. Which of these is most likely to be your analysis of the situation?

A. The children have poor intelligence

B. The children are not interested in studies and want to create indiscipline

C. The children should not have been promoted to your class

D. The children have not yet gained conceptual clarity and there is need for you to reflect on your pedagogy

10. A student highlights the main points in a chapter, draws a visual representation and poses questions that arise in her mind at the end of the chapter. She is

A. Trying to regulate her own thinking by organization ofideas

B. Trying to use strategy of maintenance rehearsal

C. Ensuring observational learning

D. Trying to use method of loci

11. How can a teacher help children become better problem solvers?

A. By giving children a variety of problems to solve and support while solving them

B. By encouraging children to look for answers to the problems in the textbook

C. By providing correct solutions to all the problems they pose to students

D. By giving tangible rewards for solving problems

12. Of the following statement, which one do you agree with?

A. Learning is completely governed by external stimuli

B. Learning cannot take place unless it is assessed externally in terms of marks

C. Learning has taken place only if it is evident in behavior

D. Learning takes place in socio- cultural context

13. Which one of these is a principle of child development?

A. Development occurs due to interaction between maturation and experience

B. Experience is the sole determinant of development

C. Development is determined by reinforcement andpunishment

D. Development can accurately predict the pace of eachindividual child

14. In a context of 'nature-nurture' debate, which one of the following statement seems appropriate to you?

A. A child is like a blank slate whose character can be moulded by the environment into any shape

B. Environmental influences only have a little value inshaping up a child's behaviors which is primarily genetically determined

C. Heredity and environment are inseparably interwoven and both influences development

D. Children are genetically predisposed to what they wouldbe like irrespective of whatever environment they grow up

15. Socialization is a process of

A. Acquiring values, beliefs and expectations

B. Assimilation and accommodation

C. Learning to critique the culture of a society

D. Socialization with friend

16. Piaget proposes that pre-operational children are unable to conserve. He attributes this inability to which of he following factors?

A. Inability of hypothetico- deductive reasoning

B. Personal fable

C. Irreversibility of thought

D. Lack of high- level abstract reasoning

17. According to Piaget's theory, children learn by

A. Memorizing information by paying due attention

B. Scaffolding provided by more able members of the society

C. Process of adaptation

D. Changing their behavior when offered appropriate rewards

18. According to Vygotsky ZPD, is

A. Zone demarking the support offered by the teacher

B. The gap between what the child can do independently and with assistance

C. The amount and nature of support provided to the child to achieve her potentialities

D. What the child can do on her own which cannot be assessed

19. A teacher in multicultural classroom would ensure that the assessment considers the following

A. Reliability and validity of her assessment

B. Expectations of the school administration by complying with the minimum levels of learning

C. Standardization of the assessment tool

D. Socio- cultural context of her students

20. An upper primary school constructivist classroom would foresee the following role of students in their own assessment

A. Make detailed guideline for how marks would be correlated to students' achievement and prestige in class

B. Students would be the sole determinants of their own assessment

C. Students would plan for assessment with the teacher

D. Denying that assessment has a role in teaching- learning

21. The rationale behind inclusive education is that

A. Society is heterogeneous and schools need to be inclusive to cater to heterogeneous society

B. We need to take pity on special children and provide them access to facilities

C. It is not cost-effective to provide for separate schools for special children

D. The benchmark for performance of each child should be uniform and standardized

22. Which one of the following would be the most effective way to identify a creative child by the teacher?

A. Observing how the child interacts with peers in team tasks

B. Administering standardized intelligence test

C. Giving objective type of question

D. Detailed observation of the child especially when she solves problems

23. A teacher can effectively respond to the needs of children from 'disadvantaged sections' of society by

A. Telling the other children to co-operate with the disadvantaged children and help them learn the ways of the school
B. Reflecting on the school system and herself about various ways in which biases and stereotypes surface
C. Ensuring that the children do not get a chance to \ interact with each other to minimize the chances of their being bullied
D. Sensitizing the disadvantaged children to the norms and structures of schools so that they can comply with those

24. Research has pointed out that several levels of discrimination exist in the schools. Which of these is not an example of discrimination at upper primary level?
A. Many teachers use only lecture method to teach
B. Dalit children are made to sit separately during mid- day meal
C. Girls are not encouraged to take up maths and science
D. Children have low expectations of children from lower socio-economic strata

25. Which of the following statements best describes why learning disability?
A. An IQ below 50
B. Bullying other children and engaging in aggressive acts
C. Doing the same motor action repeatedly
D. Difficulty in reading fluently and reversing words

26. Which one of the following statement best describes why children should be encouraged to ask questions in the class?
A. Questions increase the curiosity of the children
B. Questions take learning forward by interactions and lead to conceptual clarity
C. Children need to practice their language skills
D. Children can be made to realize that they lack intelligence by making them think of all the things they don't know about.

27. Which one of the following assessment practices will bring out the best in students?
A. When students are required to reproduce facts as tested via multiple choice questions
B. When conceptual change and students' alternative solutions are assessed through several different methods of assessment
C. When the marks obtained and the position secured by the students in the class are the ultimate determinants of success
D. When the emphasis is laid upon positive correlation between test scores and students ability

28. As per an upper primary school mathematics teacher you believe that

A. Students error provide insight into their thinking

B. Students need to possess procedural knowledge even if they don't understand conceptual basis.

C. Not all children have the ability to study mathematics in upper primary school

D. Boys will learn mathematics without much effort since they are born with it and you need to pay more attention to girls

29. Which one of these statements do you agree with?

A. A child falls because the government is not giving enough technological resources in schools

B. A child's failure is primarily due to lack of parent's education and economic status

C. A child's failure can be attributed directly to the genetic material he/ she has acquired form his/her parents

D. A child's failure is a reflection on the system and its inability to respond to the child

30. The amount and type of scaffolding to a child would change depending on the

A. Mood of the teacher

B. Child's innate abilities

C. Rewards offered for the task

D. Level of the child's performance

My Notes

Answer Key

1.	*(B)*	*11.*	*(A)*	*21.*	*(A)*
2.	*(C)*	*12.*	*(D)*	*22.*	*(A)*
3.	*(C)*	*13.*	*(A)*	*23.*	*(B)*
4.	*(D)*	*14.*	*(C)*	*24.*	*(A)*
5.	*(C)*	*15.*	*(A)*	*25.*	*(D)*
6.	*(A)*	*16.*	*(C)*	*26.*	*(B)*
7.	*(B)*	*17.*	*(C)*	*27.*	*(B)*
8.	*(B)*	*18.*	*(B)*	*28.*	*(A)*
9.	*(D)*	*19.*	*(D)*	*29.*	*(D)*
10.	*(A)*	*20.*	*(C)*	*30.*	*(D)*

CTET-2016

Held on: 21st February, 2016

Paper-1

1. Most classrooms in India are multilingual and this needs to be seen as .... by the teacher.

A. A problem
B. A resource
C. An obstacle
D. A bother

2. Mistakes and errors made by students

A. Are indicative of the failure of the teacher and the students
B. Should be seen as opportunities to understand their thinking
C. Should be severely dealt with
D. Are a wonderful opportunity to label children as weak or outstanding

3. .... views children as active builders of knowledge and little scientists who can construct their own theories of the world.

A. Pavlov
B. Jung
C. Piaget
D. Skinner

4. Child-centered pedagogy means

A. Asking the children to follow and imitate the teacher
B. Giving primacy to the children's voice and their active participation
C. Letting the children to be totally free
D. Giving moral education to the children

5. A teacher can help the children to process a complex situation by

A. Not offering any help at all so that children learn to help on their own
B. Giving a lecture on it
C. Breaking the task into smaller parts and writing down the instructions
D. Encouraging competition and offering a high reward to the child who completes the task first

6. Expecting students to reproduce knowledge in the same way as it is received

A. Is an effective assessment strategy
B. Is problematic, because individuals interpret experiences and do not reproduce knowledge as it is received
C. Is good, since we record everything as it is in our brains
D. Is good, since it is easy for the teacher to access

7. When students are given an opportunity to discuss a problem in groups, their learning curve

A. Remains stable
B. Declines
C. Remains the same
D. Becomes better

8. The pace of development varies from one individual to another, but it follows .... pattern.

A. A haphazard B. An unpredictable
C. A sequential and orderly D. A toe-to-head

9. Which one of the following is correct about development?

A. Socio-cultural context plays an important role in development
B. Development is uni-dimensional
C. Development is discrete
D. Development begins and ends at birth

10. Why do individuals differ from one another

A. Due to the inborn characteristics
B. Due to the interplay between heredity and environment
C. Because each individual has received a different gene set from his/her parents
D. Because of the impact of the environment

11. Family plays .... role in socialization of the child.

A. An exciting B. A primary
C. A secondary D. A not-so important

12. Which one of the following is a correctly matched pair?

A. Formal operational child- imitation begins, imaginary play
B. Infancy- applies logic and is able to infer
C. Pre-operational child- deductive thought
D. Concrete operational child- is able to conserve and classify

13. A child says, "clothes dry faster in the sun." she is showing an understanding of

A. Egocentric thinking B. Cause and effect
C. Reversible thinking D. Symbolic thought

14. According to Piaget, children thinking differ in .... from adults than in ....

A. size; correctness B. kind; amount
C. size; type D. amount; kind

15. Which one of the following is an example of scaffolding?

A. Giving motivational lectures to students
B. Offering explanations without encouraging questioning
C. Offering both material and non-material rewards
D. Giving prompts and cues, and asking questions at critical juncture

16. According to Vygotsky, children learn

A. By maturation B. By imitation

C. By interacting with adults and peer
D. When reinforcement is offered

17. Kohlberg has given

A. The stages of physical development
B. The stage of emotional development
C. The stages of moral development
D. The stages of cognitive development

18. Which one of the following situations is illustrative of a child-centre classroom?

A. A class in which the textbook is the only resource the teacher refer to
B. A class in which the students are sitting in groups and the teacher takes turns to go to each group
C. A class in which the behavior of students is governed by the rewards and punishments the teacher would give them
D. A class in which the teacher dictates and the students are asked to memorize the notes

19. Intelligence is

A. A singular and generic concept B. The ability to imitate other
C. A specific ability D. A set of capabilities

20. Early childhood is .... period for language development.

A. An unimportant B. A sensitive
C. A neutral D. A not-so significant

21. Teacher remarks in a co-education class to boys, "be boys and don't behave like girls." This remark

A. A good example of dealing with boys and girls
B. Reflects stereotypical behavior of discrimination between boys and girls
C. Highlights the biological superiority of boys over girls
D. Reflects caste discrimination

22. Assessment

A. Should actively promote competitive spirit among children
B. Should generate tension and stress to ensure learning
C. Is a way to improve learning
D. Is a good strategy to label and categorize students

23. Which one of the following statements best describes 'Inclusion'?

A. It is the belief that some children cannot learn at all
B. It is the philosophy that all children have a right to get equal education in a regular school system

C. It is the philosophy that special children are a special gift of God
D. It is a belief that children need to be segregated according to their abilities

24. To cater to the children from 'disadvantaged' background, a teacher should
A. Try to find out more about them and involve them in class discussions
B. Make them sit separately in the class
C. Ignore them as they cannot interact with other students
D. Give them a lot of written work

25. Which one of the following behaviors is an identifier of a child with the learning disability?
A. Abusive behavior
B. Writing 'b' as 'd', 'was' as 'saw', etc
C. Low attention span and high physical activity
D. Frequent mood swings

26. A child who can see partially
A. Should not be given education, since it is not of any use to him
B. Needs to be put in separate
C. Should be put in a regular school while making special provisions
D. Should be put in a regular school with no special provisions

27. Learning
A. Has very little connection with emotions
B. Is independent of a learner's emotions
C. Is influenced by a learner's emotions
D. Is not affected by a learner's emotions

28. To enable students to make conceptual changes in their thinking, a teacher should
A. Discourage children from thinking on their own and ask them to just listen to her and follow that
B. Offer an explanation in a lecture mode
C. Make clear and convincing explanations and have discussions with the students
D. Offer reward for children who change their thinking

29. In the context of a primary school classroom, what does active engagement mean?
A. Imitation and copying the teacher
B. Enquiry, questioning and debate
C. Copying answers given by the teachers
D. Memorizing, recall and reciting

30. Children are most creative when they participate in an activity

A. Under stress to do well in front of others

B. Of interest

C. For rewards

D. To escape their teacher's scolding

My Notes

Answer Key

1.	*(B)*	*11.*	*(B)*	*21.*	*(B)*
2.	*(B)*	*12.*	*(D)*	*22.*	*(C)*
3.	*(C)*	*13.*	*(B)*	*23.*	*(B)*
4.	*(B)*	*14.*	*(B)*	*24.*	*(A)*
5.	*(C)*	*15.*	*(D)*	*25.*	*(B)*
6.	*(B)*	*16.*	*(C)*	*26.*	*(C)*
7.	*(D)*	*17.*	*(C)*	*27.*	*(C)*
8.	*(C)*	*18.*	*(B)*	*28.*	*(C)*
9.	*(A)*	*19.*	*(D)*	*29.*	*(B)*
10.	*(B)*	*20.*	*(B)*	*30.*	*(B)*

CTET-2016

Held on: 21st February, 2016

Paper-2

1. Which one of the following is a good example of scaffolding (learning of a problem-solving task till the student is able to do it by herself)?

A. Offering a reward for solving the problem quickly
B. Telling her that she can do it by trying again and again
C. Providing a half- solved example
D. Telling her she cannot go home till she solves the problem

2. Your class has learners with different learning styles. To assess them, you would give them.

A. A uniform set of instructions and subsequently label the children according to their marks in the test
B. The same set of tasks and tests
C. A variety of tasks and tests
D. The same time to perform on the tests

3. Nowadays, there is a tendency to refer to 'wrong concepts' of children as 'alternative conceptions'. This could be attributed to

A. Children's understanding being nuanced and their being passive in their own learning
B. Recognition that children are capable of thinking and their thinking is different from that of adults
C. Using fancy terms to describe children's error
D. Children being thought of as adult like in their thinking

4. Which one of the following best describes a teacher's role in a middle school classroom?

A. Discouraging multiple perspectives and focusing on uni-dimensional perspectives
B. Using power point presentation to give lectures
C. Providing opportunity for discussions
D. Promoting students to compete amongst themselves for the first position

5. Which one of the following statements about motivation and learning is correct?

A. Motivation does not have any role to play in learning
B. Learning is effective only when the students are motivated using external rewards
C. Learning is effective only when the students have intrinsic motivation - a desire to leran from inside
D. Learning is effective only when the students are extrinsically motivated - motivated by external factors

6. **Which one of the following statements about learning is correct?**
   A. Learning is a passive receptive process
   B. Learning does not depend on learner's previous knowledge
   C. Learning is equivalent to acquisition of skills
   D. Learning is facilitated by social actions

7. **Which one of the following is an important activity to enable children to learn?**
   A. Reward B. Dialogue
   C. Lecture D. Instruction

8. **Which one of the following statements about development is correct?**
   A. Development proceeds from birth to adolescence
   B. Development changes go forward in a straight line
   C. Development occurs at a different rate among different individuals
   D. Development occurs at a very first pace from birth till adolescence and then it stops

9. **Middle child-hood is the period from**
   A. 10 years onward B. Birth to 2 years
   C. 2 years to 6 years D 6 years to 11 years

10. **"Environmental factors do not play any role in shaping an individual, since growth of each individual is determined by his genetic makeup". This statement is**
    A. Incorrect, since there have been several researches to prove that environment can have a major influence on development
    B. Correct, since genetic makeup of an individual is very strong
    C. Correct, since there have been several researches to prove that genetic material alone predicts and individual' development
    D. Incorrect, since environmental factors contribute little in an individual's growth and development

11. **.................. is a process through which a human infant begins to acquire the necessary skills to perform as a functioning member of the society**
    A. Development B. Socialization
    C. Learning D. Maturation

12. **According to Piaget, which one of the following factors plays an important role in influencing development?**
    A. Reinforcement B. Language
    C. Experience with physical world D. Imitation

13. **The cognitive ability that comes in pre-operational period is**

A. Hypothetico- deductive thinking
B. Ability for abstract thinking
C. Ability for a goal directed behavior
D. Ability to take other's perspective

14. Which one of the following is a correctly matched pair?
A. Social contract orientation - physical consequences of an action determine whether it is good or bad
B. Punishment and obedience orientation - laws are not fixed, but can be changed for the good society
C. Good boy and good girl orientation - one earns approval by being nice
D. Law and order orientation - ethical principles are self chosen on the basis of the value of human rights

15. The concept of private speech of children as proposed by Vygotsky
A. Shows that children are stupid and thus need guidance of adults
B. Illustrates that children are egocentric
C. Shows that children love themselves
D. Illustrates that children use speech to guide their own activities

16. According to Vygotsky, learning cannot be separated from
A. Perception and attention processes
B. Its social context
C. Reinforcement
D. A measurable change in behavior

17. Progressive education entails that the classrooms
A. In full control of the teacher, who is dictatorial
B. Democratic and there is space given to children for understanding
C. Authoritarian, where the teacher dictates and the students follow meekly
D. Free for all with the teacher absent from it

18. Which one of the following illustrates a person with linguistic intelligence?
A. The ability to handle long chains of reasoning
B. Sensitivity to the meaning and order of words and varied uses of language
C. Sensitivity to, pitch, melody and tone
D. The ability to notice and make distinctions among others

19. Language thought processes.
A. Cannot determine
B. Does not influence
C. Totally govern our
D. Has an influence on our

20. A textbook of class has following illustrations - women as teacher and maids while men as doctors and pilots. This type of depiction is likely to promote

A. Gender empowerment B. Gender stereotype

C. Gender role play D. Gender constancy

21. There are vast differences among the students of these, a teacher needs to be sensitive to

I. Differences based on cognitive capabilities and learning levels

II. Differences based on diversity of language, caste, gender, religion community

A. Neither I nor II B. Only I

C. Only II D. Both I, and II

22. Assessment by only paper- pencil tests

A. Promotes holistic assessment

B. Limits assessment

C. Facilitates comprehensive evaluation

D. Facilitates continuous evaluation

23. A teacher has a hearing impaired child in her middle school class. It is important for her to

A. Ask the school counselor to talk to the child's parents and tell them to withdraw their child from the school

B. Make the child sit at a place where she can see the teacher's lips and facial expressions clearly

C. Keep pointing to what the child cannot do over and over again

D. Ridicule the child and make her sit separately so that she joins an institution for learning impaired

24. A teacher can effectively respond to the needs of the children 'disadvantaged sections' of society by

A. Adapting her pedagogy to the needs of every child in the classroom

B. Ignoring their background and asking them to do chores in the class

C. Making them sit separately in the classroom so that they do not mix with other children

D. Telling other children to treat the children from disadvantaged background with sympathy

25. Children with learning disability

A. Are very active, but have a low IQ

B. Are very wise and mature

C. Cannot learn anything

D. Struggle with some aspects of learning

26. Teachers cam encourage children to think creatively by

A. Giving them multiple- choice questions

B. Asking them to think of different ways to solve a problem

C. Asking them to memorize answers

D. Asking the recall- based questions

27. Which one of the following philosophical perspectives needs to be followed to deal with children with special needs?

A. They have a right to inclusive education and study in regular school

B. They do not need any education at all

C. They should be segregated and put in separate educational institutions

D. They should be given only vocational training

28. Learner- centered approach means

A. Use of methods in which teachers are the main actor

B. Methods where learners' own initiative and efforts are involved in learning

C. That teachers draw conclusions for the learners

D. Traditional expository method

29. Which one of the following is central to learning?

A. Imitation
B. Meaning- making
C. Conditioning
D. Rote memorization

30. In constructivist classroom as envisioned by Piaget and Vygotsky learning

A. Is offering of reinforcement by the teacher

B. Is constructed by the students themselves who play an active role

C. Is dictated by the teacher and the students are passive recipient of the same

D. Happens by pairing of a stimulus and a response

My Notes

Answer Key

1.	*(C)*	*11.*	*(B)*	*21.*	*(D)*
2.	*(C)*	*12.*	*(C)*	*22.*	*(B)*
3.	*(B)*	*13.*	*(C)*	*23.*	*(B)*
4.	*(C)*	*14.*	*(C)*	*24.*	*(A)*
5.	*(C)*	*15.*	*(D)*	*25.*	*(D)*
6.	*(D)*	*16.*	*(B)*	*26.*	*(B)*
7.	*(B)*	*17.*	*(B)*	*27.*	*(A)*
8.	*(C)*	*18.*	*(B)*	*28.*	*(B)*
9.	*(D)*	*19.*	*(D)*	*29.*	*(B)*
10.	*(A)*	*20.*	*(B)*	*30.*	*(B)*

CTET-2016

Held on: 18th September, 2016

Paper-1

1. **Which of the following is the most effective method to encourage conceptual development in students?**
   A. Give students multiple examples and encourage them to use reasoning
   B. Use punishment till students have made the required conceptual changes
   C. New concepts need to be understood on their own without any reference to the old ones
   D. Replace the student's incorrect ideas with correct ones by asking them to memorize

2. **Primary schoolchildren will learn most effectively in an atmosphere -**
   A. Where the focus and stress are only on mastering primary cognitive skills of reading, writing and mathematics
   B. Where the teacher leads all the learning and accepts students to play a passive role
   C. Where their emotional needs are met and they feel that they are valued
   D. Where the teacher is authoritative and clearly dictates what should be done

3. **A child sees a crow flying past the window and says, "A bird." What does this suggest about the child's thinking?**
   (1) The child has previously stored memories.
   (2) The child has developed the concept of a 'bird'.
   (3) The child had developed some tools of language to communicate her experience.
   A. 1,2 and 3 B. Only 2
   C. 1 and 2 D. 2 and 3

4. **What should a teacher tell her students to encourage them to do tasks with intrinsic motivation?**
   A. "Complete the task fast and get a toffee"
   B. Try to do it, you will learn"
   C. "Come on, finish it before she does."
   D. "Why can't you be like him? See, he has done it perfectly."

5. **How can a teacher encourage her students to be intrinsically motivated towards learning for the sake of learning?**
   A. By supporting them in setting individual goals and their mastery
   B. By offering tangible rewards such as toffees
   C. By inducing anxiety and fear
   D. By giving competitive tasks

6. **In an elementary classroom, an effective teacher should aim at the students to be motivated -**
   A. By using punitive measures so that they respect the teacher
   B. To perform so that they get good marks in the ends of the year examination
   C. To learn so that they become curious and love learning for its own sake
   D. To rote memorize so that they become good at recall

7. **Which of the following is an example of effective school practice?**
   A. Individualized learning
   B. competitive classroom
   C. Constant comparative evaluation
   D. Corporal punishment

8. **The cephalocaudal principle of development explains how development proceeds from -**
   A. Head to toe
   B. Rural to urban areas
   C. General to specific functions
   D. Differentiated to integrated functions

9. **Which of the following is a sensitive period pertaining to language development?**
   A. Adulthood
   B. Early Childhood period
   C. Prenatal period
   D. Middle childhood period

10. **A 6-year old girl shows exceptional sporting ability. Both of her parents are sports-persons, send her for coaching everyday and train her on weekends. Her capability are most likely to be the result of an interaction between:**
    A. Health and training
    B. Discipline and nutrition
    C. Heredity and environment
    D. Growth and development

11. **Which of the following are secondary agents of socialisation?**
    A. School and immediate family members
    B. Family and relatives
    C. Family and neighbourhood
    D. School and neighbourhood

12. **According to Lev Vygotsky, the primary cause of cognitive development is -**
    A. Adjustment of mental schemas
    B. Stimulus-response pairing
    C. Equilibration
    D. Social interaction

13. In the context of Kohlberg' stages of moral reasoning, under which stage would be given typical response of a child fall? "Your parents will be proud of you if you are honest. So, you should be honest."

A. Good girl-good boy orientation

B. Law and order orientation

C. Punishment-obedience orientation

D. Social contract orientation

14. According to Jean Piaget, which of the following is necessary for learning?

A. Belief in immanent justice

B. Reinforcement by teachers and parents

C. Active exploration of the environment by the learner

D. Observing the behaviour of adults

15. According to Jean Piaget, schema building occurs as a result of modifying new information to fit existing schemes and by modifying old schemes as per new information. These two processes are known as:

A. Equilibration and modification

B. Assimilation and accommodation

C. Accommodation and adaptation

D. Assimilation and adaptation

16. In a progressive classroom setup, the teacher facilitates learning by providing an environment that:

A. Discourages inclusion   B. Encourages repetition

C. Promotes discovery   D. Is restrictive

17. Howard Gardner's theory of Multiple Intelligence (MI) suggests that:

A. Teachers should use MI as a framework for devising alternative ways to teach the subject matter

B. Ability is destiny and does not change over a period of time

C. Every child should be taught every subject in eight different ways in order to develop all of the intelligences

D. Intelligence is solely determined by IQ tests

18. A 5-year-old girl talks to herself while trying to fold a T-shirt. Which of the following statements is correct in the context of the behaviour display by the girl?

A. Jean Piaget would explain this as social interaction, while Lev Vygotsky would explain this as an exploration.

B. Jean Piaget and Lev Vygotsky would explain this as the child's attempt to imitate her mother.

C. Jean Piaget and Lev Vygotsky would explain this as egocentric nature of the child's thoughts.

D. Jean Piaget would explain this as egocentric speech, while Lev Vygotsky would explain this as the child's attempt to regulate her actions through private speech.

19. 'Gender' is a/an:

A. Innate quality B. Social construct

C. Biological entity D. Physiological construct

20. As a teacher, who firmly believes in social constructivist theory of Lev Vygotsky, which of the following methods would you prefer for assessing your students?

A. Fact-based recall questions

B. Objective multiple-choice type questions

C. Collaborative projects

D. Standardized tests

21. To cater in individual differences in his classroom, a teacher should:

A. Engage in a dialogue with students and value their perspectives

B. Impose strict rules upon his students

C. Have uniform and standard ways of teaching and assessment

D. Segregate and label children based on their marks

22. Assessment is purposeful if:

A. It is done only once at the end of the year

B. Comparative evaluations are made to differentiate between the students' achievements

C. It induces fear and stress among the students

D. It serves as a feedback for the students as well as the teachers

23. According to NCF, 2005, the role of a teacher has to be:

A. Permissive B. Facilitative

C. Authoritative D. Dictatorial

24. Research suggests that in a diverse classroom, a teacher's expectations from her students .... their learning.

A. Should not be correlated with

B. Do not have any effect on

C. Have a significant impact on

D. Are the sole determinant of

25. Inclusion of children with special needs :

A. Will increase the burden on schools

B. Requires a change in attitude, content and approach to teaching

C. Is an unrealistic goal

D. Is detrimental to children without disabilities

26. "Having a diverse classroom with children from varied social, economic and cultural backgrounds enriches the learning experiences of all students." This statement is :

A. Correct, because it makes the classroom more hierarchical

B. Incorrect, because it leads to unnecessary competition

C. Incorrect, because it can confuse the children and they may feel lost

D. Correct, because children learn many skills from their peers

27. Child with hearing impairment:

A. Can do very well in a regular school if suitable facilitation and resources are provided

B. Will never be able to perform on a par with classmates in a regular school

C. Should be sent only to a school for the hearing impaired and hot to a regular school

D. Will not benefit from academic education only and should be given vocational training instead

28. Which of the following is a characteristic of a gifted learner?

A. He is highly temperamental.

B. He engages in ritualistic behaviour like hand flapping rocking, etc.

C. He gets aggressive and frustrated.

D. He can feel under stimulated and bored if the class activities are not challenging enough.

29. A teacher can enhance effective learning in her elementary classroom by:

A. Encouraging competition amongst her students

B. Connecting the content to the lives of the students

C. Offering rewards for small steps in learning

D. Drill and practice

30. Which of the following statements about children are correct?

(1)Children are passive recipients of knowledge.

(2)Children are problem solvers.

(3)Children are scientific investigators.

(4)Children are active explorers of the environment.

A. 1, 2, 3 and 4 B. 1, 2 and 3

C. 1, 2 and 4 D. 2, 3 and 4

My Notes

Answer Key

1.	*(A)*	*11.*	*(D)*	*21.*	*(A)*
2.	*(C)*	*12.*	*(D)*	*22.*	*(D)*
3.	*(A)*	*13.*	*(A)*	*23.*	*(B)*
4.	*(B)*	*14.*	*(C)*	*24.*	*(C)*
5.	*(A)*	*15.*	*(B)*	*25.*	*(B)*
6.	*(C)*	*16.*	*(C)*	*26.*	*(D)*
7.	*(A)*	*17.*	*(A)*	*27.*	*(A)*
8.	*(A)*	*18.*	*(D)*	*28.*	*(D)*
9.	*(B)*	*19.*	*(B)*	*29.*	*(B)*
10.	*(C)*	*20.*	*(C)*	*30.*	*(D)*

CTET-2016

Held on: 18th September, 2016

Paper-2

1. Two students read the same passage yet construct entirely different interpretations of its meaning. Which of the following is true about them?

A. It is not possible and the students need to re-read the passage.

B. It is possible because the teacher has not explained the passage.

C. It is possible because different factors affect learning of individuals in varied ways.

D. It is not possible because learning is not meaning-making.

2. According to the National Curriculum Framework, 2005, learning is .... and .... in its character.

A. Active; social

B. Passive; simple

C. Passive; social

D. Active; simple

3. To enable students to think independently and become effective learners, it is important for a teacher to:

A. Offer rewards for each success achieved by the students

B. Teach students how to monitor their own learning

C. Give information in small units or chunks

D. Present information in an organized manner to make it easier to recall

4. If a teacher wants her students to acquire problem-solving skills, the students should be engaged in activities that involve:

A. Structured worksheets containing multiple-choice questions

B. Recall, memorization and comprehension

C. Drill and practice

D. Inquiring, reasoning and decision making

5. Knowing the naive conceptions that students bring to the classroom:

A. Pulls down the teacher's morale since it increases his work

B. Does not serve any purpose of the teacher

C. Helps the teacher to plan teaching more meaningfully

D. Hampers the teacher's planning and teaching

6. Which of the following factors affect learning?

1 Motivation of the learner

2 Maturation of the learner

3 Teaching strategies

4 Physical and emotional health of the learner

A. 1, 2, 3 and 3　　　B. 1 and 2

C. 1 and 3　　　D. 1, 2 and 3

7. **Meaningful learning is:**
   A. Pairing and association between the stimulus and the response
   B. Imitation of adults and more able peers
   C. Passive receiving of the given information
   D. Active creation of knowledge structures from personal experience

8. **Which of the following is not one of the primary tasks of a teacher for effective student learning?**
   A. Transmitting information to the students in a didactic manner
   B. Knowing the concepts that students bring to the classroom
   C. Requiring students to respond to higher-order questioning
   D. Teaching students how to monitor and improve their own learning by effort

9. **Which of the following statements about principles of development is incorrect?**
   A. Development depends on maturation and learning.
   B. Development takes place due to a constant interaction between heredity and environment.
   C. Every child goes through stages of development, yet there are wide individual differences among children.
   D. Development is a quantitative process which can be measured precisely.

10. **The unique interaction of .... and ....can result in different paths and outcomes of development.**
   A. Challenges; limitations   B. Heredity; environment
   C. Stability; change   D. Exploration; nutrition

11. **Which of the following is true of school and socialization?**
   A. School is an important agent of socialization.
   B. School does not play any role in socialization.
   C. School plays very little role in socialization.
   D. School is the first primary agent of socialization.

12. **Which of the following statements is correct about Jean Piaget's theory of cognitive development?**
   A. Piaget argues that instead of progressing through stages, cognitive development is continuous.
   B. Piaget has proposed five distinct stages of cognitive development.
   C. The stages are invariant which means that no stage can be skipped.
   D. The sequence of the stages can vary according to the cultural context of children.

13. **The concept of 'conservation' as proposed by Jean Piaget means that:**

A. It is important to protect wildlife and forests
B. Certain physical properties remain the same even when outward appearances change
C. One can arrive at the correct conclusion by systematically testing hypothesis
D. Taking the perspective of others into consideration is an important cognitive ability

14. Match the following in the light of Howard Gardner's theory of Multiple Intelligence:

Type of Intelligence	
(a) Musical	(i) Therapist
(b) Linguistic	(ii) Poet
(c) Interpersonal	(iii) Athlete
(d) Spatial End State	(iv) Violinist
	(v) Sculptor

A. a-v, b-ii, c-iv, d-i   B. a-ii, b-iv, c-i, d-v
C. a-iv, b-ii, c-i, d-v   D. a-iv, b-ii, c-v, d-iii

15. According to Lev Vygotsky:
A. Interaction with adults and peers does not influence language development
B. Language development changes the nature of human thought
C. Culture plays a very small role in language development
D. Children learn language through a language acquisition device

16. Lawrence Kohlberg's theory of moral reasoning has been criticized on several counts. Which of the following statements is correct in the context of this criticism?
A. Kohlberg has not given typical responses to each stage of moral reasoning.
B. Kohlberg has duplicated Piaget's methods of arriving at his theoretical framework.
C. Kohlberg's theory does not focus on children's responses.
D. Kohlberg has based his study primarily on a male sample.

17. Which of the following highlights assessment for learning?
A. The teacher assesses conceptual understanding of the students besides focusing on the processes of thinking.
B. The teacher assesses the students by comparing their responses to 'standard' responses.
C. The teacher assesses the students based on the information given in the textbooks.

D. The teacher assesses a student based on his/her performance in comparison to others.

18. 'Child-centred' pedagogy means:

A. The teacher dictating the children what should be done
B. Giving primacy to children's experiences and their voices
C. Enabling the children to follow prescribed information
D. The teacher leading all the learning in the classroom

19. Which of the following statements describes Piaget and Vygotsky's views on language and thought correctly?

A. According to Vygotsky, thought emerges first and according to Piaget, language has a profound effect on thought.
B. According to Piaget, thought emerges first and according to Vygotsky, language has a profound effect on thought.
C. Both view thought as emerging from the child's language.
D. Both view language as emerging from the child's thought.

20. Watching her granddaughter arguing with her father for going on a school trip, the grandmother says, "Why can't you be obedient like a good girl? Who will marry you if you behave like a boy?" This statement reflects which of the following?

A. Gender constancy
B. Gender stereotypes about attributes of girls and boys
C. Improper gender identification of the girl
D. Difficulties faced by families in child-rearing

21. Which of the following statements about assessment are correct?

1. Assessment should help students see their strengths and gaps and help the teacher fine-tune her teaching accordingly.
2. Assessment is meaningful only if comparative evaluations of students are made.
3. Assessment should assess not only memory but also understanding and application.
4. Assessment cannot be purposeful if it does not induce fear and anxiety.

A. 2 and 3 B. 1 and 2
C. 2 and 4 D. 1 and 3

22. According to the Right to Education Act, 2009, children with special needs should study:

A. At home with their parents and caregivers providing necessary support
B. In special schools created exclusively for them
C. In inclusive education setups with provisions to cater to their

individual needs

D. In vocational training centres which would prepare them for life skills

23. An effective teacher in a classroom, where students come from diverse backgrounds, would:

A. Push students from deprived backgrounds to work hard so that they can match up with their peers

B. Focus on their cultural knowledge to address individual differences among the group

C. Ignore cultural knowledge and treat all his students in a uniform manner

D. Create group of students with those from the same economic background put together

24. Match the following principles of development with their correct descriptions:

Principle

(a) Proximo-distal trend (b) Cephalocaudal trend

(c) Inter-individual differences (d) Intra-individual differences

Description

(i) Different children develop at different rates

(ii) Head to toe sequence

(iii) In a single child, the rate of development can vary from one domain of development to the other

(iv) From the centre of body to outwards

(v) Progression from simple to complex

A. a-v, b-ii, c-i, d-iii B. a-ii, b-iv, c-i, d-iii

C. a-ii, b-iv, c-iii, d-i D. a-iv, b-ii, c-I, d-iii

25. Which of the following statements about cognition and emotions is correct?

A. Cognition and emotions are intertwined and affect each other.

B. Cognition and emotions are processes independent of each other.

C. Cognition affects emotions but emotions do not affect cognition.

D. Emotions affect cognition but cognition does not affect emotions.

26. In an inclusive classroom with diverse learners, cooperative learning and peer-tutoring

A. Should be used only sometimes since it promotes comparison with classmates

B. Should be actively discouraged and competition should be promoted

C. Should be actively promoted to facilitate peer-acceptance

D. Should not be practiced and students should be segregated based on their abilities.

27. A teacher can address diversity in her class by:

1. accepting and valuing differences
2. using socio-cultural background of children as a pedagogic resource
3. accommodating different learning styles
4. giving standard instruction and setting uniform benchmarks for performance

Select the correct answer using the code given below.

A. 1, 2, 3 and 4　　B. 1, 2 and 4
C. 2, 3 and 4　　D. 1, 2 and 3

28 A teacher asks her class to cover sharp edges of furniture with cotton and use 'Touch and Feel' notice boards and books. The needs of which category of special learners is she attempting to cater to?

A. Visually-impaired learners
B. Hearing-impaired learners
C. Learning-impaired learners
D. Socially disadvantaged learners

29 Gifted children are best catered to by educational programmes at:

A. Make use of gifts and rewards to motivate them to perform according to minimum standards of learning
B. Emphasize mastery of knowledge by recall
C. Stimulate their thinking and give them opportunities to engage in divergent thinking
D. Control their aggressive behaviour

30 Which of the following statements about students' failure in schools are correct?

1. Students belonging to certain castes and communities fail since they do not have ability.
2. Students fail in schools because appropriate rewards are not offered for their learning.
3. Students fail because teaching is not done in a manner in which it is meaningful to them.
4. Students fail because school system does not cater to individual child's needs and interests.

A. 3 and 4　　B. 1 and 2
C. 2 and 3　　D. 2 and 4

My Notes

Answer Key

1.	*(C)*	*11.*	*(A)*	*21.*	*(D)*
2.	*(A)*	*12.*	*(C)*	*22.*	*(C)*
3.	*(B)*	*13.*	*(B)*	*23.*	*(B)*
4.	*(D)*	*14.*	*(C)*	*24.*	*(D)*
5.	*(C)*	*15.*	*(B)*	*25.*	*(A)*
6.	*(A)*	*16.*	*(D)*	*26.*	*(C)*
7.	*(D)*	*17.*	*(A)*	*27.*	*(D)*
8.	*(A)*	*18.*	*(B)*	*28.*	*(A)*
9.	*(D)*	*19.*	*(B)*	*29.*	*(C)*
10.	*(B)*	*20.*	*(B)*	*30.*	*(A)*

CTET-2018

Held on: 9th December, 2018

Paper-1

1. **Which of the following statements is true about the role of heredity and environment?**
   A. Certain aspects of development are influenced more by heredity and others more by environment
   B. A child's ability to learn and perform is completely decided by the genes
   C. Good care and a nutritious diet can fight off any disorder a child is born with
   D. Environment plays a significant role only in the child's language development

2. **Which one of the following statements cannot be attributed to Piaget's theory?**
   A. Development occurs in qualitative stages
   B. Children construct and use knowledge about their world
   C. Learning takes place through constant practice
   D. Children act on their environment

3. **Which one of the following is not a limitation of the preoperational thought?**
   A. Tendency to concentrate
   B. Development of the symbolic thought
   C. Egocentrism
   D. Irreversibility

4. **Play has a significant role in development of young children for the following reasons, except -**
   A. They gain mastery over their body
   B. It stimulates their senses
   C. It is just a pleasant way to spend time
   D. They acquire new skills and learn when to use them

5. **Which one of the following questions invites children to think critically?**
   A. Do you know the answer to this?
   B. What is the right answer?
   C. Can you think of a similar situation?
   D. What are the different ways in which we can solve this?

6. **Which one of the following option best describes progressive education?**
   A. Learning by doing, project method, cooperative learning
   B. Thematic units, regular unit tests, ranking
   C. Personalized learning, ability grouping, labeling students
   D. Project method, ability grouping, ranking

7. Which one of the following statements about progressive education explains - Education is life itself?

A. School education should continue as long as possible

B. Schools are not required, children can learn from their life experiences

C. Education in schools should reflect the social and natural world

D. Life is the true educator

8. Which of the following can be considered as a contribution of Kohlberg's theory?

A. His theory has supported an association between cognitive maturity and moral maturity

B. The theory has elaborate testing procedures

C. It establishes a clear relationship between moral reasoning and action

D. His belief is that children are moral philosophers

9. The Zone of Proximal Development refers to -

A. The phase when maximum development is possible

B. The developmental phase when child takes complete responsibility for learning

C. A context in which children can almost perform a task on their own with right level of support

D. The point in learning when support can be withdrawn

10. An androgynous personality -

A. Refers to men with feminine traits

B. Has a balance of what are generally considered masculine and feminine traits

C. Tends to be assertive and arrogant

D. Adheres to stereotypical gender roles prevalent in the society [74]

11. Children acquire gender roles through all of the following except -

A. Media	B. Socialization
C. Culture	D. Tutoring

12. One of the critiques of standardized tests has been that -

A. They represent largely the mainstream culture and are therefore biased

B. Their language is difficult to understand

C. The tests cannot be administered on large populations

D. They do not give a clear picture of a child's ability

13. The theory multiple intelligence says that-
A. Intelligence can be rapidly accelerated
B. Intelligence can be of several kinds
C. Paper-pencil tests are not helpful
D. Intelligence can be multiplied with effective pedagogy

14. Teacher can utilize both assessment for learning and assessment of learning to -
A. Know children's progress and achievement level
B. Know learning needs of child and select teaching strategy accordingly
C. Assess child's performance at periodic intervals and certify his/ her performance
D. Monitor children's progress and set appropriate goals to fill their learning gaps

15. Which one of the following is not related to Continuous and Comprehensive Evaluation?
A. It has been mandated by the Right to Education Act of India
B. It is an integral part of teaching- learning process
C. It focuses on child's achievement in different learning areas
D. It is useful to label children as slow, poor or intelligent

16. Giftedness in children can be attributed to-
A. An interplay between heredity and environment
B. A resource- rich environment
C. Successful parents
D. A disciplined routine

17. Children coming from socioeconomically disadvantaged backgrounds need a classroom environment which -
A. Teaches them good behavior
B. Values and uses their cultural and linguistic knowledge
C. Discourages the use of their language so that they learn the mainstream language
D. Categorizes children based on their abilities

18. The intervention needed for creative and talented children in the classroom rests on¬
A. Use of customized and simulating instructional methods by the teacher
B. Giving extra time to them
C. Being affectionate towards them
D. Giving them the responsibility of teaching other children

19. Which one of the following ways is not a suitable way to help hyperactive children learn?

A. Breaking up a task into small, manageable segments

B. Offering alternative ways of learning

C. Including physical activity in their daily scheduled

D. Reprimanding them often for being restless

20. Patterns of divergent thinking identify children, who are -

A. Disabled B. Dyslexic

C. Creative D. Resilient

21. Which one of the following does not describe the ways in which a teacher can model problem solving for children in the classroom?

A. Discuss your thought processes about solving a particular problem

B. Be honest about making mistakes while solving something

C. Use vocabulary like think, ideas, trial and different answers

D. Ask questions with convergent answers

22. Which one of the following is an emotion?

A. Memory B. Fear

C. Attention D. Stimulus

23. A three year old child explains that milk is produced by a machine at the milk booth. Which one of the following offers the best explanation of the child's understanding?

A. The child has very limited exposure of the world

B. The child's answer is based on his/her experience of buying milk from the milk booth

C. The child has never seen cows

D. The child's family does not offer a stimulating environment to the child

24. Which one of the following best describes a teacher's role?

A. Teacher's most important role in the classroom is to maintain discipline

B. A teacher should adhere to the prescribed textbook

C. Completing the syllabus on time leaving enough time for revision is important

D. Creating a relaxed space where children learn through dialogue and enquiry

25. Which one of the following classrooms encourages rich learning?

A. A classroom with a variety of material displayed in the class beyond the reach of children so that the material lasts longer

B. A classroom with open activity corners and a variety of children's literature in open shelves accessible any time of the day
C. A classroom with neatly organized material in cupboards brought out once a week for free play
D. A classroom with structured and planned learning driven by textbook content

26. Which one of the following best describes the role of textbooks in the classroom?
A. They are one of the resource and reference materials available in the class
B. They maintain homogeneity in learning across a state or the nation
C. They provide guidance to teachers and parents about the course of study
D. They form the most essential learning resource in a resource-starved context

27. The National Curriculum Framework- 2005 derives its understanding from -

A. Humanism	B. Behaviourism
C. Constructivism	D. Cognitive theories

28. The children in a class can be considered to be motivated if -
A. They come to school neatly dressed in uniform
B. They maintain discipline in the class
C. All are regular in attendance
D. They ask questions seeking clarification from the teacher

29. Which one of the following is the most suitable to improve children's learning?
A. Regular assessment test should be conducted
B. Teacher should explain the content using different examples and illustrations
C. All types of learning material should be there in the class
D. Teacher should facilitate children to interact with each other on real- life situations

30. The discipline which has a significant role in a learning environment is of the kind which helps -
A. Children to regulate and monitor their own learning
B. To create silence
C. Teachers to give instructions
D. Children rote memorize their lessons

My Notes

Answer Key

1.	*(A)*	*11.*	*(D)*	*21.*	*(D)*
2.	*(C)*	*12.*	*(A)*	*22.*	*(B)*
3.	*(B)*	*13.*	*(C)*	*23.*	*(B)*
4.	*(C)*	*14.*	*(D)*	*24.*	*(D)*
5.	*(D)*	*15.*	*(D)*	*25.*	*(B)*
6.	*(A)*	*16.*	*(A)*	*26.*	*(A)*
7.	*(C)*	*17.*	*(B)*	*27.*	*(C)*
8.	*(A)*	*18.*	*(A)*	*28.*	*(D)*
9.	*(C)*	*19.*	*(D)*	*29.*	*(D)*
10.	*(B)*	*20.*	*(C)*	*30.*	*(A)*

CTET-2018

Held on: 9th December, 2018

Paper-2

1. The development from central part of the body towards peripheries or extremities denotes the -

A. Principles of radiated development
B. Principles of decentralized development
C. Principles of proximodistal development
D. Principles of cascade development

2. School is an institution of socialization of children where-

A. School children occupy the central position
B. School routines occupy the central position
C. School activities occupy the central position
D. School teachers occupy the central position

3. If you join a teacher fraternity and choose to dress like most of the others in your group, you are exhibiting-

A. Group identity. B. Obedience
C. Compliance D. Conformity

4. The concept of object permanence is attained during Piaget's stage of development

A. Sensorimotor B. Preoperational
C. Concrete operational D. Formal operational

5. Individualized Education Programme is planned from the perspective of -

A. Special Education Programme
B. Child- centered Education Programme
C. Open School Education Programme
D. e-learning Education Programme

6. Between .... months of age, most children begin to combine words into short sentences while speaking.

A. 12 and 18 B. 18 and 24
C. 24 and 30 D. 30 and 36

7. The concept of Intelligence Quotient or IQ was developed by -

A. Galton B. Binet
C. Stern D. Terman

8. Creativity is thought to be related to the concept of -

A. Fluid intelligence B. Crystallized intelligence
C. Convergent thinking D. Divergent thinking

9. The acceptable sound combinations of a language are specified in its .... rules.

A. Phonological B. Grammatical

C. Syntactic D. Inflection

10. The position where thought patterns are influenced by language is called

A. Cultural tendency B. Linguistic determination

C. Cognitive bias D. Sociolinguistic genesis

11. Ravi repairs appliances by testing hypothesis about the cause of the malfunction based on his experiences with the symptoms. He uses-

A. Insight B. Algorithms

C. Mental set D. Heuristics

12. Divya often divides the assigned job into small tasks which she can handle easily. She is using -

A. Reductionism B. Secondary elaboration

C. Sub-goal analysis D. Functional fixedness

13. "Society determines the roles of male and female." This statement articulates-

A. Gender as an inherent construct

B. Gender as a hereditary endowment

C. Gender as an intuitive construct

D. Gender as a social construct

14. Grading, coding, marking and credit accumulation systems are some of the examples of -

A. Evaluation procedure of answer sheets of the examination

B. Symbolizing position of children in the class

C. Depicting the academic progress in report card

D. Scoring procedure of assessment of learners' achievement

15. Assessment of learners' achievement helps the teachers to -

A. Maintain the performance record of learners

B. Evaluate the effectiveness of pedagogy

C. Make ability grouping of learners in the classrooms

D. Prepare activity log for teaching

16. Inclusive education is based on the principle of -

A. Social equilibrium

B. Equity and equal opportunities

C. Social existence and globalization

D. World brotherhood

17. The Rights of Persons with Disabilities Act has been enacted in the year-

A. 1992 B. 1995
C. 1999 D. 2016

18. Children with individual differences should be taught in a school having teachers -

A. To teach in different sections of classrooms based on their individual differences
B. Trained to use different pedagogy to meet their diverse learning needs
C. Trained to teach children with specific individual differences
D. Trained to make them homogeneous learners

19. The Rights of Children to Free and Compulsory Education Act, 2009 ensures the rights of children with disabilities to free education from-

A. 6 years to 18 years B. 3 years to 18 years
C. 6 years to 14 years D. 6 years to 22 years

20. Providing teaching- learning materials in accessible formats to the diverse learners implies -

A. Universal Inclusive Education Ethical Considerate
B. Universal Code of Teaching Practices
C. Universal Humanistic Approach of Teaching
D. Universal Design of Learning

21. .... involves self- awareness and control of cognitive abilities, e.g., planning, reviewing and revising, etc.

A. Centration B. Metacognition
C. Cognition D. Accommodation

22. When children think to interpret the received information according to their experiences, it is called -

A. Reflective thinking B. Creative thinking
C. Abstract thinking D. Concrete thinking

23. Teaching learner at varying levels of difficulty based on the ability of individual learner is known as -

A. Differentiated instruction B. Selective instruction
C. Precision teaching D. Errorless instruction

24. Maintenance is the specific stage of learning which is antecedent to .... stage of learning.

A. Acquisition B. Motivation
C. Independent D. Generalization

25. Zajonc believes that cognition and emotion are -

A. Interdependent B. Independent
C. Interrelated D. Integrated

26. A teacher is teaching children by demonstration of task to correct the performance of an already learned task. He is using method of teaching.

A. Imitation B. Observation
C. Correction D. Modeling

27. According to Mann and Janis, decision makers children analyze the problem, list the alternatives and weigh each option for its advantages and disadvantages -

A. Surveillance B. Vigilant
C. Outgoing D. Autocratic

28. In .... thinking, a child as a problem solver evaluates the truth or likelihood of statements.

A. Creative B. Aesthetic
C. Abstract D. Logical

29. The task in which children get experience while enjoying themselves is known as -

A. Drill and practice task B. Consumer type task
C. Producer type task D. Problem type task

30. Multisensory approach in teaching learning is the simultaneous use of visual, auditory, tactile and .... senses to enhance learning.

A. Kinesthetic B. Vestibular
C. Perceptual D. Observational

My Notes

Answer Key

1.	*(C)*	*11.*	*(D)*	*21.*	*(B)*
2.	*(A)*	*12.*	*(C)*	*22.*	*(D)*
3.	*(D)*	*13.*	*(D)*	*23.*	*(A)*
4.	*(A)*	*14.*	*(D)*	*24.*	*(D)*
5.	*(B)*	*15.*	*(B)*	*25.*	*(B)*
6.	*(B)*	*16.*	*(B)*	*26.*	*(D)*
7.	*(C)*	*17.*	*(D)*	*27.*	*(B)*
8.	*(D)*	*18.*	*(B)*	*28.*	*(D)*
9.	*(A)*	*19.*	*(C)*	*29.*	*(B)*
10.	*(B)*	*20.*	*(D)*	*30.*	*(A)*

CTET-2019

Held on: 7th July, 2019

Paper-1

1. Which of the following constructs does Right to Education Act, 2009 advocate?

(A) Inclusive education (B) Segregation

(C) Mainstreaming (D) Integrated education

2. .... is the philosophy that all children have a right to get equal education in a regular school system.

(A) Mainstreaming (B) Special Education

(C) Multi-cultural education (D) Inclusion

3. A teacher should -

(A) promote students belonging to certain cultures.

(B) ignore cultural differences and diversity amongst students.

(C) communicates that she respects and values all cultures in the classroom.

(D) maximize comparisons amongst students.

4. Children learn effectively when -

(A) they memorise facts given in the textbook.

(B) they copy answer written by the teacher on the blackboard.

(C) they actively participate in different activities and tasks.

(D) the teacher fully controls everything that happens in the class including the children.

5. Children should .... questions in the class.

(A) be discouraged to ask (B) not be allowed to ask

(C) be stopped from asking (D) be encouraged to ask

6. Which of the following is NOT a key process through which meaningful learning occurs?

(A) Repetition and practice (B) Instruction and direction

(C) Exploration and interaction (D) Memorization and recall

7. Which of the following represent the correct matching of children in column-A with their primary characteristic in column-B ?

Column-A	**Column B**
i. Gifted	a. Lacks reading fluency
ii. Learning disabled	b. Can think of original solutions
iii. Creative	c. Tendency to get distracted easily
iv. Attention Deficit Hyperactivity Disorder (ADHD)	d. Ability to learn quickly and independency

	i	ii	iii	iv
(A)	d	a	b	c
(B)	d	c	a	b
(C)	a	b	d	c
(D)	d	d	b	a

8. Children's errors -

(A) should be immediately corrected by asking them to do repeated practice.

(B) are a part of learning and give an insight into their thinking.

(C) are insignificant in the teaching-learning process.

(D) reflect how careless children are.

9. Assessment-

(A) should be a part of the teaching-learning process.

(B) should be done only in terms of marks.

(C) should be based on objective type written tasks.

(D) should be undertaken as a separate activity.

10. In a constructivist frame, learning is -

(A) passive and individualistic.

(B) the process of acquisition of knowledge.

(C) a change in behaviour as a result of experience.

(D) active and social in its character.

11. When teacher have positive beliefs about students and their abilities, the students-

(A) become relaxed and stop putting in any efforts to learn.

(B) become demotivated and stressed.

(C) are not affected in any way.

(D) are eager and motivated to learn.

12. A teacher can encourage children to become effectively problem solvers by-

(A) giving them plenty of opportunities to answer similar kinds of questions from the textbook.

(B) emphasizing on rote memorisation of the information given in the textbook.

(C) encouraging children to make intuitive guesses and to look at multiple solutions to the problem.

(D) writing step-by-step solution to all the questions in the textbook.

13. Use of methods where learner's own initiative and efforts are involved is an example of -

(A) Deductive method (B) Learner-centered method

(C) Traditional method (D) Inter-personal intelligence

14. What principle does the following highlight

"Student who do not perform well, feel that they are not 'good enough' and feel demotivated. They are then likely to give up easily without trying or persisting in doing tasks."

(A) Cognition and emotions are not related.

(B) Heredity and environment are not separable.

(C) Heredity and environment are not related.

(D) Cognition and emotions are not separable.

15. Which of the following is the primary socialising agency ?

(A) School (B) Government

(C) Media (D) Family

16. The major proposition of Jean Piaget's theory is that -

(A) Children's thinking is superior to adults.

(B) Children's thinking is quantitatively different from adults.

(C) Children's thinking is qualitatively different from adults.

(D) Children's thinking is inferior to adults.

17. Gender is a/an -

(A) psychological entity (B) social construct

(C) economic concept (D) biological determinant

18. Which of the following correctly identifies the broad domains of dovelopment?

(A) Emotional; intellectual; spiritual and self

(B) Physical; personality; spiritual and emotional

(C) Social; physical; personality; self

(D) Physical; cognitive; social and emotional

19. Which of the following statements about intelligence is correct?

(A) Intelligence is a relatively permanent change in behaviour as a result of experience.

(B) Intelligence is hereditary trait that involves mental activities such as memory and reasoning.

(C) Intelligence is multi-dimensional involving several abilities not entirely measureable by intelligence test.

(D) Intelligence is the ability to think convergently.

20. In progressive education children are seen as-

(A) Passive imitators (B) Active explorers

(C) Blank slates (D) Miniature adults

21. According to Lev Vygotsky, learning is-

(A) An individual activity (B) A passive activity

(C) A conditioned activity (D) A social activity

22. Which of the following characterizes a child in the preoperational stage?

(A) Goal-directed behaviour (B) Deferred Imitation

(C) Irreversibility of thought (D) Circular reactions

23. Which of the following statements regarding children and their learning is correct?

(A) Children's motivation to learn and their capability to learn is pre-determined by heredity only.

(B) Children's socio-economic background determines and limits their motivation and learning capability.

(C) Children have to be rewarded and punished to make them motivated for learning.

(D) All children are naturally motivated to learn and are capable of learning.

24. There are Individual variations in the rate of motor development, yet the sequence of motor development is from to ....

(A) Proximodistal; Cephalocaudal.

(B) Gross motor development; fine motor development.

(C) Fine motor development; gross motor development.

(D) Cephalocaudal; proximodistal

25. The period that initiates the transition to adulthood is -

(A) Middle childhood. (B) Pre-operational period.

(C) End childhood. (D) Adolescence.

26. According to Jean Piaget, children-

(A) learn by observing others following a process of observational learning.

(B) can be conditioned to behave in particular was by carefully controlled stimulus-response associations.

(C) can be taught to behave and learn in specific manner using principles of rewards and punishments.

(D) actively construct knowledge as they manipulate and explore the world.

27. Lev Vygotsky refers to the verbal dialogues that children have with themselves as-

(A) Private speech. (B) Distorted speech.
(C) Problematic speech. (D) Egocentric speech.

28. Associating toys, articles of clothing, household items, occupations and colours with specific sex, is a demonstration of-

(A) Gender stereotyping. (B) Gender theory.
(C) Gender relevance. (D) Evolved gender identity.

29. In an elementary classroom it is important to .... the experiences that a child brings with her.

(A) Neglect. (B) Ignore.
(C) Build on. (D) Deny.

30. A child argues that Heinz shouldn't steal the drug (medicine that can save his wife) because he will be caught and sent to jail if he does so. According to kohlberg, which stage of moral understanding does the child fall under?

(A) The social-order maintaining orientation.
(B) The punishment and obedience orientation.
(C) The universal ethical principle orientation.
(D) The instrumental purpose orientation.

My Notes

Answer Key

1.	*(A)*	*11.*	*(D)*	*21.*	*(D)*
2.	*(D)*	*12.*	*(C)*	*22.*	*(C)*
3.	*(C)*	*13.*	*(B)*	*23.*	*(D)*
4.	*(C)*	*14.*	*(D)*	*24.*	*(B)*
5.	*(D)*	*15.*	*(D)*	*25.*	*(D)*
6.	*(D)*	*16.*	*(C)*	*26.*	*(D)*
7.	*(A)*	*17.*	*(B)*	*27.*	*(A)*
8.	*(B)*	*18.*	*(D)*	*28.*	*(A)*
9.	*(A)*	*19.*	*(C)*	*29.*	*(C)*
10.	*(C)*	*20.*	*(B)*	*30.*	*(B)*

CTET-2019

Held on: 7th July, 2019

Paper-2

1. To understand individual differences in development it is important

(A) to look at the environmental factors that affect individuals.

(B) to consider maturation of the body and the brain.

(C) to consider both inherited characteristics as well as environmental factors and their interplay.

(D) to look at the inherited characteristics that give each person a special start in life.

2. Which of the following is not a principle of development?

(A) Development is relatively orderly.

(B) Development takes place gradually over a period of time.

(C) Exact course and nature of development is determined at the time of birth itself.

(D) Individuals develop at different rates.

3. Several research studies show that teachers have more overall interaction with boys than girls. What is the correct explanation for this?

(A) Boys need more attention than girls.

(B) This is an example of gender bias in teaching.

(C) Boys are easier to manage than girls in the classroom.

(D) Boys have much more academic capabilities than girls.

4. Which of the following is central to the concept of progressive education?

(A) Belief in the capability and potential of every child

(B) Standard instruction and assessment

(C) Extrinsic motivation and uniform assessment parameter

(D) Textbook centric learning

5. What instructional adaptation should a teacher make while working with students who are 'Visually Challenged'?

(A) Use a variety of visual presentation.

(B) Orient herself so that the students can watch her closely.

(C) Focus on a a variety of written tasks especially worksheets.

(D) Speak clearly and use a lot of touch and feel material.

6. Co-operative learning and peer-tutoring .... in an inclusive classroom.

(A) should be actively discouraged

(B) should be occasionally used

(C) should not be used

(D) should be actively promoted

7. Which of the following is most important in an inclusive classroom?

(A) Standardized testing

(B) Promoting competitive learning

(C) Individualized education plan

(D) Uniform instruction

8. Which of the following is a correctly matched pair of learner and their primary characteristics ?

(A) 'Dyslexic' learners -Lack reading and writing fluency

(B) Creative learner-Hyperactive; slow in completing work

(C) Attention deficit learners-High motivation; can sustain attention for long period of time.

(D) Hearing impaired learners-Cannot comprehend visual information

9. The ability to come up with original and divergent solutions to a problem is a primary characteristic of

(A) Impaired children

(B) Creative children

(C) Children with learning disability

(D) Egocentric children

10. Which of the following would not be consistent with a constructivist environment?

(A) Students work collaboratively and are given support to engage in task-oriented dialogue with each other

(B) Teacher elicit students ideas and experiences in relationship to key topics and plants teaching-learning to elaborate or restructure their current knowledge.

(C) Teacher employ specific end of the term assessment strategies and give feedback on products rather than processes.

(D) Students are given frequent opportunities to engage in complex, meaningful, problem based activities.

11. A teacher should encourage students to set .... rather than ....

(A) performance goal; learning goals

(B) failure avoiding goals; marks seeking goals

(C) marks seeking goals; failure avoiding goals

(D) learning goals; performance goals

12. Which of the following does not result in meaningful facilitation of learning?

(A) Promoting repetition and recall

(B) Use of examples and non-examples
(C) Encouraging multiple ways of looking at a problem
(D) Connecting new knowledge to pre-existing knowledge

13. Which of these is an example of extrinsic motivation?
(A) "I learn so much when I do my homework."
(B) "Doing homework makes me understand my concept better."
(C) "I complete my homework because the teachers gives us marks for each assignment."
(D) "I enjoy doing my homework because it is so much fun."

14. In a primary classroom a teacher should
(A) Give only non-examples
(B) Give both examples and non-examples
(C) Not give any examples and non-examples
(D) Give only examples

15. Which of the following strategies would promote meaning-making in children ?
(A) Transmission of information
(B) Using punitive measures
(C) Uniform and standardized testing
(D) Exploration and discussion

16. Which of the following are examples of effective learning strategies?
(i) Setting goals and time tables
(ii) Making organizational charts and concept maps
(iii) Thinking of examples and non-examples
(iv) Explaining to a peer
(v)Self-questioning
(A) (i), (iv), (v) (B) (i), (ii), (iii), (v)
(C) (i), (ii), (iii), (iv), (v) (D) (i), (ii), (iii)

17. In the constructivist frame child is viewed as
(A) 'tabula rasa' or 'blank slate' whose life is shaped entirely by experience.
(B) a 'passive being' who can be shaped and molded into any form through conditioning
(C) a 'problem solver' and a 'scientific investigator'
(D) 'miniature adult' who is less than adult in all aspects such as size, cognition, emotions.

18. A teacher's role while using co-operative learning in her class -
(A) is to leave the class and let children work on their own

(B) is to be supportive and monitor each group
(C) is to support the group which has the 'bright' and 'talented' children.
(D) is to be a silent spectator and let children do what they want.

19. Children's errors and misconceptions-
(A) are a hindrance and obstacle to the teaching-learning process
(B) should be ignored in the teaching-learning process
(C) signify that children's capabilities are far inferior than that of adults.
(D) are a significant step in the teaching-learning process.

20. According to Piaget, specific psychological structures (organized ways of making sense of experience) are called
(A) Schemes (B) images
(C) mental maps (D) mental tools

21. "With an appropriate question/suggestion, the child's understanding can be extended far beyond the point which she could have reached alone." Which construct does the above statement highlight ?
(A) Equilibration
(B) Conservation
(C) Intelligence
(D) Zone of proximal development

22. According to Lev Vygotsky, basic mental capacities are transformed into higher cognitive processes primarily through
(A) Social cultural theory
(B) Stimulus-response association
(C) Adaptation and organization
(D) Rewards and Punishment

23. Which of the following statements denotes the relationship between development and learning correctly ?
(A) Learning takes place irrespective of development
(B) Rate of learning far exceeds the rate of development
(C) Development and learning are inter-related and inter-dependent
(D) Development and learning are not related

24. One of the major accomplishments of concrete operational stage is
(A) Ability to conserve
(B) Hypothetic -deductive reasoning

(C) Secondary circular reactions
(D) Animistic thinking

25. Constructivists such as Jean Piaget and Lev Vygotsky view learning as
(A) Conditioning of responses
(B) Passive repetitive process
(C) Process of meaning-making by active engagement
(D) Acquisition of skills

26. Selecting and presenting stories and clippings from newspaper that portray both men and women in non-traditional roles is an effective strategy to
(A) Promote gender constancy
(B) Encourage stereotypical gender roles
(C) Counter gender stereotypes
(D) Promote gender bias

27. Read the following description and identify the stage of moral reasoning of kohlberg.

Description:

Right action is defined by self-chosen ethical principles of conscience that are valid for all humanity, regardless of law and social agreement.
(A) The social-contract orientation
(B) The social-order maintaining orientation
(C) The universal ethical principle orientation
(D) The instrumental purpose orientation

28. As per Howard Gardner's theory of multiple intelligence, how would the intelligence of a person with the following characteristics be categorized ?
(A) Intrapersonal
(B) Interpersonal
(C) Therapeutic
(D) Naturalistic

29. Which of the following should be the reasons for assessment of children ?
(i) To separate and label children into 'non-achievers', 'low-achievers', 'average' and 'high-achievers'.
(ii) To improve teaching-learning processes in the classroom.
(iii) To find out what changes and progress in learning that takes place in the child over a period of time.

(iv) To discuss the capabilities, potential, strengths and challenging areas of the child with the parents.

(A) (i), (ii), (iii)
(B) (ii), (iii), (iv)
(C) (ii), (iv)
(D) (i), (ii), (iii), (iv)

30. Which of the following play an important role in a child's socialization?

(i) Media
(ii) School
(iii) Family
(iv) Neighbourhood

(A) (ii), (iii)
(B) (i), (iii), (iv)
(C) (i), (ii), (iii), (iv)
(D) (iii), (i)

My Notes

Answer Key

1.	*(C)*	*11.*	*(D)*	*21.*	*(D)*
2.	*(C)*	*12.*	*(A)*	*22.*	*(A)*
3.	*(B)*	*13.*	*(C)*	*23.*	*(C)*
4.	*(A)*	*14.*	*(B)*	*24.*	*(A)*
5.	*(D)*	*15.*	*(D)*	*25.*	*(C)*
6.	*(D)*	*16.*	*(C)*	*26.*	*(C)*
7.	*(C)*	*17.*	*(C)*	*27.*	*(C)*
8.	*(A)*	*18.*	*(B)*	*28.*	*(B)*
9.	*(B)*	*19.*	*(D)*	*29.*	*(B)*
10.	*(C)*	*20.*	*(A)*	*30.*	*(C)*

CTET-2021

Held on: 1st January, 2021

Paper-1

1. **After getting hurt during a play activity, Rohan started crying. Seeing this, his father responded, "Don't behave like girls, boys don't cry". This statement by the father-**
   (A) Reflects gender stereotype.
   (B) Challenges gender stereotype.
   (C) Reduces gender bias.
   (D) Promotes gender equality.

2. **In a progressive classroom-**
   (A) A teacher should follow fixed curriculum.
   (B) The emphasis should be on competition among students.
   (C) Ample opportunities should be provided for construction of knowledge.
   (D) Students should be labelled on the basis of their academic scores.

3. **After observing that students are struggling to proceed further on an ongoing activity, a teacher decides to provide cues and hints in form of what, why, how. According to Lev Vygotsky's theory, this strategy of teacher will**
   (A) Demotivate the children to learn.
   (B) Act as a scaffold for learning.
   (C) Cause withdrawal tendency among students.
   (D) Be meaningless in process of learning.

4. **Which of the following is correct in the context of socialization of children?**
   (A) School is a secondary socialization agent and family is a primary socialization agent.
   (B) School is a primary socialization agent and peers are secondary socialization agents.
   (C) Peers are primary socialization agents and family is a secondary socialization agent.
   (D) Family and mass-media both are secondary socialization agents.

5. **Theory of multiple intelligence emphasizes that-**
   (A) Intelligence Quotient (IQ) can be measured only by objective tests.
   (B) Intelligence in one domain ensures intelligence in all other domains.
   (C) There are several forms of intelligences.
   (D) There are no individual differences in intelligence.

6. **According to Lawrence Kohlberg's theory, "Performing an act and doing something because others approves it", represents**

.... stage of morality.

(A) Pre-conventional (B) Conventional

(C) Post-conventional (D) Formal conventional

7. **Lev Vygotsky's social-cultural perspective of learning emphasizes importance of .... in the learning process.**

(A) Cultural tools (B) Attribution

(C) Motivation (D) Equilibration

8. **In his theory of cognitive development, Jean Piaget explains cognitive structures in terms of ....**

(A) Psychological tools

(B) Stimulus-response association

(C) Zone of proximal development

(D) Schemas

9. **Pre-operational stage in Jean Piaget's theory of cognitive development characterizes ....**

(A) Development of abstract thinking

(B) Centration in thought

(C) Hypothetico deductive thinking

(D) Ability to conserve and seriate objects.

10. **Which of the following statement is correct in context of development?**

(A) Development has the same rate of growth across cultures for everyone.

(B) Development occurs only through learning that takes place in school.

(C) Development occurs only during the period of childhood.

(D) Development is multidimensional.

11. **Sequence of development among children from birth to adolescence is**

(A) Sensory, concrete, abstract.

(B) Abstract, sensory, concrete.

(C) Concrete, abstract, sensory.

(D) Abstract, concrete, sensory.

12. **Individual differences in a progressive classroom should be treated as-**

(A) A hindrance to the process of learning.

(B) A failure on the part of teacher.

(C) Criteria for making ability-based groups.

(D) Important for planning of teaching-learning process.

13. In an Inclusive classroom emphasis should be on

(A) Performance oriented goals.
(B) Undifferentiated instructions.
(C) Segregation of students based on their social identity.
(D) Providing opportunities aiming at maximizing potential of individual children.

14. According to Right of Persons with Disabilities Act (2016), which of the following term is appropriate to use ?

(A) Retarded student
(B) Handicapped student
(C) Student with physical disability
(D) Student with crippled body

15. In order to address the needs of students who are facing learning difficulties, a teacher should NOT

(A) Use multiple audio-visual aids.
(B) Use constructive pedagogical approaches.
(C) Do individualized educational planning.
(D) Practice rigid structures for pedagogy and assessment.

16. .... is the primary identifying feature of creativity.

(A) Low comprehension (B) Divergent thinking
(C) Hyperactivity (D) Inattentiveness

17. In order to address learners from diverse backgrounds, a teacher should-

(A) Avoid talking about aspects related to diversity.
(B) Draw examples from diverse settings.
(C) Use standardized assessment for all.
(D) Use statements that strengthen negative stereotypes.

18. Problem-solving abilities can be facilitated by

(A) Focusing on drill and practice.
(B) Encouraging fixed process of solving the problems.
(C) Encouraging use of analogies.
(D) Generating fear among students.

19. Motivation to learn can be sustained by-

(A) Punishing the child.
(B) Focusing on mastery-oriented goals.
(C) Giving very easy tasks to children.
(D) Focusing on rote-memorisation.

20. Shame ....

(A) Has no relation to cognition.

(B) Can have negative impact on cognition.
(C) Is very effective to motivate the children to learn.
(D) Should be generated frequently in teaching-learning process.

21. Which of the following is most effective mode of teaching-learning?
(A) Rote memorization of content
(B) Exploration of relationships between concepts
(C) Observation without analysis (D) Imitation and repetition

22. A teacher should analyse the various errors made by students on a given task because
(A) She can decide degree of punishment accordingly.
(B) Understanding of errors are meaningful in the teaching learning process.
(C) She can segregate those who made more errors in comparison to others.
(D) learning is solely based on correction of errors.

23. It is difficult for children to learn when
(A) Information is presented in disconnected chunks.
(B) They are intrinsically motivated.
(C) Learning is socially contextualized.
(D) Content is represented through multiple ways.

24. Best state of learning is
(A) High arousal, high fear. (B) Low arousal, high fear.
(C) Moderate arousal, no fear. (D) No arousal, no fear.

25. Constructivist view of learning suggests that children .... construction of their own knowledge.
(A) Have no role to play in
(B) Are solely dependent on adults for
(C) Play an active role in
(D) Are solely dependent on textbooks in

26. Which of the following belief is good for learning?
(A) Ability is improvable. (B) Ability is fixed.
(C) Efforts don't make any difference.
(D) Failure is uncontrollable.

27. Conceptual understanding among students is likely to improve in the settings which emphasise on
(A) Competitions. (B) Textbook-centric pedagogy.
(C) Frequent examinations. (D) Inquiry and dialogue.

28. During a task, Saina is talking to herself about ways she can proceed on the task. According to Lev Vygotsky's ideas on language and thought; this kind of'private speech' is a sign of -

(A) Cognitive immaturity. (B) Self-regulation.

(C) Ego-centricism. (D) Psychological disorder.

29. Evaluation practices should aim at

(A) Labelling of students.

(B) Segregation of students for ability based groups.

(C) Identifying students' needs and requirements.

(D) Identification of high-achievers for prize distribution.

30. Individual differences in development of children can be attributed to

(A) Heredity only.

(B) Environment only.

(C) Neither heredity nor environment.

(D) Interplay of heredity and environment.

My Notes

Answer Key

1. (A)	11. (D)	21. (B)
2. (C)	12. (D)	22. (B)
3. (B)	13. (D)	23. (A)
4. (A)	14. (C)	24. (C)
5. (C)	15. (D)	25. (C)
6. (B)	16. (B)	26. (A)
7. (A)	17. (B)	27. (D)
8. (D)	18. (C)	28. (B)
9. (B)	19. (B)	29. (C)
10. (D)	20. (B)	30. (D)

CTET-2021

Held on: 1st January, 2021

Paper-2

1. **During the period of childhood, development-**
   (A) is slow and cannot be measured.
   (B) is multi-layered and complex.
   (C) consists only of quantitative changes.
   (D) is disorderly and disjointed.

2. **'Zone of proximal development' is**
   (A) the area between a child's current level of independent performance and the level of performance that the child could achieve with the help of adults and more skilled peers.
   (B) a range of tasks that the child should be able to do as per her age but cannot.
   (C) the process where two individuals who begin with different understandings arrive at a shared understanding.
   (D) the process in which children learn to perform tasks as set by the elder members in a society.

3. **According to Jean Piaget, children in formal operational stage**
   (A) are capable of hypotheticodeductive reasoning and propositional thought.
   (B) are bound by centration and irreversibly of thought.
   (C) cannot conserve, classify and seriate.
   (D) begin to engage in make-believe and symbolic play.

4. **At which stage of Lawrence Kohlberg's theory of moral development do individuals believe that actively maintaining the current social system ensures positive human relationships and societal order ?**
   (A) The punishment and obedience orientation
   (B) The social-order maintaining orientation
   (C) The instrumental purpose orientation
   (D) The universal ethical principle Orientation

5. **Which of the following is a correctly matched pair of type of intelligence and end-state performance possibilities as per Howard Gardner's theory of multiple intelligences ? Types of Intelligence End-state performance possibility**
   (A) Spatial - Therapist
   (B) Intra-personal - Salesperson
   (C) Linguistic - Sculptor
   (D) Bodily-kinesthetic - Athlete

6. **According to Lev Vygotsky -**
   (A) language plays an important role in cognitive development of children.

(B) children learn language through a 'language acquisition device'.
(C) children's cognitive development occurs in stages.
(D) maturation of schemas leads to cognitive development in children.

7. In a progressive classroom, assessment of learners during the process of teaching-learning -
(A) is not at all helpful in children's learning.
(B) creates a hindrance in the process of children's learning.
(C) is helpful in identifying 'high', 'low' and 'non' achievers for the purposes of giving feedback to the parents.
(D) is very important since it gives insights into children's understanding and helps the teacher to reflects on her pedagogy.

8. An effective classroom strategy to reduce gender stereotyping and broadening developmental possibilities for all sexes is
(A) to ignore and dismiss biological differences among the sexes.
(B) to reinforce gender roles as portrayed in the society.
(C) forming same-sex ability groupings.
(D) forming mixed-sex activity groups and promote discussion.

9. Multilingualism in a classroom needs to be understood as .... by the teachers.
(A) an asset and resource (B) a hindrance
(C) a problem (D) a systemic issue

10. A child-centered classroom is one in which
(A) the teacher uses the textbook as the only source of knowledge.
(B) the teacher segregates the children based on their abilities.
(C) the teacher uses rewards and punishments to direct children's behaviour.
(D) the teacher is flexible and caters to needs of individual children.

11. According to which theorist 'cultural tools' play an important role in cognitive development of children?
(A) Lev Vygotsky
(B) Jean Piaget
(C) Albert Bandura
(D) B.F. Skinner

12. Which of the following is NOT a suitable learning material for students who are partially sighted ?
(A) Large-print books
(B) Three dimensional maps and charts
(C) Talking books, felt bulletin boards
(D) Small-print worksheets

13. The underlying belief behind 'inclusive education' is
- (A) segregation of children on the basis of their abilities and provisioning of vocational training accordingly.
- (B) diagnostic labelling of children based on their handicaps for identification of their limitations.
- (C) provisioning of special education institutions for children with different handicaps.
- (D) the philosophy that all children have a right to get equal education in a regular school.

14. Needs of gifted and creative children can be addressed by
- (A) giving challenging tasks and activities to prevent boredom.
- (B) giving questions that require convergent thinking.
- (C) providing specific instructions to solve problems.
- (D) administrating memory based tests.

15. Children with 'dyslexia' can be identified by
- (A) finding out their social and cultural context.
- (B) a thorough physical health checkup.
- (C) analyzing their reading and writing skills.
- (D) assessing their ability to solve complex higher-order problems.

16. Which of the following is NOT an effective strategy to address learners from disadvantaged and deprived backgrounds?
- (A) Talk to the learners to understand their needs and challenges faced by them.
- (B) Asking the learners to enroll for tuition outside of school so that the teacher does not have to pay much attention to them.
- (C) Motivate the students to set moderately challenging goals and provide appropriate instructional support.
- (D) Form collaborative groups to work on activities and encourage students to support each other.

17. Physical and emotional health of children .... their learning
- (A) does not have any influence on
- (B) plays an important role in
- (C) is not related to
- (D) has an insignificant role in

18. To promote meaningful learning in the classrooms, a teacher should-
- (i) help students to regulate their own emotions and motivation.
- (ii) categorize and label students according to their performance and make ability-grouping.
- (iii) promote dialogue and discussion among children to build multiple perspectives.

(iv) ignore diversity in the classroom and follow standard methods of instruction.

(A) (i), (iii)
(B) (ii), (iii)
(C) (i), (iii), (iv)
(D) (i), (ii), (iii), (iv)

19. Learning is a .... and .... process.

(A) complex; active
(B) simple; linear
(C) simple; individual
(D) complex; passive

20. A teacher should .... the social, cultural, religious and linguistic diversity in her classroom to facilitate meaningful learning.

(A) dismiss
(B) ignore
(C) understand
(D) neglect

21. It is important to create .... learning environment in the classroom rather than .... one.

(A) collaborative; competitive
(B) competitive; collaborative
(C) fearful; facilitative
(D) competitive; facilitative

22. Which of the following is an example of effective motivational strategy to encourage students to learn?

(A) Providing scaffolding especially when students learn a new skill
(B) Emphasis on completion of work rather than learning.
(C) Giving tasks that are very easy.
(D) Creating a lot of opportunities for competition.

23. Which of the following statements about children's thinking is NOT correct?

(A) Children construct their own theories about various phenomenon around them.
(B) Children cannot think of concepts on their own and the primary role of teachers is to provide information.
(C) Children actively think about various phenomenon around them and have an urge to explore.
(D) Children are born with curiosity to learn about the world around them.

24. Children's failure in school

(A) suggests that children from deprived backgrounds are not capable of learning.

(B) indicates that school has not been able to cater to the needs and interests of these children.

(C) proves that these children have genetic birth defects and hence should be pulled out from school.

(D) signifies that parents have not been able to support their children to learn.

25. By working in groups, teaching and helping each other, children

(A) are able to reflect on their own thought processes and shift to a higher level of cognitive activity.

(B) can develop misconceptions which interferes with their learning.

(C) get distracted and hence it is an ineffective pedagogical strategy.

(D) develop competitive tendencies that hinder learning.

26. In a .... classroom teachers adapt their pedagogy and vary assessment to cater to individual students.

(A) teacher-centric

(B) progressive

(C) textbook-centric

(D) behaviouristic

27. Which of the following statements about development is correct?

(A) There is a lot of cultural diversity in the development of children.

(B) Children across the world follow the same sequence and exact time of development.

(C) Development occurs in a neat, orderly set of stages predetermined by genetic factors.

(D) Development is simple and unidimensional.

28. Which of the following is a major hallmark of the period of middle childhood?

(A) Emergence of make-believe play.

(B) Development of logical thought that is concrete in nature.

(C) Rapid development of motor skills and overall physical growth.

(D) Development of scientific reasoning and ability to think abstractly.

29. School .... socialization of children.

(A) does not play any role in

(B) plays very little role in

(C) is a primary agency of

(D) is a secondary agency of

30. Which of the following theorists proposed that children's thinking is qualitatively different from that of adults?

(A) Jean Piaget
(B) Lev Vygotsky
(C) Howard Gardner
(D) Lawrence Kohlberg

My Notes

Answer Key

1. (B)

2. (A)

3. (A)

4. (B)

5. (D)

6. (A)

7. (D)

8. (D)

9. (A)

10. (D)

11. (A)

12. (D)

13. (D)

14. (A)

15. (C)

16. (B)

17. (B)

18. (A)

19. (A)

20. (C)

21. (A)

22. (A)

23. (B)

24. (B)

25. (A)

26. (B)

27. (A)

28. (B)

29. (D)

30. (A)

CTET-2022

Held on: 28 December, 2022

Paper-1

1. Which period marks the transition from childhood to adulthood?

(A) Early childhood

(B) Middle childhood

(C) Preoperational period

(D) Adolescence

2. Which of the following would require use of gross motor skills ?

(A) Painting on a paper using brush

(B) Cutting and pasting bits of paper

(C) Threading the needle

(D) Walking and running

3. The first primary agent of socialization is.

(A) family

(B) school

(C) friends

(D) media

4. The belief that physical objects such as dolls, cars, etc have life-like qualities is called -

(A) animistic thinking

(B) hierarchical thinking

(C) centration

(D) categorization

5. Assertion (A):

Four-year-old Riya cannot take into consideration the height and width of the two beakers at the same time while pouring the same amount of water into tall and wide beakers.

Reason(R):

Riya is at Preoperational stage of cognitive development as per Jean Piaget.

Choose the correct option.

(A) Both (A) and (R) are true and (R) is the correct explanation of (A).

(B) Both (A) and (R) are true but (R) is not the correct explanation of (A).

(C) (A) is true but (R) is false.

(D) Both (A) and (R) are false.

6. Giving cues and offering support to children as and when required is an example of

(A) Scaffolding (B) Reinforcement

(C) Conditioning (D) Cognitive conflict

7. The application of Vygotsky's theory to children's education proposes

(A) collaborative learning (B) operant learning

(C) rote learning (D) passive learning

8. In Kohlberg's of moral development the individual strives to maintain the expectations of others rather than focus on the consequences of one's actions.

(A) Preoperational level (B) Pre-conventional level

(C) Conventional level (D) Post-conventional level

9. A progressive classroom is

(A) Examination-centric (B) Textbook-centric

(C) Teacher-centric (D) Learner-centric

10. Renu is a counsellor at a school. Which intelligence should she have to be an effective counsellor as per Howard Gardners theory?

(A) Linguistic (B) Spatial

(C) Interpersonal (D) Intra person al

11. According to NEP 2020, which language should a teacher use for interacting with primary school children during the teaching-learning process ?

(A) Only the regional language

(B) Only Hindi language

(C) Only English language

(D) Mother tongue of the children

12. Five-year-old Vaishali told her mother. "Mother, I want a football like Amit." Responding to Vaishali, her mother said, "Only boys play with football, I will bring a small cute doll for you." The mother's response illustrates

(A) Gender Role Flexibility

(B) Gender Equity

(C) Gender Stereotyping

(D) Gender Relevance

13. Labelling of children and placing them in categories

(A) enhances and facilitates meaningful learning.

(B) creates a sense of helplessness and inferiority amongst a group of children.

(C) is a positive strategy to manage the learning needs of all children.

(D) does not have any impact on the self-esteem and performance of children.

14. Continuous and comprehensive evaluation means

(A) comparing the students with each other

(B) assessment covering all aspects of school activities related to child's overall development

(C) evaluation of child's performance on the basis of scholastic activities only

(D) evaluation of the children at the end of the year to determine promotion to the next class

15. Effective teachers often use probing questions during the course of teaching-learning processes in the classroom. This would enable the teacher to undertake

(A) Summative assessment

(B) Formative assessment

(C) Standardised assessment

(D) Norm-referenced assessment

16. Role of teacher in an inclusive classroom is to

(A) address and respond to the diverse needs of all children

(B) give attention to some special students ony

(C) identify and segregate children based on their academic abilities

(D) refer special needs children to a specialist and ensure that they are taught in a separate section

17. What should a teacher keep in mind while teaching a diverse group of learners?

(i) Acknowledge and respect every student

(ii) Ignore cultural differences

(iii) Maintain consistent communication

(iv) Give indirect instructions

(v)Give students autonomy and flexibility

(A) (i) (ii) (iii) (B) (ii) (iii) (iv)

(C) (i) (iii) (v) (D) (iii)(iv) (v)

18. To cater to the specific needs of child with visual disability, the teacher should

(A) focus on a variety of visual presentations

(B) use a variety of tactile manipulative and materials

(C) show a lot of silent films

(D) give a lot of structured worksheets with pictures

19. Difficulties in social interaction and verbal communication is a typical characteristics of

(A) Autism

(B) Attention Deficit Hyperactivity Disorder

(C) Dyslexia

(D) Dyscalculia

20. The teacher gives clays of different colours to the children and asks them to make whatever comes to their mind from that clay. Through this, she wants to promotein children.

(A) Creativity (B) Rote memorisation

(C) Non-cooperation (D) Indiscipline

21. The early primary years of childhood should focus on the development of

(i) physical skills

(ii) social skills

(iii) cognitive capabilities

(iv) emotional skills

(v) abstract reasoning

(1) (i) (ii) (2) (i) (iii)

(3) (i) (ii) (iii) (iv) (4) (i) (ii) (iii) (iv) (v)

22. In a constructivist classroom, meaningful learning

(A) refers to the storage and retrieval of information.

(B) is the process of discovery through exploration and interaction.

(C) occurs through the use of rewards and punishment.

(D) takes place through repeated practice and drill.

23. A teacher begins to works together, by giving cues and prompts, with a student who is unable to understand a concept. This process is referred to as

(A) scaffolding

(B) teacher-centered pedagogy

(C) maintainance rehearsal

(D) direct instruction

24. ***Assertion (A)*:**

A teacher tries to include examples from the immediate environment of children to make the classes interactive.

Reason(R):

Socio-cultural context plays an important role in learning.

Choose the correct option.

(A) Both (A) and (R) are true and (R) is the correct explanation of (A).

(B) Both (A) and (R) are true but (R) is not the correct explanation of (A).

(C) (A) is true but (R) is false.

(D) Both (A) and (R) are false.

25. What will pose as a hindrance to a child in solving a problem ?

(A) Identifying the problem correctly

(B) Defining the problem clearly

(C) Thinking of similar problems that one has solved

(D) Remaining fixed at using objects in a conventional manner

26. Assertion (A)

Mistakes and errors made by the students are indicative of the failure of the teachers and the students.

Reason (R):

Children do not have the ability to think on their own and need to be constantly instructed to ensure learning.

Choose the correct option.

(A) Both (A) and (R) are true and (R) is the correct explanation of (A).

(B) Both (A) and (R) are true but (R) is not the correct explanation of (A).

(C) (A) is true but (R) is false.

(D) Both (A) and (R) are false.

27. Which of the following is not an emotion ?

(A) Memory

(B) Anger

(C) Love

(D) Fear

28. What strategies can a teacher use to increase intrinsic motivation in her primary grade students ?

(A) Praise each and every effort made by every student

(B) Punish undesirable behaviour

(C) Promote competition amongst students

(D) Encourage children to experience joy of learning

29. Overall physical and mental well-being of the childlearning.

(A) does not affect

(B) hinders

(C) is not related to

(D) facilitates

30. Ruhi believes that she did not study properly which is why she did not get good marks in her science test though she can do science quite well. She is attributing her performance to

(A) environmental factors

(B) lack of ability

(C) lack of effort

(D) tough luck

My Notes

Answer Key

1.	*(D)*	*11.*	*(D)*	*21.*	*(C)*
2.	*(D)*	*12.*	*(C)*	*22.*	*(B)*
3.	*(A)*	*13.*	*(B)*	*23.*	*(A)*
4.	*(A)*	*14.*	*(B)*	*24.*	*(A)*
5.	*(A)*	*15.*	*(B)*	*25.*	*(D)*
6.	*(A)*	*16.*	*(A)*	*26.*	*(D)*
7.	*(A)*	*17.*	*(C)*	*27.*	*(A)*
8.	*(C)*	*18.*	*(B)*	*28.*	*(D)*
9.	*(D)*	*19.*	*(A)*	*29.*	*(D)*
10.	*(C)*	*20.*	*(A)*	*30.*	*(C)*

CTET-2022

Held on: 28 December, 2022

Paper-2

1. **Assertion (A):** The physical development of children is important as it also influences a child's social and cognitive development.

   Reason (R): All aspects of development are inter related in childhood and greatly influence each other.

   Choose the correct option.

   (A) Both (A) and (R) are true and (R) is the correct explanation of (A).

   (B) Both (A) and (R) are true but (R) is not the correct explanation of (A).

   (C) (A) is true but (R) is false.

   (D) Both (A) and (R) are false.

2. **The principle that suggests growth follows a pattern beginning from head and then proceeding to the rest of the body is :**

   (A) Proximodistal principle

   (B) Cephalocaudal principle

   (C) Principle of individuality

   (D) Principle of uniformity

3. **..................... refers to the process of predetermined unfolding of genetic dispositions.**

   (A) Vatu ration (B) Scaffolding

   (C) Adaptation (D) Socialisation

4. **According to Jean Piaget which of the following factors are influential in determining the course of cognitive development ?**

   (i) Maturation

   (ii) Conditioning

   (iii) Punishment

   (iv) Activity

   (v) Social experience

   (A) (i), (ii), (iv), (v) (B) (ii), (iii), (iv)

   (C) (iii), (iv), (v) (D) (i), (ii), (iii), (iv), (v)

5. **According to Jean Piaget a cliild who believes that water when poured from one container to another, gains or looses in quantity depending on the shape of the second container:**

   (A) has not attained conservation

(B) has not mastered object permanence
(C) is limited in drinking due to animism
(D) is unable to perform seriation

6. The correct sequence of stages of cognitive development given by Piaget is:

(A) Sensorimotor stage, Pre-Operational stage, Concrete Operational stage, and Formal Ope rational stage
(B) Pre-Operational stage, Concrete Operational stage, Sensorimotor stage, and Formal Operational stage
(C) Formal Operational stage, Concrete Operational stage, Pre-Operational stage, and Sensorimotor stage
(D) Sensorimotor stage, Concrete Operational stage, Pre-Operational stage, and Formal Operational stage

7. Neha resists eating sweets her mother has got for guests because she might get caught. According to Kohlberg's theory Neha is at which stage of moral development?

(A) Instrumental purpose orientation
(2) Punishment and obedience orientation
(C) Universal ethical principles
(D) Good boy-good girl orientation

8. As per .... theory children learn through interaction with more knowledgeable peers and adults.

(A) Lev Vygotsky's (B) Jean Piaget's
(C) Howard Gardner's (D) Lawhrence Kohlberg

9. What plays an important role in cognitive development according to Lev Vygotsky?

(A) Conditioning (B) Reinforcement
(C) Cultural context (D) Heredity

10. In Howard Gardner's theory of intelligence, the ability to manipulate both the body and objects is referred to as :

(A) Logico-mathematical intelligence
(B) Bodily-kinaesthetic intelligence
(C) Interpersonal intelligence
(D) Linguistic intelligence

11. Visual-spatial intelligence includes :

(A) The capacity to think in images and pictures, to visualise accurately and abstractly.

(B) Sensitivity to rhythm, pitch, meter, tone, melody.

(C) Ability to comprehend and create stories and poems.

(D) Ability to classify natural forms such as animal and plant species and rocks and Mountain types.

12. A teacher's remark to boys in a co-education class, "Be strong and don't behave meekly like girls" would encourage :

(A) gender equity

(B) gender stereotyping

(C) gender role flexibility

(D) gender equality

13. What should be the pedagogical strategies m a classroom with diverse learners?

(A) Reasonable accommodation

(B) Standardized assessment

(C) Decontextualized curriculum

(D) Inflexibility in approach

14. Which of the following is an important aspect related to assessment for learning?

(A) Single strategy of assessment can provide complete information about a child's progress and learning

(B) It serves to observe changes in learning progress over time

(C) It does not identify individual and specific needs of all children

(D) It helps teachers to identify children who are mentally retarded

15. Aim of Assessment should be to:

(A) Induce fear and stress in the students.

(B) Create feeling of insecurity and inferiority.

(C) Enable comparison among students.

(D) Aid in the process of teaching learning.

16. Assertion (A): Only special children benefit from inclusive education.

Reason (R): The concept of inclusive education is based on the philosophy of addressing only learners with some impairment.

Choose the correct option.

(A) Both (A) and (R) are true and (R) is the correct explanation of (A)

(B) Both (A) and (R) are true but (R) is not the correct explanation of (A)

(C) (A) is true but (R) is false

(D) Both (A) and (R) are false

17. To cater to students from disadvantaged backgrounds teachers should practise

(A) Social exclusion

(B) Social marginalization

(C) Standardized curriculum

(D) Differentiated instruction

18. .... is an example of assistive technology to aid mobility for students with locomotor disability.

(A) Wheelchair

(B) Large print books

(C) Word prediction software

(D) Tactile materials

19. Difficulties in mathematical concepts and computation are typical characteristics of students with :

(A) Dyscalculia

(B) Dyslexia

(C) Dysgraphia

(D) Autism

20. Typical identifying characteristics of creative children include:

(A) Rigidity for ideas

(B) High tolerance for boredom

(C) Preference for complexity

(D) Convergent thinking

21. Meaningful learnmg involves :

(A) Provisions of rewards and punishment

(B) Opportunities to interact with each other

(C) Reflections on learning how to learn

(D) Opportunites for competition with peers

22. **Assertion (A):** Learner-centred approach is one where textbook is the centre of all learning.

Reason (R): Students in middle school learn best when asked to reproduce the textbook as it is.

Choose the correct option.

(A) Both **(A)** and **(R)** are true and **(R)** is the correct explanation of **(A)**.

(B) Both **(A)** and **(R)** are true but **(R)** is not the correct explanation of **(A)**.

(C) **(A)** is true but **(R)** is false.

(D) Both **(A)** and **(R)** are false.

23. **In a soao-construchvist classroom, learning:**

(A) Is a permanent measurable change in the child's behaviour

(B) Is a process of co-construction of knowledge

(C) Happens by pairing of a stimulus and response

(D) Takes place when the students are offered positive reinforcement

24. **................. should be the basis for a conducive classroom environment for learning.**

(A) Principles of conditioning and reinforcement

(B) Competition and individualism

(C) Cooperation and collaboration

(D) Segregation and labelling

25.

Assertion (A): Encouraging middle school children to make intuitive guesses and prompting them to look for different ways is an effective strategy to promote problem-solving skills.

Reason (R): Children learn through the processes of discussion and thinking of multiple perspectives.

Choose tire correct option.

(A) Both **(A)** and **(R)** are true and **(R)** is the correct explanation of **(A)**.

(B) Both **(A)** and **(R)** are true but **(R)** is not the correct explanation of **(A)**.

(C) **(A)** is true but **(R)** is false.

(D) Both **(A)** and **(R)** are false.

26. Questions in the classrooms:

(A) Should be asked by the students and answered by the teacher only.

(B) Should be asked by the teacher and answered by tire students only.

(C) Should not be asked or responded by anyone.

(D) Should be asked and answered both by tire students and teachers.

27. Intrinsic motivation amongst students can be increased by:

(A) Offering materialist rewards

(B) Negative reinforcement

(C) Fear of punishment

(D) Focusing on the joy of learning

28. Students in middle school construct knowledge and make meaning through:

(i) Active exploration

(ii) Working on abstract problems

(iii) Enquiry and experimentation

(iv) Interaction with teachers and peers

(A) (i) (iii)

(B) (i) (ii) (iv)

(C) (ii) (iii) (iv)

(D) (i) (ii) (iii) (iv)

29. Teachers should encourage children to think of ability as .... and failure as ....

(A) Fixed; shameful and humiliating.

(B) Incremental; an oppportunity for improvement.

(C) Fixed; an opportunity for improvement.

(D) Incremental; shameful and humiliating.

30. .... would be a contributing factor for children's academic failure.

(A) Collaborative learning

(B) Inclusive classroom

(C) Decontextualised curriculum

(D) Meaningful leitrning

My Notes

Answer Key

1.	*(A)*	*11.*	*(A)*	*21.*	*(B,C)*
2.	*(B)*	*12.*	*(B)*	*22.*	*(D)*
3.	*(A)*	*13.*	*(A)*	*23.*	*(B)*
4.	*(*)*	*14.*	*(B)*	*24.*	*(C)*
5.	*(A)*	*15.*	*(D)*	*25.*	*(A)*
6.	*(A)*	*16.*	*(D)*	*26.*	*(D)*
7.	*(B)*	*17.*	*(D)*	*27.*	*(D)*
8.	*(A)*	*18.*	*(A)*	*28.*	*(D)*
9.	*(C)*	*19.*	*(A)*	*29.*	*(B)*
10.	*(B)*	*20.*	*(C)*	*30.*	*(C)*

CTET-2023

Held on: 20 August, 2023

Paper-1

Directions: Answer the following questions by selecting the correct/ most appropriate option.

1. **As per Lev Vygotsky, ... plays a significant role in the development of conceptual abilities among children.**
   (A) Standardized curriculum
   (B) Tangible rewards
   (C) Peer collaboration
   (D) Social isolation

2. **Four-year-old Aparna says that a button is alive because it helps tie her shirt together. According to Jean Piaget, her thinking is characterized by:**
   (A) Hypothetical-deductive thinking
   (B) Transductive reasoning
   (C) Animistic thinking
   (D) Centration

3. **According to Lev Vygotsky's theory, inner speeph:**
   (A) is a way for children to regulate their own thinking.
   (B) is a way for children to communicate with an imaginary friend.
   (C) is a sign of cognitive immaturity.
   (D) is a sign of developmental delay.

4. **According to Howard Gardner, a philosopher has .... type of intelligence and a sculptor has more .... type of intelligence.**
   (A) interpersonal; linguistic
   (B) linguistic; interpersonal
   (C) spatial; intrapersonal
   (D) intrapersonal; spatial

5. **Which of the following is an example of an internal attribution for failure?**
   (A) I failed the test because my friends were . distracting me.
   (B) I received a low grade because the Reacher is a tough grader.
   (C) I failed the test because I didn't study enough.

(D) I didn't get good marks because the teacher was biased.

6. Which of the following is an example of a question that requires students to reflect on their own thinking?

(A) How has your thinking about the use of verbs changed since the beginning of the class?

(B) What is the relationship between nouns and verbs in a sentence?

(C) What is the definition of a verb?

(D) How do you change a verb to the present tense?

7. Read the following statements and choose the correct option :

Assertion (A):

At a very early age, girls in most cultures across the world choose dolls as toys while boys prefer to play with cars.

Reason (R):

Children organize information about what is considered appropriate for a boy or a girl on the basis of what a particular culture expects and behave accordingly.

(A) (A) is true, but (R) is false.

(B) Both (A) and (R) are false.

(C) Both (A) and (R) are true and (R) is the correct explanation of (A).

(D) Both (A) and (R) are true, but (R) is *not* the correct explanation of (A).

8 Read the following statement's and choose the g. correct option:

Assertion (A):

Interaction with more knowledgeable others, such as teachers and peers, can provide the necessary support and guidance to help learners develop their understanding and skills.

Reason (R):

Social interaction is a key component of learning and development.

(A) (A) is true, but (R) is false.

(B) Both (A) and (R) are false.

(C) Both (A) and (R) are true and (R) is the correct explanation of (A).

(D) Both (A) and (R) are true, but (R) is ***not*** the correct explanation of (A).

9. According to Lev Vygotsky :

(A) Language development facilitates cognitive development.

(B) Social factors influence language development, but not cognitive development.

(C) Cognitive development facilitates language development.

(D) Language development and cognitive development advance independent from each other.

10. At which level of Lawrence Kohl berg's moral reasoning, do children typically believe that people should live up to the expectations of the society and behave in "good ways?

(A) Pre-operational level

(B) Post-operational level

(C) Pre-conventional level

(D) Conventional level

11. Which of the following is an effective method to enhance problem-solving skills in children?

(A) Giving them opportunities to brainstorm and make intuitive guesses

(B) Discouraging independent thinking and focusing on declarative knowledge

(C) Encouraging them to avoid difficult problems

(D) Providing them with ready-made solutions to problems

12. Experiential learning stresses on:

(A) learning as a product rather than a process.

(B) control of teacher on the learning of children.

(C) the role of reinforcement in learning.

(D) importance of critical reflection.

13. Read the following statements and choose the correct option :

Assertion (A):

Teachers should create a meaningful environment which seeks active participation and engagement of all children.

Reason (R):

All children are intrinsically motivated to learn and are capable of learning.

(A) (A) is true, but (R) is false.

(B) Both (A) and (R) are false.

(C) Both (A) and (R) are true and (R) is the cprrect explanation of (A).

(D) Both (A) and (R) are truc, but (R) is ***not*** the correct explanation of (A).

14. Which of the following process does not contribute to the course of learning?

(A) Decontextualization

(B) Organization

(C) Categorization

(D) Conceptualization

15. Which of the following is a gross motor skill ?

(A) Cutting along the outline of a big rectangle on a paper

(B) Knitting

(C) Swimming

(D) Cutting along the outline of a circle on a paper

16. Physical growth and development follow the .... and .... principles of development.

(A) differentiation (simple to complex); integration (complex to simple)

(B) integration (simple to complex); differentiation (complex to simple)

(C) cephalocaudal (top-down); proximodistal (inner to outer)

(D) proximodistal (top-down); cephalocaudal (inner to outer)

17. In early childhood, growth .... and thinking is ...., while in middle childhood, growth ....and thinking is...........

(A) slows, logical; is steady, egocentric

(B) slows, somewhat egocentric; is steady, logical

(C) is steady, somewhat egocentric; slows,- logical

(D) is steady, logical; slows, egocentric

18. One of the main characteristics of pre-operational thought

according to Jean Piaget is .... which refers to the tendency to focus on one aspect of a situation and neglect others.

(A) Transduction

(B) Causation

(C) Centration

(D) Decentration

19. What is the main goal of 'assessment for learning'?

(A) To compare student performance to a standard or benchmark

(B) To identify students who can be categorised as 'slow learners'

(C) To evaluate student performance and assign grades

(D) To provide feedback to students that can be used to improve their learning

20. At which age can children engage in word play and like jokes and riddles that involve a play on words?

(A) Seven years

(B) Twelve years

(C) One year

(D) Three years

21. Carol Gilligan has critiqued Kohlberg's theory of moral development:

(A) for using case study as the research method.

(B) from a social cognitive perspective.

(C) from a feminist perspective.

(D) for not giving adequate importance to genetic factors.

22. While .... agencies of socialisation are predominantly important in infancy, ... agencies of socialization also become important in early childhood.

(A) secondary; tertiary

(B) tertiary, secondary

(C) primary; secondary

(D) secondary, primary

23. Dysgraphia is a:

(A) Psychological disorder characterized by lack of attention and impulsive behaviour.

(B) Speech disorder characterized by stuttering and errors in articulation.

(C) Locomotor disorder characterized by gross motor impairment.

(D) Neurological disorder characterized by trouble in forming letters and shapes.

24. The approach to educating gifted children which moves them through curriculum at an unusually rapid pace is known as:

(A) Immersion

(B) Differentiated instruction

(C) Enrichment

(D) Acceleration

25. Which of the following is a typical characterstic of students having autism?

(A) Higher level of communication skills

(B) Superior ability of differentiating fiction from fact

(C) Advanced socio-emotional reciprocity

(D) Frequent repetitive and recurring behaviour

26. Teachers who are working towards inclusive classrooms:

(i) Create curriculum adaptations

(ii) Incorporate diverse perspectives

(iii) Examine their own implicit bias

(iv) See diversity as an obstacle Which of the above are correct?

(A) (ii), (iii), (iv)

(B) (i), (ii), (iii), (iv)

(C) (i), (ii), (iii)

(D) (i), (iii), (iv)

27. Variability in learning styles of students:

(A) should be seen as a barrier and hindrance toj,p aching-learning process.

(B) should be valued and seen as a reflection . of human diversity.

(C) should be ignored and attempts should be made to bring uniformity in learning styles.

(D) should not be taken into consideration during teaching-learning process.

28. Read the following statements and choose the correct option:

Assertion (A):

To facilitate critical thinking among learners, teachers should expose them to diverse situations and differing perspectives. .

Reason (R):

Students learn and enrich their abilities to think critically and creatively as they engage in conversations across differences.

(A) (A) is true, but (R) is false.

(B) Both (A) and (R) are false.

(C) Both (A) and (R) are true and (R) is the correct explanation of (A).

(D) Both (A) and (R) are true, but (R) is not the correct explanation of (A).

29. Theprimary goal of learning should be:

(A) development of critical thinking.

(B) memorization of facts.

(C) becoming excellent at rote rehearsal.

(D) competing with peers.

30. Children learn more effectively if a concept proceeds from:

(A) Rational to Empirical.

(B) Generic to Specific.

(C) Abstract to Concrete.

(D) Complex to Simple.

My Notes

Answer Key

1.	*(C)*	*11.*	*(A)*	*21.*	*(C)*
2.	*(C)*	*12.*	*(D)*	*22.*	*(C)*
3.	*(A)*	*13.*	*(C)*	*23.*	*(D)*
4.	*(D)*	*14.*	*(A)*	*24.*	*(D)*
5.	*(C)*	*15.*	*(C)*	*25.*	*(D)*
6.	*(A)*	*16.*	*(C)*	*26.*	*(C)*
7.	*(C)*	*17.*	*(B)*	*27.*	*(B)*
8.	*(C)*	*18.*	*(C)*	*28.*	*(C)*
9.	*(A)*	*19.*	*(D)*	*29.*	*(A)*
10.	*(D)*	*20.*	*(D)*	*30.*	*(B)*

CTET-2023

Held on: 20 August, 2023

Paper-2

Directions: Answer the following questions by selecting the correct/ most appropriate option.

1. **According to Piaget, the four qualitatively differpm stages:**
   (A) are dependent upon the genetic codes of the children.
   (B) represent universal patterns of development of children.
   (C) illustrate that children's minds are miniature adult minds.
   (D) vary vastly across the various cultures in theworid.
2. **Lev Vegotsky believed that development:**
   (A) results directly from maturation.
   (B) results directly from social interaction.
   (C) is an unfolding of genetic programming.
   (D) is discontinuous in nature.
3. **Which of the following is a limitation of Piaget's theory of cognitive development?**
   (A) It doss not account for the role of biological factors in cognitive development.
   (B) It does not account for the influence of culture and social factors on cognitive development.
   (C) It does not account for individual differences in cognitive development.
   (D) It overemphasizes the role of language in cognitive development.
4. **Read the following statements and choose the correct option:**
   Assertion (A):
   Every year Lata, a Class VII teacher invites a female maths professor and a male nurse to her class to discuss careers in these fields.
   Reason (R):
   Gender differences are innate and not acquired through society.
   (A) Both (A) and (R) are false.
   (B) Both (A) and (R) are true and (R) is the corredf explanation of (A).
   (C) Both (A) and (R) are true, but (R) is ***not*** the correct

explanation of (A).

(D) (A) is true, but (R) is false.

5. Which of the following questiions promotes critical and cretive thinking in children?

(A) How many states and how many capitls are there in your country?

(B) What it the name of your country and its geographical location on the map

(C) Where does water come from in your city

(D) Which can be the beat way to save water and why?

6. What does inclusive education entail?

(A) Provisioning of only vocational education to learners with special need?

(2) Flexibility in the curriculum as a result of recognition of individual differences

(C) Segregation and categorisation of students on the basis of their abilities

(D) Standard curriculum for all learners

7. What is the role of evidence in critical thinking?

(A) Evidence is irrelevant to critical thinking.

(B) Evidence should be ignored in favour of personal opinion.

(C) Evidence should he accepted without analysis

(D) Evidence should be evaluated in a logical and systematic way

8. Read the following statements and choose the correct option:

Assertion (A):

Jean Piaget and Lev Vygotsky differ in their perspective on the influence of language on cognitive development in children.

Reason (R):

In discovery learning, teacher provides opportunities and students derive information for themselves.

(A) Both (A) and (R) are false.

(B) Both (A) and (R) are true and iR) is the correct explanation of (A).

(C) Both (A) and (R) are true, but (R) is ***not*** tlie correct explanation of (A).

(D) (A) is true, but (R) is false.

9. Read the following statements and choose the 9. correct option:

Assertion (A):

Considerable variations exist in developmental rates among children.

Reason (R):

Developmental differences are an inevitable result of complex interaction of genetic and experiential variations.

(A) Both (A) and (R) are false.

(B) Both (A) and (R) are true and (R) is the correct explanation of (A).

(C) Both (A) and (R) are true, but (R) is ***not*** the correct explanation of (A).

(D) (A) is true, but (R) is false.

10. Sibling relationships:

(A) play an important role only during early childbed.

(B) do not have much role in socialization.

(C) are similar to relationships with parents and peers and play an important role in socialization throughout childhood.

(D) are different than relationships with parents and peers and play an important role in socialization throughout childhood.

11. Which principle of development is illustrated in the following statement ?

"Children who are deprived of a conducive environment for learning language in their early years have some difficulty in picking language later in life."

(A) Development of language is totally dependent on genetics.

(B) Development is a disorderly and unpredictable.

(C) There is a sensitive period of language development.

(D) Language and cognition are complexly interrelated.

12. Read the following statements and choose the 12 correct option:

Assertion (A):

Teachers should ask students to identify their own examples and non-exampies of the concept for strengthening the concept.

Reason (R):

Thinking of examples leads to strengthening of the concept while non-examples tend to confuse the students.

(A) Both (A) and (R) are false.

(B) Both (A) and (R) are true and (R) is the correct ex-planation of (A).

(C) Both (A) and (R) are true, but (R) is ***not*** the correct explanation of (A).

(D) (A) is true, but (R) is false.

13. General Principles of learning suggest that studeoiR learn better if a teacher:

(A) first introduces the concept overall and then moves on to the intricacies of it.

(B) first discusses the concepts in terms of logic and reason and then grants opportunity to verify the ideas.

(C) first discusses what is not known to the student and then comes to what the student alreadj' knows.

(D) first introduces the concept in its symbolic form and then moves to its physical form.

14. A teacher wants to help her students develop metacognitive skills. Which of the following strategies would be most effective?

(A) Assigning texts to students to memorize and encouraging them to repeat information from the textbook

(B) Providing students with detailed and prescriptive instructions for all learning tasks

(C) Encouraging students to reflect on their own learning and evaluate their progress.

(D) Providing frequent grades and feedback to motivate students

15. In the context of inclusion, curriculum learning expectations are the same in .... while in ...., they are different.

(A) acceleration; enrichment

(B) accommodation; modification

(C) modification; accommodation

(D) enrichment; acceleration

16. Which of the following set correctly mentions the characteristics on which students who are gifted typically differ from other students in the class?

(A) Advanced depth of understanding

(B) Fast pace of learning

(C) Higher dependence on others for understanding

(D) Rapid physical development

Choose the.correct option:

(A) C and D

(B) A and B

(C) B and C

(D) A and C

17. Which of the following statements is correct in the context of hearing impairment?

(A) Hearing impairment of a child can be reliably tested by making loud noises near the child.

(B) Hearing impairment is always due to a physical problem with the ear.

(C) All children with hearing impairment need to use 'sign language' to communicate.

(D) Hearing impairment can affect a child's ability to communicate effectively.

18. According to constructivist theorists, which of the following statements would not be correct?

(l) Learners need to be extrinsically motivated to ensure effective learning.

(B) Knowledge is pluralistic and multiple.

(C) Learners construct knowledge in their social and cultural context.

(D) Knowledge is subjective.

19. How can a teacher help Aman who is struggling with complex problems develop problem-solving skills?

(A) Discourage him from experimenting and taking risks

(B) Provide him with the answers

(C) Tell him to give up on the problem

(D) Encourage him to brainstorm and generate ideas

20. The underlying principle of 'understanding-based teaching' is the belief that:

(A) learners can construct knowledge when provided with a facilitativc environment to do so.

(B) learners know little and leaching involves transmission of facts to students.

(C) learners are passive recipients and the teacher has the 'right' knowledge.

(D) learners' abilities and needs are diverse which cannot be catered to without focusing on standard instructions.

21. A conducive classroom environment for learning in middle classes centres around ....

(A) competitive ethos

(B) conditioning and reinforcement

(C) co-operative learning

(D) fear of punishment and embarrassment

22. Students struggling with dyslexin' can be taught to read:

(A) through use of strict punishment to ensure corrective reading.

(B) through systemic phonological training.

(C) by providing higher grade level reading texts

(D) by encouraging them to study in multiple distractions.

23. Read the following statements and choose the correct option:

Assertion (A):

Teachers should work hard to break down students' stereotypes of particular ethnic groups.

Reason (R):

A key educational objective is to enable student? to engage in critical self-reflection.

(A) Both (A) and (R) are false.

(B) Both (A) and (R) are true and (R) is the correct explanation of (A).

(C) Both (A) and (R) are true, but (R) is ***not*** the correct explanation of (A).

(D) (A) is true, but (R) is false.

24. What is the difference between mastery goals and performance goals?

(A) Mastery goals are focused on gaining approval from others, while performance goals are focused on avoiding failure.

(B) Mastery goals are focused on achieving a certain level of performance for competing with others, while performance goals are focused on improving one's own skills and understanding of a task.

(C) Mastery goals are focused on improving one's own skills and understanding of a task, while performance goals are focused on amieving a high grade or receiving external rewards.

(D) Mastery goals are focused on avoiding failure, while performance goals are focused on gaining approval and recognition from others.

25. Which of the following is an example of intrinsic motivation?

(A) Studying to avoid being scolded

(B) Participating in a competition for the prize money

(C) Playing a musical instrument for personal enjoyment

(D) Completing the project to impress the teacher

26. In a progressive classroom, the students:

A. do not ask many questions.

B. ask questions to the teacher.

C. ask questions to each other.

D. ask themselves questions.

Choose the correct option:

(A) B, C and D

(B) A

(C) B and C

(D) B and D

27. Expectations associated with being male or female are referred to as .... and these are learned ....

(A) gender stereotypes; only during middle childhood

(B) gender bias; mainly during early childhood

(C) gender constancy; initially during adolescence

(D) gender roles; throughout childhood and into adulthood

28. Lawrence Kohlberg's theory has been critiqued by Carol Gilligan for:

(A) presenting a stage-theory of moral development.

(B) collecting data by means of real-life situations.

(C) not applying quantitative methods of analysis.

(D) ignoring gender differences in moral reasoing

29. Which of the following views about intelligence supports the respectful consideration of diversity among learners?

(A) IQ tests are the only measure of intelligence.

(B) Intelligence is multidimensional and can change over time.

(C) Intelligence is not influenced by genetic factors.

(D) Intelligence is not influenced by environmental factors.

30. Who among the following critiqued the concept of 'general' intelligence and proposed an alternative theory of intelligence?

(A) Lev Vygotsky

(B) Charles Spearman

(C) Howard Gardner

(D) Jean Piaget

My Notes

Answer Key

1.	*(A)*	*11.*	*(C)*	*21.*	*(C)*
2.	*(B)*	*12.*	*(D)*	*22.*	*(D)*
3.	*(B)*	*13.*	*(A)*	*23.*	*(B)*
4.	*(D)*	*14.*	*(C)*	*24.*	*(B)*
5.	*(D)*	*15.*	*(D)*	*25.*	*(C)*
6.	*(B)*	*16.*	*(B)*	*26.*	*(A)*
7.	*(D)*	*17.*	*(C)*	*27.*	*(D)*
8.	*(C)*	*18.*	*(A)*	*28.*	*(D)*
9.	*(B)*	*19.*	*(D)*	*29.*	*(B)*
10.	*(C)*	*20.*	*(A)*	*30.*	*(B)*

CTET-2024

Held on: 07 July, 2024

Paper-1

Directions: Answer the following questions by selecting the correct/ most appropriate option.

1. **Which of the following would support continuous and comprehensive evaluation ?**
   (A) Best works portfolio
   (B) Growth and learning progress portfolio
   (C) Standardized achievement test
   (D) Standardized intelligence test

2. **Assertion (A) :** Teachers should constantly examine their own attitudes and biases while working with children.

   Reason (R) : The process of problem-solving is hindered by functional fixedness.

   Choose the correct option.
   (A) Both (A) and (R) are true and (R) is the correct explanation of (A).
   (B) Both (A) and (R) are true but (R) is not the correct explanation of (A).
   (C) (A) is true but (R) is false.
   (D) Both (A) and (R) are false.

3. **While talking about her poor marks in mathematics Avi says "I just don't have the sense for numbers" Avi is attributing his performance to :**
   (A) Luck
   (B) Task difficulty
   (C) Lack of effort
   (D) Lack of ability

4. **According to Lev Vygotsky's theory, which of the following is a recommended approach in order to optimize students' learning experience ?**
   (A) Providing students with work that is completely unrelated to their current level of understanding.
   (B) Providing students with work that is just beyond their current level of understanding, with appropriate support and guidance.

(C) Providing no support to students and leaving them to struggle on their own.

(D) Providing students with work that they can manage and complete individually.

5. Which of the following statement best describes the role of the teacher in progressive education ?

(A) The teacher is the primary source of knowledge.

(B) The teacher serves as a facilitator.

(C) The teacher implements the prescribed curriculum 'as it is'.

(D) The teacher leaves the children on their own to work independently.

6. Howard Gardner's concept of Intelligence implicates that :

(A) Everyone processes and understands the world in the same way.

(B) Human beings differ in their abilities in different domains.

(C) Intelligence has only one dimension.

(D) Intelligence is only about 'practical' learning.

7. Which of the following sequence of representation of concept is in accordance with children's gradual development of cognitive abilities ?

(A) action-based, image-based, symbol-based

(B) image-based, symbol-based, action-based

(C) symbol-based, action-based, image-based

(D) symbol-based, image-based, action-based

8. Assertion (A) : Teachers should provide emotional support to children in the classrooms to ensure effective learning.

Reason (R) : Emotions and cognition are related to each other in complex ways.

Choose the correct option.

(A) Both (A) and (R) are true and (R) is the correct explanation of (A).

(B) Both (A) and (R) are true but (R) is not the correct explanation of (A).

(C) (A) is true but (R) is false.

(D) Both (A) and (R) are false.

9. Which of the following statement about development is correct ?

(A) Development is a discontinuous process.

(B) Development occurs in a spiral manner, not linear.

(C) Development proceeds from specific to general.

(D) Different aspects of development are independent to each other.

10. According to Lev Vygotsky, children regulate their own behaviour through the :

(A) Processes of adaptation

(B) Use of inner speech

(C) Process of equilibration

(D) Use of self-reinforcement

11. Which pedagogical approach would be adopted by teachers who firmly believe in constructivism to teach concepts of floating and sinking to class V children ?

(A) Lecture method

(B) Showing videos

(C) Showing power point presentation

(D) Guided discovery

12. Which of the following is not an effective memory technique for meaningful learning ?

(A) Rote Rehearsal

(B) Mnemonics

(C) Concept Mapping

(D) Elaborative Rehearsal

13. Which of the following is not a characteristic of a well-formulated critical thinking question ?

(A) It is open-ended and allows for multiple answers.

(B) It is based primarily on factual information.

(C) It requires analysis and evaluation of information.

(D) It promotes higher-level thinking and problem-solving skills.

14. Assertion (A) : Classroom pedagogy should be culturally responsive to meet the needs of students from diverse cultural backgrounds.

Reason (R) : Equity in classroom can be ensured only through standardized curriculum and assessment.

Choose the correct option.

(A) Both (A) and (R) are true and (R) is the correct explanation of (A).

(B) Both (A) and (R) are true but (R) is not the correct explanation of (A).

(C) (A) is true but (R) is false.

(D) Both (A) and (R) are false.

15. Jagriti has learned that her dog, Rusty, is a Golden Retriever. When she sees another dog that looks similar to Rusty but is a different breed, she calls it a dog too. According to Jean Piaget's theory of cognitive development, which concept does this demonstrate ?

(A) Egocentrism

(B) Object permanence

(C) Conservation

(D) Assimilation

16. Heredity totally determine an individual's :

(i) Sex

(ii) Gender

(iii) Academic Success

(iv) Learning Style

Choose the correct option.

(A) (i)

(B) (ii)

(C) (i), (iii), (iv)

(D) (ii), (iii), (iv)

17. Assertion (A) : Teachers should focus on asking questions in classroom and encouraging children also to ask questions rather than giving instructions.

Reason (R) : Child-centred pedagogy means giving opportunities to children's voices and ensuring their participation.

Choose the correct option.

(A) Both (A) and (R) are true and (R) is the correct explanation of (A).

(B) Both (A) and (R) are true but (R) is not the correct explanation of (A).

(C) (A) is true but (R) is false.

(D) Both (A) and (R) are false.

18. Repetitive and ritualistic behaviour is an identifying characteristic of :

(A) Autism Spectrum Disorder

(B) Learning Disabilities

(C) Attention Deficit Hyperactivity Disorder

(D) Cerebral palsy

19. Learners feel engaged and actively involved in process of learning when :

(A) Activities are related to their context.

(B) Focus of learning is repetition and memorization.

(C) Socio-emotional needs of learners are ignored.

(D) Their prior knowledge is discarded and negated.

20. Children with 'learning difficulties' typically :

(A) Have difficulties in reading due to their poor sight.

(B) Have problems in regulating their emotions.

(C) Have confusion with letter and alphabets that look alike.

(D) Have very low IQ as diagnosed through standard intelligence tests.

21. Feral children, those who experienced severe (human) social deprivation since very young age usually have delayed or hindered development and despite rehabilitation the improvement in certain domains of development is likely to be subordinate. This period wherein development is significantly influenced by environmental support is called _________.

(A) Deductive period

(B) Intuitive period

(C) Native period

(D) Sensitive period

22. Preconceived generalizations about behaviour of various gender are called :

(A) Gender stereotypes

(B) Gender discriminations

(C) Gender identity

(D) Gender typing

23. In an inclusive classroom :

(A) 'Special children' always work on their own curriculum.

(B) All children have access to and are included in classroom activities.

(C) 'Special' children are looked upon as needy and dependent.

(D) All children follow same curriculum and uniform pedagogy is adopted for all learners.

24. What is the primary purpose of asking critical thinking questions ?

(A) To enable students to develop procedural knowledge.

(B) To assess students' knowledge and understanding skills.

(C) To promote higher-level thinking and problem-solving skills.

(D) To encourage students to memorize information.

25. Which of the following is correct about the process of learning, according to socio-constructivist theories ?

(A) Learning is an individualistic process that occurs in isolation.

(B) Learning occurs only in a classroom or formal educational setting.

(C) Learning is a passive process that occurs solely through observation.

(D) Learning is a social process of meaning making.

26. Assertion (A) : While some children start babbling and uttering two word sentences at 12 months, others don't do this till they are 20 months old.

Reason (R) : Development milestones are only suggestive and development of individual children can be quite varied.

Choose the correct option.

(A) Both (A) and (R) are true and (R) is the correct explanation of (A).

(B) Both (A) and (R) are true but (R) is not the correct explanation of (A).

(C) (A) is true but (R) is false.

(D) Both (A) and (R) are false.

27. Growth in height and weight of children is an example of :

(A) Quantitative change

(B) Qualitative change

(C) Change in affective domain

(D) Change in cognitive domain

28. When presented with Heinz's dilemma, Arunima reasons : "The law wasn't set up for these circumstances. Taking the drug in this situation isn't really right, but it's justified."

Which stage of moral development is Arunima according to the theory of Lawrence Kohlberg ?

(A) Social concern and conscience

(B) Morality of contrast, of individual rights and of democratically

(C) Orientation towards punishment and obedience accepted law

(D) Instrumental purpose and exchange

29. Which of the following is correct in context of gifted children ?

(A) Gifted children are free from risk of learning disability.

(B) Gifted children certainly excel in all areas academic, social and emotional.

(C) Gifted students are always happy, popular and well adjusted.

(D) Gifted students learn at comparatively advanced pace than other students.

30. As per Jean Piaget, pre-operational stage is characterized by abilities to perform :

(A) Classification and seriation

(B) Conservation and abstract thinking

(C) Imitation and reversibility

(D) Symbolic play and animism

My Notes

Answer Key

1.	*(B)*	*11.*	*(D)*	*21.*	*(D)*
2.	*(C)*	*12.*	*(A)*	*22.*	*(A)*
3.	*(D)*	*13.*	*(B)*	*23.*	*(B)*
4.	*(B)*	*14.*	*(C)*	*24.*	*(C)*
5.	*(B)*	*15.*	*(D)*	*25.*	*(D)*
6.	*(B)*	*16.*	*(A)*	*26.*	*(A)*
7.	*(A)*	*17.*	*(A)*	*27.*	*(A)*
8.	*(A)*	*18.*	*(A)*	*28.*	*(B)*
9.	*(A)*	*19.*	*(A)*	*29.*	*(D)*
10.	*(B)*	*20.*	*(C)*	*30.*	*(D)*

CTET-2024

Held on: 07 July, 2024

Paper-2

Directions: Answer the following questions by selecting the correct/ most appropriate option.

1. In progressive education children are perceived as :

(A) Innocent and dependent

(B) Compliant and capable of only consuming knowledge

(C) Knowledgeable and meaning-makers

(D) Vulnerable and in need of protection

2. Feedback to the students in a classroom is most effective when:

(A) It assigns comparative ranks to the students.

(B) It occurs during as well as after the learning activity.

(C) It focuses on what the child cannot do rather than what they can do.

(D) It centres around tests and exams at the end of the year.

3. **Assertion (A) :** During adolescence the pressures to conform to gender expectations and follow conventions of feminity or masculinity increases.

Reason (R) : Gender and gender roles are determined biologically.

Choose the correct option.

(A) Both (A) and (R) are true and (R) is the correct explanation of (A).

(B) Both (A) and (R) are true but (R) is not the correct explanation of (A).

(C) (A) is true but (R) is false.

(D) Both (A) and (R) are false.

4. Sunita, a 12 year old girl, shows exceptional musical ability. Both her parents are accomplished singers, and they send her for classes for voice training after school. Her capabilities are most likely to be the result of an interaction between :

(A) Growth and maturation

(B) Nutrition and discipline

(C) Heredity and environment

(D) Gender identity and genetic make-up

5. Sensitive periods are those time periods during which certain _________ are especially important for course of 'normal' development.

(A) Genetic predispositions

(B) Ethnic factors

(C) Environmental factors

(D) Hereditary factors

6. In order to develop critical thinking among students a teacher should :

(A) Ask only those questions which carry single answers.

(B) Discourage the students from asking doubts and questions.

(C) Give questions that involve inferences and explanations.

(D) Avoid questions which need inference and analysis.

7. A teacher asks herself - "How can I provide experiences that require students to classify different types of objects in the environment and analyse their classification schemes ?" Which intelligence is she trying to promote in students ?

(A) Linguistic Intelligence

(B) Inter-personal Intelligence

(C) Naturalistic Intelligence

(D) Bodily- Kinesthetics Intelligence

8. How does setting mastery goals impact a student's motivation and views of ability ?

(A) It often implies enhanced intrinsic motivation and belief in the entity view of ability.

(B) It often implies enhanced intrinsic motivation and belief in the incremental view of ability.

(C) It often implies enhanced extrinsic motivation and belief in the entity view of ability.

(D) It often implies enhanced extrinsic motivation and belief in the incremental view of ability.

9. Rama is a teacher who is implementing Vygotsky's theory in her classroom and she assigns her students to work in groups to complete a challenging task. During the task, one student struggles to understand a key concept. What would be the most effective way for Rama to help this student ?

(A) Provide the student with the answer to the problem so the group can move on.

(B) Encourage the student to try to solve the problem on her own.

(C) Assign a different task to the student that is better suited to her abilities.

(D) Work through the problem with the student and providing guidance and feedback as needed while involving other group members.

10. Assertion (A) : Teachers should encourage debates, discussions and collaborations among students.

Reason (R) : Knowledge production is an inactive process and engagement in group activities hinders meaningful learning.

Choose the correct option.

(A) Both (A) and (R) are true and (R) is the correct explanation of (A).

(B) Both (A) and (R) are true but (R) is not the correct explanation of (A).

(C) (A) is true but (R) is false.

(D) Both (A) and (R) are false.

11. Change and stability in emotions, personality and social relationships together constitute :

(A) Personality development

(B) Emotional development

(C) Psychosocial development

(D) Cognitive development

12. Which of the following correctly describes 'culturally responsive teaching' to cater to diverse groups of students ?

(i) Intentional

(ii) Adaptive

(iii) Differentiated

(iv) Standardized

Choose the correct option.

(A) (i), (iv)

(B) (ii), (iii)

(C) (i), (ii), (iii)

(D) (i), (ii), (iii), (iv)

13. **Assertion (A) :** Schools should function within frameworks which assess the finished product and learning outcomes.

Reason (R) : Learning is tightly sequential and hierarchical.

Choose the correct option.

(A) Both (A) and (R) are true and (R) is the correct explanation of (A).

(B) Both (A) and (R) are true but (R) is not the correct explanation of (A).

(C) (A) is true but (R) is false.

(D) Both (A) and (R) are false.

14. **According to Lev Vygotsky what is the relationship between language and thought ?**

(A) Language does not shape thought

(B) Thought shapes language

(C) Language and thought are independent of each other

(D) Language and thought are complex interrelated processes of development

15. **Which of the following is a correctly matched pair ?**

(A) Criterion - referenced assessment : includes mastery of specific topics

(B) Norm - references assessment : compares performance to that of peers

(C) Formative assessment : determining what the students can do before and after the class

(D) Summative assessment : involves paper - pencil tests as well as detailed accounts of nonwritten behaviours

16. **Which of the following hinders the participation of students with visual impairment in classroom ?**

(A) Electronically formatted lecture transcriptions

(B) Printed textbooks and notes

(C) Raised-line drawings and maps

(D) Tactile models of graphic materials

17. Which method did Lawrence Kohlberg used to study moral development of children ?

(A) Quantitative research approach

(B) Posing moral dilemmas to children and analyzing responses

(C) Conducting observations of children during play

(D) Experimental method

18. Constructivist teaching leads to __________ learning by students.

(A) Discovery

(B) Meaningless

(C) Rote

(D) Receptive

19. Students struggling with dyslexia can be taught to read :

(A) Through systematic phonological training.

(B) By providing higher grade level reading texts.

(C) By giving long and complex passages.

(D) Through association method of conditioning.

20. Jean Piaget's theory of cognitive development implicates that :

(A) Behaviour should be conditioned using rewards and punishments.

(B) Concepts should be taught in a sequence of complex to simple.

(C) Curriculum should be designed keeping children's age-group and stage in mind.

(D) Focus of teaching should be the outcome of the activity instead of the process of thinking.

21. You are a teacher who wants to help your students develop metacognitive skills. Which of the following strategies is most likely to foster this type of thinking ?

(A) Giving students marks instead of qualitative feedback on their performance.

(B) Encouraging students to reflect on their own learning and thinking processes.

(C) Providing students with summarised notes for assignments.

(D) Assigning homework that requires memorization and recall.

22. Which of the following statement is correct about 'Autism' ?

(A) All autistic people have at least one exceptional skill.

(B) Autism is a neuro-developmental disorder.

(C) Autism is caused solely by environmental factors.

(D) Autism can be cured and improves with age.

23. A key commonality in Piaget and Vygotsky's theories is :

(A) Their views of relationship between language and thought.

(B) Focus on stage-like progression in children's development.

(C) Involvement and engagement of children in their own learning.

(D) The role of culture in the cognitive processes.

24. Assertion (A) : Teachers should respect the individual differences among learners and adapt their teaching to cater to needs of all students.

Reason (R) : Collaborations, group works and interactions among students should be avoided while teaching a class of diverse learners.

Choose the correct option.

(A) Both (A) and (R) are true and (R) is the correct explanation of (A).

(B) Both (A) and (R) are true but (R) is not the correct explanation of (A).

(C) (A) is true but (R) is false.

(D) Both (A) and (R) are false.

25. Which learning strategy involves children teaching others what they have learned ?

(A) Conditioned learning

(B) Rote learning

(C) Expository teaching

(D) Reciprocal teaching

26. Assertion (A) : In Asian cultures which stress social harmony, expressions of 'anger' are discouraged and 'shame' is encouraged.

Reason (R) : Emotions are subjective and do not play any role in learning.

Choose the correct option.

(A) Both (A) and (R) are true and (R) is the correct explanation of (A).

(B) Both (A) and (R) are true but (R) is not the correct explanation of (A).

(C) (A) is true but (R) is false.

(D) Both (A) and (R) are false.

27. According to Jean Piaget how are children different from adults ?

(A) Children are dependent on adults while adults are independent.

(B) Adults are much more knowledgeable than children.

(C) Children's thinking is qualitatively different from that of adults.

(D) Children's thinking is quantitatively different from that of adults.

28. Which of the following question promotes analytical thinking ?

(A) The capital city of India is ________

(B) How many States are there in India ?

(C) What is the total population of India ?

(D) What are the various causes of increase of population in India ?

29. Inclusive classrooms :

(A) Recognize that every child will learn at the same rate and at the same time.

(B) Is an educational program offered to cater to the needs of 'special children'.

(C) Are meant to offer differentiated instructions as per individual differences.

(D) Aim to remove all kinds of differences among the children.

30. Assertion (A) : Teachers should give lot of opportunities to children for experimentation and discuss examples and non-examples.

Reason (R) : A constructive way of dealing with misconceptions in children is to provide counter examples.

Choose the correct option.

(A) Both (A) and (R) are true and (R) is the correct explanation of (A).

(B) Both (A) and (R) are true but (R) is not the correct explanation of (A).

(C) (A) is true but (R) is false.

(D) Both (A) and (R) are false.

My Notes

Answer Key

1.	*(C)*	*11.*	*(C)*	*21.*	*(B)*
2.	*(B)*	*12.*	*(C)*	*22.*	*(B)*
3.	*(C)*	*13.*	*(D)*	*23.*	*(C)*
4.	*(C)*	*14.*	*(D)*	*24.*	*(C)*
5.	*(C)*	*15.*	*(B)*	*25.*	*(D)*
6.	*(C)*	*16.*	*(B)*	*26.*	*(C)*
7.	*(C)*	*17.*	*(B)*	*27.*	*(C)*
8.	*(B)*	*18.*	*(A)*	*28.*	*(D)*
9.	*(D)*	*19.*	*(A)*	*29.*	*(C)*
10.	*(C)*	*20.*	*(C)*	*30.*	*(A)*

CTET-2024

Held on: 14 December, 2024

Paper-1

Directions: Answer the following questions by selecting the correct/ most appropriate option.

1. Mastery Oriented learners typically attribute success to __________ and failure to __________.

(A) Ability and good luck; task difficulty

(B) Ability and effort; bad luck

(C) Ability and good luck; low ability

(D) Ability and effort; insufficient effort

2. Which of the following statement represents 'Proximodistal' principle of development ?

(A) Development is multidirectional and multidimensional.

(B) Identical twins living in different cultures can develop at different rates.

(C) Children develop ability to grasp the ball before putting beads in thread.

(D) Children develop ability to sit up before standing.

3. According to Vygotsky children speak to themselves :

(A) To aid thought and for self-regulation.

(B) To provide self-reinforcement when adults are ignoring them.

(C) Because they are egocentric.

(D) Because their thought is illogical.

4. Challenges in social communication are evident in :

(A) Attention deficit hyperactivity disorder

(B) Cerebral palsy

(C) Autism Spectrum Disorder

(D) Learning Disabilities

5. According to Vygotsky's theory of learning and development, which of the following is an example of scaffolding ?

(A) Breaking a task down into smaller steps and providing support as needed.

(B) Providing a student with a grade for their work as motivation.

(C) Providing a student with a reading assignment and asking them to answer questions independently.

(D) Demonstrating a skill to a student and then having them master it on their own.

6. **Dysgraphia is characterised by :**

(A) Delayed motor skills

(B) Difficulties in writing

(C) Lack of reading fluency

(D) Repetitive behavioural patterns

7. **In order to help students to become good problem solvers, a teacher should emphasize on the practice of :**

(A) Focusing on information that confirms existing beliefs and preconceptions.

(B) Approaching problems in a particular fixed fashion.

(C) Breaking large complex problems into smaller manageable problems.

(D) Centering only on one particular piece of information related to problem.

8. **Assertion (A) :** Teachers should use multisensory materials to cater to needs of students in an inclusive classroom.

Reason (R) : Inclusive classrooms should adopt standardization of curricular materials as well as assessment strategies.

Choose the correct option.

(A) (A) is true but (R) is false.

(B) Both (A) and (R) are false.

(C) Both (A) and (R) are true and (R) is the correct explanation of (A).

(D) Both (A) and (R) are true but (R) is not the correct explanation of (A).

9. **In the constructivist view :**

(A) Individuals are passively influenced by environmental events.

(B) Individuals are conditioned to learn new behaviours.

(C) Learning is extending and transforming the current understanding.

(D) Learning is simply writing associations on the blank slates of our brains.

10. **Assertion (A) :** Effective teachers familiarize themselves with daily lives and socio-cultural backgrounds of learners.

Reason (R) : Learning takes place in a social context.

Choose the correct option.

(A) (A) is true but (R) is false.

(B) Both (A) and (R) are false.

(C) Both (A) and (R) are true and (R) is the correct explanation of (A).

(D) Both (A) and (R) are true but (R) is not the correct explanation of (A).

11. **Meaningful learning is primarily NOT about :**

(A) Memorizing information

(B) Understanding the concept

(C) Constructing knowledge

(D) Developing skills

12. **Assertion (A) :** Teacher should encourage boys of her class to participate in sports while assigning art decoration to girls.

Reason (R) : Children acquire gender roles primarily because of the underlying biological differences.

Choose the correct option.

(A) (A) is true but (R) is false.

(B) Both (A) and (R) are false.

(C) Both (A) and (R) are true and (R) is the correct explanation of (A).

(D) Both (A) and (R) are true but (R) is not the correct explanation of (A).

13. **Kinesthetic learners prefer to learn through __________.**

(A) Seeing

(B) Touching

(C) Doing and moving

(D) Listening

14. According to Howard Gardner while a scientist would exhibit high _________ Intelligence, a sculptor would have high _________ Intelligence.

(A) Naturalistic; Spatial

(B) Transductive; Spatial

(C) Logical-mathematical; Bodily Kinesthetic

(D) Spatial; Bodily Kinesthetic

15. Inclusion needs to be promoted through :

(i) Flexible curriculum

(ii) Cooperative learning

(iii) Segregation and labelling

(iv) Accessibility of building

Choose the correct option.

(A) (ii) (iii) (iv)

(B) (i) (ii) (iii) (iv)

(C) (i) (ii) (iii)

(D) (i) (ii) (iv)

16. Children learn better if they experience :

(A) Low level of alertness during activity

(B) Moderate level of excitement to learn

(C) High degree of anxiety to perform

(D) Learned helplessness

17. Assertion (A) : Children below the age of 5 - 6 years should not be pressurized to write 'properly' and 'within the lines'.

Reason (R) : Children gain a control of finer motor skills from 5 - 6 years onwards.

Choose the correct option.

(A) (A) is true but (R) is false.

(B) Both (A) and (R) are false.

(C) Both (A) and (R) are true and (R) is the correct explanation of (A).

(D) Both (A) and (R) are true but (R) is not the correct explanation of (A).

18. Children often come up with their own explanations of events around them. On being probed as to why does it rain Sia says - "God was tired of carrying the buckets of water on his shoulders".

Such explanations :

(A) Depict that children have an egocentric view and cannot consider other's viewpoint.

(B) Illustrate that children are not capable of any reasoning.

(C) Prove that children's thinking is much lesser than adults quantitively.

(D) Indicate that children have naïve understanding rooted in their cultural context with which they try to understand events.

19. Piaget described cognitive development as occurring in :

(A) A continuous continuum

(B) Four overlapping culture specific stages

(C) Four qualitatively different stages

(D) Three progressive levels

20. During play time at school, Rishab, a 7-year-old boy picked a doll to play with. Some of his peers made fun of him for his choice of toy. As a teacher who wants his students to grow up with gender role flexibility, which of the following would be the best response to the situation by the teacher ?

(A) Talk to Rishabh that dolls are suitable for girls and boys should not play with dolls.

(B) Tell Rishabh that he should play with something else because his friends won't approve of him playing with doll.

(C) Let Rishabh play with doll and tell other children that they can also choose any toy of their choice.

(D) Quitely take away the doll and give a car toy to Rishabh without saying anything.

21. In developmental terms, a time frame where an individual upholds an amplified sensitivity to particular incentives for developing particular skills to function in an efficient manner is referred to as __________ of development.

(A) Incentive period

(B) Stimulus period

(C) Critical period

(D) Encoding period

22. In order to cater to needs of students struggling with Attention Deficit Hyperactivity Disorder teachers should avoid :

(A) Creating distractions and making noises

(B) Flexibility in curricular materials and instructions

(C) Breaking the task into small easily manageable parts

(D) Using multi-sensory materials

23. Lawrence Kohlberg argued that :

(A) Moral development in children occurs in a continuous manner.

(B) There are cultural differences in moral reasoning of children.

(C) Moral development occurs progressively in stages.

(D) There are gender differences in moral reasoning of children.

24. At which level of Kohlberg's moral development does individual's ethical behavior mainly depends on the mindset that "what do people think of me"?

(A) Postconventional

(B) Non-conventional

(C) Preconventional

(D) Conventional

25. According to Jean Piaget a child who is unable to understand the logic behind simple mathematical reversals such as 4 + 5 = 9 so 9–5=4, it is because of :

(A) Animistic thinking

(B) Irreversibility

(C) Egocentrism

(D) Perceptual centration

26. Assertion (A) : Teachers should distance themselves from students and place primary responsibility for learning on them only.

Reason (R) : Learning takes place affectively in an authoritative rather than a democratic environment.

Choose the correct option.

(A) (A) is true but (R) is false.

(B) Both (A) and (R) are false.

(C) Both (A) and (R) are true and (R) is the correct explanation of (A).

(D) Both (A) and (R) are true but (R) is not the correct explanation of (A).

27. **Assertion (A) :** Scaffolding provided by the teachers hinders the learning process of children.

Reason (R) : Lev Vygotsky proposed that children learn independently by acting upon and manipulating the environment.

Choose the correct option.

(A) (A) is true but (R) is false.

(B) Both (A) and (R) are false.

(C) Both (A) and (R) are true and (R) is the correct explanation of (A).

(D) Both (A) and (R) are true but (R) is not the correct explanation of (A).

28. **Which of the following correctly describes extrinsic motivation?**

(A) Motivation that comes from environmental consequences.

(B) Motivation that comes from a sense of personal satisfaction.

(C) Motivation that comes from personal enjoyment of the task.

(D) Motivation that comes from internal factors.

29. **Two important cognitive development milestones of sensorimotor stage of Piaget's theory of cognitive development are :**

(A) Animism and Transformation

(B) Classification and seriation

(C) Object permanence and deferred imitation

(D) Reversibility of thought and hypothetic-deductive reasoning

30. **Children -**

(A) Are born unruly and need to be socialized.

(B) Come into this world with genetic codes that determine their destiny.

(C) Are greatly influenced by the social cultural context they grow up in.

(D) Come into this world as tabula rasa or blank slate.

My Notes

Answer Key

1.	*(D)*	*11.*	*(A)*	*21.*	*(B)*
2.	*(D)*	*12.*	*(B)*	*22.*	*(A)*
3.	*(A)*	*13.*	*(C)*	*23.*	*(C)*
4.	*(A)*	*14.*	*(A)*	*24.*	*(D)*
5.	*(A)*	*15.*	*(D)*	*25.*	*(B)*
6.	*(B)*	*16.*	*(B)*	*26.*	*(B)*
7.	*(C)*	*17.*	*(C)*	*27.*	*(B)*
8.	*(D)*	*18.*	*(D)*	*28.*	*(A)*
9.	*(C)*	*19.*	*(C)*	*29.*	*(C)*
10.	*(C)*	*20.*	*(C)*	*30.*	*(C)*

CTET-2024

Held on: 14 December, 2024

Paper-2

Directions: Answer the following questions by selecting the correct/ most appropriate option.

1. **Which of these statements would advocates of progressive education agree with ?**
   (A) Children are a distinct life-stage that hold importance because of 'what they would become as adults' rather than 'what they are as children'.
   (B) Children are naturally 'good' and society corrupts them.
   (C) Children are naturally 'uncivilized' and socialization is necessary to make them moral human beings.
   (D) Children are born in a social, cultural, economic context and this background influences their development.

2. **Changes in emotion, self-perception and interpersonal relationships with families, peers and friends are studied under __________ domain of development.**
   (A) Psycho-social
   (B) Physical
   (C) Cognitive
   (D) Linguistic

3. **The behaviours, interests, attitudes, skills and personality traits that a culture considers appropriate for specific gender are referred to as __________ and are __________.**
   (A) Gender identity; genetically determined
   (B) Gender roles; culturally defined
   (C) Gender roles; genetically determined
   (D) Gender identity; culturally defined

4. **Assertion (A) :** In an inclusive classroom, all curriculum adaptations should be directed to lower the educational standards for 'Special children'.

   Reason (R) : 'Special children' do not have any potential for learning in mainstream classroom.

   Choose the correct option.
   (A) Both (A) and (R) are false.

(B) Both (A) and (R) are true and (R) is the correct explanation of (A).

(C) Both (A) and (R) are true but (R) is not the correct explanation of (A).

(D) (A) is true but (R) is false.

5. As per Jean Piaget's theory of Cognitive Development :

(A) Previous knowledge doesn't play any role in the process of learning.

(B) Biological factors such as maturation don't play any role in cognitive development.

(C) Learning experiences depend on children's current level of cognitive functioning.

(D) Memorization should be prioritized over learning through experience.

6. Lev Vygotsky views cognitive development as :

(A) Effective adoption to the environment process

(B) A collaborative process

(C) An individual activity

(D) A unified process

7. While proposing the relationship between language and thinking process, Lev Vygotsky conceptualized language as a/an :

(A) Independent domain which is not related to cognition.

(B) Cultural tool which facilitates cognition in multiple ways.

(C) Form of egocentric speech used to only fulfill basic needs.

(D) Hinderance to the development of cognitive abilities.

8. Which of the following is an example of a performance goal orientation ?

(A) A student studies hard to further her own growth.

(B) A student studies hard to achieve a deep understanding of a topic.

(C) A student studies hard to get a good grade and be better than others.

(D) A student studies hard to learn as much as possible from the teacher.

9. Following Lev Vygotsky's ideas, a teacher should :

(A) Practice reciprocal teaching with her students.

(B) Discourage the use of cultural tools by students.

(C) Disseminate the knowledge to be memorized by the students.

(D) Encourage students to compete with each other.

10. Which of the following are effective strategies to teach new concepts ?

(i) Presenting examples

(ii) Presenting non-examples

(iii) Promoting thinking about relationships amongst concepts.

(iv) Giving a definition and encouraging students to rote memorize it.

Choose the correct option.

(A) (iii), (iv), (i)

(B) (i), (ii)

(C) (i), (iii)

(D) (i), (ii), (iii)

11. In which of the following method teacher and student interchange their roles ?

(A) Reciprocal teaching

(B) Conditioned learning

(C) Receptive learning

(D) Expository teaching

12. Fiza analyzes that she has more problems in learning topic X than in learning topic Z because she is interested in topic Z and is paying focused attention to it. Which of the following construct describes Fiza's abilities to analyze her thinking ?

(A) Cognitive conflict

(B) Metacognition

(C) Memory

(D) Cognition

13. Howard Gardner's theory of multiple intelligence proposes that:

(A) Intelligence can successfully predict academic success.

(B) Intelligences change over time.

(C) Intelligence is primarily inherited.

(D) Intelligence can be measured accurately and predicated precisely.

14. While there exists a possibility of intra-group individual differences, yet most students with Autism :

(A) Perform superior skills of imaginative play.

(B) Acquire advanced socio-emotional reciprocity.

(C) Demonstrate advanced communication skills.

(D) Express strict adherence to routine or steps.

15. Assertion (A) : Creating an environment of fear and stress keeps students 'on their' toes and facilitates meaningful learning.

Reason (R) : Learning is governed only by extrinsic factors.

Choose the correct option.

(A) Both (A) and (R) are false.

(B) Both (A) and (R) are true and (R) is the correct explanation of (A).

(C) Both (A) and (R) are true but (R) is not the correct explanation of (A).

(D) (A) is true but (R) is false.

16. An example of 'class inclusion' :

Assertion (A) : Lokesh has trouble with classifying one concept (Delhi) as a subset of another (India).

Reason (R) : Understanding how emotions affect memory and learning can lead to selfregulated learning.

Choose the correct option.

(A) Both (A) and (R) are false.

(B) Both (A) and (R) are true and (R) is the correct explanation of (A).

(C) Both (A) and (R) are true but (R) is not the correct explanation of (A).

(D) (A) is true but (R) is false.

17. Which of the following statement aptly describes the purpose of a diagnostic assessment ?

(A) To identify the areas where students may need additional support or instruction.

(B) To give students the opportunity to critically assess the work of their peers.

(C) To identify the attitude patterns of students and design a career guidance programme as per their needs.

(D) To provide feedback to the teacher about their teaching methods.

18. Ten year old Kakuli is struggling with a difficult math problem. What can her teacher do to enhance her problem-solving skills?

(A) Give severe punishment so that it is not repeated in future

(B) Give her the solution to the problem

(C) Tell her to skip the problem and move on to the next one

(D) Encourage her to keep trying and offer scaffolding when needed

19. Jean Piaget perceives __________ to be __________. Lev-Vygotsky believes __________ to be __________.

(A) Private speech, effective in self-regulation; egocentric speech, a sign of cognitive immaturity

(B) Egocentric speech, a sign of cognitive immaturity; private speech, effective in self-regulation

(C) Egocentric speech, effective in self-regulation; private speech, a sign of cognitive immaturity

(D) Private speech, a sign of cognitive immaturity; egocentric speech, effective in self-regulation

20. Universal design for learning does NOT involve :

(A) Practicing forms of labelling and categorization of learners.

(B) Giving all learners various ways of acquiring information and knowledge.

(C) Providing all learners alternatives for demonstrating what the learners know.

(D) Tapping into all learners' interests and offering challenges accordingly.

21. Which of the following statements about Lawrence Kohlberg's theory is correct ?

(A) It takes into account effects of culture and gender on moral reasoning.

(B) It does not specify exact stages for progression of moral development in children.

(C) It is based on the study done through experimental methods.

(D) It presents conflicting situations to children.

22. Assertion (A) : Each child finds opportunities to play, experiment and discover their world.

Reason (R) : Childhood is a universal construct.

Choose the correct option.

(A) Both (A) and (R) are false.

(B) Both (A) and (R) are true and (R) is the correct explanation of (A).

(C) Both (A) and (R) are true but (R) is not the correct explanation of (A).

(D) (A) is true but (R) is false.

23. Which of the following is an example of a question that promotes analytical thinking ?

(A) Who was the leader of Germany during World War II ?

(B) In which year did World War II end ?

(C) Which countries were directly involved in the World War II ?

(D) Which factors contributed to the outbreak of World War II ?

24. While engaging students who are visually challenged, teachers should use __________ which __________.

(A) Frequency modulated transmission devices; are an auditory system.

(B) Braille, is a tactile system.

(C) Braille, is an auditory system.

(D) Frequency modulated transmission devices; are a tactile system.

25. You are a teacher who wants to encourage your students to think critically and creatively. Which of the following strategies is most likely to foster this type of thinking ?

(A) Lecturing on the topic and providing students with detailed notes.

(B) Assigning a project in which students must memorize and present information on a topic.

(C) Providing students with open-ended questions to come up with their own solutions.

(D) Giving students multiple-choice tests to assess their knowledge.

26. Which of the following is an example of assessment for student's learning ?

(A) A rubric given to students at the beginning of a project, outlining what they need to do to achieve a certain grade.

(B) A final exam that covers all the material learned throughout the term.

(C) A quiz and brainstorming at the beginning of class to check for prior knowledge.

(D) A standardized test used to compare students across the country.

27. Assertion (A) : As compared to boys, girls have an innate tendency to be affected more by social and cultural factors.

Reason (R) : Girls are genetically more sensitive and emotionally weaker than boys, making it more likely for them to conform to societal expectations.

Choose the correct option.

(A) Both (A) and (R) are false.

(B) Both (A) and (R) are true and (R) is the correct explanation of (A).

(C) Both (A) and (R) are true but (R) is not the correct explanation of (A).

(D) (A) is true but (R) is false.

28. Assertion (A) : 12-year Amana gets scared every time the teacher asks her to answer or solve the maths problem on the blackboard because she fears that the teacher will scold her and she would be embarrassed.

Reason (R) : When students feel unsafe and anxious their learning is adversely affected.

Choose the correct option.

(A) Both (A) and (R) are false.

(B) Both (A) and (R) are true and (R) is the correct explanation of (A).

(C) Both (A) and (R) are true but (R) is not the correct explanation of (A).

(D) (A) is true but (R) is false.

29. A teacher wants to enable meaningful and analytical learning in her class by providing opportunities for students to connect their prior knowledge to new concepts. Which of the following teaching strategies would be most effective ?

(A) Providing students with a step-by-step guide on how to complete a task related to the new material.

(B) Lecturing on new material and providing students with a list of key terms to memorize.

(C) Assign students to read the textbook chapter and answer questions at the end.

(D) Ask students to share their own experiences related to the new material and then connect them to the topic.

30. In an inclusive classroom the teacher :

(A) Tries to encourage children to do better by promoting competitive spirit.

(B) Identifies 'deficits' in children and correctly labels them.

(C) Segregates children based on differing academic capabilities.

(D) Modifies the curriculum and pedagogical strategies to suit varied needs of children.

My Notes

Answer Key

1.	*(D)*	*11.*	*(A)*	*21.*	*(D)*
2.	*(A)*	*12.*	*(B)*	*22.*	*(A)*
3.	*(B)*	*13.*	*(B)*	*23.*	*(D)*
4.	*(A)*	*14.*	*(D)*	*24.*	*(B)*
5.	*(C)*	*15.*	*(A)*	*25.*	*(C)*
6.	*(B)*	*16.*	*(C)*	*26.*	*(A)*
7.	*(B)*	*17.*	*(A)*	*27.*	*(A)*
8.	*(C)*	*18.*	*(D)*	*28.*	*(B)*
9.	*(A)*	*19.*	*(B)*	*29.*	*(D)*
10.	*(D)*	*20.*	*(A)*	*30.*	*(D)*

CTET-2026

Held on: 7th February, 2026

Paper-1

1. **Rama was mean to her brother Tahir. Next day Tahir got sick. Rama concluded that she made her brother sick. According to Piaget, which stage of cognitive development is Rama in?**

   A. Preoperational stage

   B. Concrete operational stage

   C. Formal operational stage

   D. Sensorimotor stage

2. **__________ is the process by which children become aware of their gender roles.**

   A. Gender equality B. Gender relatedness

   C. Gender homogeneity D. Gender typing

3. **Which of the following scenarios is aptly describing the application of Lev Vygotsky's concept of 'scaffolding'?**

   A. A teacher has strictly prohibited students to have any kind of collaborations and communication with their peers.

   B. A teacher has written answers on the blackboard and has asked the students to copy the answers passively in their notebooks.

   C. A teacher has made it mandatory for her students to solve problems on their own in a set time period.

   D. A teacher gave half-solved problems to her students who were finding it difficult to solve them otherwise.

4. **Progressive education is an educational philosophy that emphasizes on**

   A. rote memorization and teacher-centred instruction

   B. standardized testing and strict curriculum guidelines

   C. competition and individual achievement

   D. student-centred learning and active participation

5. **Read the following statements:**

   Assertion (A) : Children progress from understanding consequences of act to determine whether they are good/bad to understanding that rules and laws are flexible and can be changed.

   Reason (R) : According to Kohlberg, children's moral development occurs in continuous manner and not a discontinuous one.

Choose the correct option.

A. Both A and R are true but R is not the correct explanation of A.

B. A is true but R is false.

C. Both A and R are false.

D. Both A and R are true and R is the correct explanation of A.

6. **According to Lev Vygotsky, cognitive development is guided by**

A. Processes of attention and perception

B. Assimilation and accommodation that change 'schemes'

C. Positive and negative reinforcement given by the environment

D. Language in the form of private speech

7. **Which of the following intelligence helps people to perceive, express, understand and regulate moods and feelings of others?**

A. Logical-mathematical

B. Musical

C. Naturalist

D. Interpersonal

8. **A child's first experience as well as expectations of what it means to be a 'girl' or a 'boy' comes from**

A. Relatives B. Neighbourhood

C. Family D. Media

9. **An essential characteristic of formative assessment is-**

A. Tests and exams at the end of the year.

B. Clarification of assessment criteria to the learners.

C. To focus on quantitative means to achieve objectivity.

D. To assign relative ranks and positions to learners.

10. **Dysgraphia is a**

A. Personality disorder

B. Physical disability

C. Learning disability

D. Neurodevelopmental disorder

11. **A teacher should cater to __________ needs of gifted children in the classrooms.**

A. Cognitive and emotional B. Cognitive and social

C. Cognitive, social and emotional D. Cognitive

12. Which of the following are examples of pedagogical approaches to teach students with learning disabilities?

(i) Use of multisensory strategies

(ii) Standardized learning goals

(iii) Flexible and sequential instructions

(iv) Breaking down tasks into smaller parts

Choose the correct option.

A. (iii) and (iv)

B. (i), (iii) and (iv)

C. (i), (ii), (iii) and (iv)

D. (i) and (ii)

13. Which of the following statements about Autism Spectrum Disorder is correct?

A. Sensory integration and regulation help children with Autism Spectrum Disorder.

B. It is primarily the ability to hear that is affected in Autism Spectrum Disorder.

C. Children with Autism Spectrum Disorder exhibit a preference for new stimuli every day.

D. Children with Autism Spectrum Disorder have excellent communication skills but very poor memory.

14. While teaching in inclusive setups, it is important that teachers-

A. Continuously examine their own implicit and preconceived bias.

B. Understand special children as needy and dependent on others.

C. Follow same curriculum and uniform pedagogy of all learners.

D. See diversity as an obstacle to effective teaching.

15. Read the following statements:

Assertion (A) : Teachers should include a variety of children's literature to create print-rich environment in the classroom.

Reason (R) : Classrooms rich in literacy materials and literacy experiences are central to effective learning.

Choose the correct option.

A. Both A and R are true but R is not the correct explanation of A.

B. A is true but R is false.

C. Both A and R are false.

D. Both A and R are true and R is the correct explanation of A.

16. In order to facilitate students' learning in a progressive classroom, a teacher should emphasize on the practice of

A. Passive replication B. Reflective thinking

C. Obedient listening

D. Behaviour conditioning

17. Seeing Raman, a 4th grade student stuck on a question, his teacher asked him to try the solution while speaking what is going on in his mind. Such verbalization is likely to be-

A. Helpful because language facilitates thought process.

B. Supportive only for students with learning disabilities because they have difficulty in auditory processing.

C. Unproductive because language and thought are not related.

D. Futile because language hinders thought process.

18. A teacher who believes in constructivist pedagogy would-

A. Avoid judgements of students solely on the basis of socio-cultural backgrounds.

B. Promote high levels of verbal instructions as primary pedagogy.

C. Promote 'ability grouping' of students.

D. Avoid connecting content to real world.

19. Active engagement of learners implies that the students-

A. Rote memorize facts and information.

B. Actively value marks and competition.

C. Consider textbook as the sole source of knowledge.

D. Inquire, explore and question.

20. Radha reasons, "Clothes dry faster in the sun than in the shade, so the sun is helping them to dry". She is showing an understanding of-

A. Reversible thinking. B. Decentration.

C. Animism. D. Cause and effect.

21. Which of the following is an example of intrinsic motivation?

A. Playing a game for the prize money

B. Playing a sport for personal enjoyment

C. Completing the homework to avoid being scolded by parents

D. Studying for a test to get good grade

22. Read the following statements:

Assertion (A) : Teachers who believe in constructivist pedagogy should provide a lot of materials to the children.

Reason (R) : Young children depend solely on verbal instructions and lectures for meaningful learning.

Choose the correct option.

A. Both A and R are true but R is not the correct explanation of A.

B. A is true but R is false.

C. Both A and R are false.

D. Both A and R are true and R is the correct explanation of A.

23. Avoiding the appearance of low ability in front of peers and teachers is an example of

A. Performance approach goals

B. Task-involved goals

C. Performance avoidance goals

D. Mastery goals

24. Which of the following is an effective way to promote critical thinking in the classroom?

A. Discouraging students from asking questions.

B. Encouraging students to think independently and questioning assumptions.

C. Providing students with a set of predetermined answers to choose from.

D. Encouraging rote memorization of facts.

25. Read the following statements:

Assertion (A) : Some children have characteristics that resemble their parents while others are markedly different from their parents.

Reason (R) : Working out how much of any characteristic is due to nature or genes and how much is due to nurture or environment is a complex issue.

Choose the correct option.

A. Both A and R are true but R is not the correct explanation of A.

B. A is true but R is false.

C. Both A and R are false.

D. Both A and R are true and R is the correct explanation of A.

26. Which of the following statements about development is correct?

A. Development is a simple and unitary process.

B. Development can always be measured precisely.

C. Development is multidimensional and multidirectional.

D. Development in children can be predicted very accurately.

27. Read the following statements:

Assertion (A) : The ability to comprehend and speak depends on the physical development of the mouth and brain.

Reason (R) : Emotional development is related to physical growth.

Choose the correct option.

A. Both A and R are true but R is not the correct explanation of A.

B. A is true but R is false.

C. Both A and R are false.

D. Both A and R are true and R is the correct explanation of A.

28. Most children can speak five-six coherent sentences at

A. Three years

B. Five years

C. Seven years

D. One year

29. As per Lev Vygotsky, as children grow, their language develops from

A. Private speech to egocentric speech

B. Silent speech to thinking aloud

C. Think out loud to inner speech

D. Inner speech to external speech

30. Piaget described cognitive development as occurring

A. At three progressive levels

B. As resolution of conflict at eight stages

C. In a continuous manner from birth through adulthood

D. In four qualitatively different stages

My Notes

Answer Key

1.	*(A)*	*11.*	*(C)*	*21.*	*(B)*
2.	*(D)*	*12.*	*(B)*	*22.*	*(B)*
3.	*(D)*	*13.*	*(A)*	*23.*	*(C)*
4.	*(D)*	*14.*	*(A)*	*24.*	*(B)*
5.	*(B)*	*15.*	*(D)*	*25.*	*(D)*
6.	*(D)*	*16.*	*(B)*	*26.*	*(C)*
7.	*(D)*	*17.*	*(A)*	*27.*	*(D)*
8.	*(C)*	*18.*	*(A)*	*28.*	*(A)*
9.	*(B)*	*19.*	*(D)*	*29.*	*(C)*
10.	*(C, D)*	*20.*	*(D)*	*30.*	*(D)*

CTET-2026

Held on: 7th February, 2026

Paper–2

1. **Read the following statements:**

   Assertion (A): The purpose of administering intelligence tests and extended observation should be to compare children in specific domains and abilities.

   Reason (R) : Intelligence is an innate ability and cannot be nurtured. Choose the correct option.

   A. Both A and R are true but R is not the correct explanation of A.

   B. A is true but R is false.

   C. Both A and R are false.

   D. Both A and R are true and R is the correct explanation of A.

2. **A teacher who consciously takes examples of scientists of all genders in her middle school classroom is trying to-**

   A. Reinforce gender discrimination.

   B. Enable gender identity.

   C. Construct gender constancy.

   D. Break gender stereotypes.

3. **Read the following statements:**

   Assertion (A): All girls are hardworking and sincere while boys are intelligent and dominating.

   Reason (R) : Two distinctive biological brains produce all differences in physical and cognitive skills as well as personalities and temperament in girls and boys. Choose the correct option.

   A. Both A and R are true but R is not the correct explanation of A.

   B. A is true but R is false.

   C. Both A and R are false.

   D. Both A and R are true and R is the correct explanation of A.

4. **Individual differences in learning preferences of students should be seen as-**

   A. Cognitive abnormality among some children.

   B. Developmental deficits among some children.

   C. Normal depiction of diversity.

   D. Abnormal parameter of their differing IQ levels.

5. The kind of assessment in which a student's scores are compared with the average performance of other students is called

A. Format-referenced. B. Norm-referenced.

C. Self-referenced. D. Criteria-referenced.

6. Which of the following statements about classroom assessment are correct?

(i) Assessments should influence the students' cognitive processes while they study.

(ii) Assessments should serve as learning experiences in themselves.

(iii) Assessments should create fear and stress among students to get them to learn.

(iv) Assessments should be standardized and norm-referenced. Choose the correct option.

A. (i), (ii) B. (ii), (iii), (iv)

C. (i), (ii), (iii), (iv) D. (i), (iii)

7. Which of the following questions would promote higher-order critical and analytical thinking skills among the students?

A. Identify the nouns mentioned in a specific newspaper article.

B. Read the newspaper articles and make a list of new words.

C. Read the newspaper article and think of a suitable title.

D. Identify the assumptions underlying two newspaper articles depicting the same event.

8. Read the following statements:

Assertion (A): Students with poor writing abilities are often stereotyped by their teachers as 'intellectually disabled'.

Reason (R) : Teachers tend to have implicit bias and hold assumptions about students' learning behaviours that can affect students' growth. Choose the correct option.

A. Both A and R are true but R is not the correct explanation of A.

B. A is true but R is false.

C. Both A and R are false.

D. Both A and R are true and R is the correct explanation of A.

9. Which of the following is not a way to promote diversity in the classroom?

A. Encouraging students to express their unique identities and cultures

B. Adapting behaviour based on stereotyping students according to their backgrounds and cultures

C. Providing opportunities for students to interact with individuals from different backgrounds and cultures

D. Incorporating a variety of perspectives and experiences in the curriculum

10. Which of the following is the correct match of learning disability and challenge caused by it?

A. Dysgraphia-Impacts fine motor skills and spelling

B. Dyslexia-Impacts ability to learn numbers and arithmetic operations

C. Dyspraxia-Impacts ability to see, hear and talk properly

D. Dyscalculia-Impacts ability to read and language processing skills

11. Students struggling with 'autism' show ease at

A. Eye contact during conversation.

B. Familiar and predictable routines.

C. Rapid transitions between activities.

D. Communication with strangers.

12. Which of the following statements is not correct about gifted children?

A. Children can be gifted in more than one kind of intelligence.

B. Gifted children are born with extraordinary abilities and potential that need to be nurtured.

C. Gifted children have lower sense of curiosity and poor imagination skills.

D. Children can be gifted at different levels and some can have some kind of disability also.

13. Error analysis by students

A. Hinders metacognitive skills of students.

B. Is a futile activity in process of learning.

C. Supports students in retaining their learning.

D. Creates further gaps in students' understanding.

14. Which of the following statements is correct regarding declarative knowledge and procedural knowledge?

A. Declarative knowledge is also known as analytical knowledge.

B. Procedural knowledge is generally process-oriented in nature.

C. Procedural knowledge tells the factual knowledge about something.

D. Declarative knowledge emphasizes how to do something.

15. Contents which require an extension or modification of existing cognitive structures take time for learning and are retained for duration.

A. Long, short

B. Short, short

C. Short, long

D. Long, long

16. Read the following statements:

Assertion (A): Teachers should encourage children to focus on questions such as "what is my learning goal and what do I need to do to get there".

Reason (R) : When students understand how to self-assess their work performance, they can use this understanding to help themselves learn and progress. Choose the correct option.

A. Both A and R are true but R is not the correct explanation of A.

B. A is true but R is false.

C. Both A and R are false.

D. Both A and R are true and R is the correct explanation of A.

17. In guided discovery approach of learning

A. No prior planning or previous knowledge is required.

B. Opportunities are provided to learners to construct knowledge for themselves.

C. Teacher acts as a dictator and learners act as listeners.

D. Learners are left on their own without any kind of intervention by teacher.

18. Which of the following strategies is not effective while developing conceptual understanding in children?

A. Presenting non-examples to show what the concept is not

B. Asking students to generate their own examples

C. Asking students to memorize the definition as it is

D. Presenting a wide range of examples in diverse contexts

19. An active middle school classroom should be founded on the theoretical principles of

A. Psychodynamism

B. Social constructivism

C. Psychoanalysis

D. Behaviourism

20. Read the following statements:

Assertion (A): Empathy depends on the ability to understand that others have feelings and to gauge their feelings.

Reason (R): Emotions and cognition are not related to each other. Choose the correct option.

A. Both A and R are true but R is not the correct explanation of A.

B. A is true but R is false.

C. Both A and R are false.

D. Both A and R are true and R is the correct explanation of A.

21. A middle school teacher can enable students become strategic self-motivated learners by-

A. Providing varied forms of reinforcement for every task completed.

B. Dictating well-prepared answers to questions in the textbook.

C. Stressing upon objective-type testing at the end of the term.

D. Encouraging students to develop their metacognitive knowledge and skills.

22. Which of the following exemplifies intrinsic motivation?

A. Motivation driven by personal interest or enjoyment of the task

B. Motivation driven by competition with others

C. Motivation driven by gaining the appreciation of others

D. Motivation driven by external rewards

23. Which debate is highlighted in the following question? "Does an individual's biologically determined sex bring with it all the characteristics that define one's socially constructed gender?"

A. Continuous-Discontinuous view of development

B. Stable-Unstable view of development

C. Entity-Incremental view of ability

D. Nature-Nurture influences on development

24. A major developmental task during is the search for identity-personal, sexual and occupational.

A. Early childhood

B. Adolescence

C. Middle adulthood

D. Middle childhood

25. Read the following statements:

Assertion (A) : Children learn values and norms of the society in overt as well as covert ways.

Reason (R) : Socialization is the simple process of passing on customs and rituals of the society. Choose the correct option.

A. Both A and R are true but R is not the correct explanation of A.

B. A is true but R is false.

C. Both A and R are false.

D. Both A and R are true and R is the correct explanation of A.

26. As per Jean Piaget's theory of cognitive development, which of the following abilities distinguishes formal operational thinking from concrete operational thinking?

A. Conservation

B. Object permanence

C. Symbolic play

D. Abstract logic

27. A significant critique of Jean Piaget is that he failed to adequately consider the influence of ....on development.

A. Culture

B. Experience

C. Activity

D. Maturation

28. Which of the following is a correctly matched pair?

A. Gond bey-Good girl orientation-Greatest good for greater numbers

B. Law and Order orientation Upholding principles of social justice for humanity

C. Social Contract orientation-Consideration of perception of others

D. Punishment and Obedience orientation-Avoidance of had consequences

29. Jean Piaget and Lev Vygotsky are similar in their belief that

A. Language infinences and determines thought.

B. Culture has a proband effect on the learning

C. Development of children takes place in stage-like progression

D. Children are involved in the process of meaning making

30. Lev Vygotsky proposed that

A. Children's thinking is 'quantitatively different from adultm

B. Children's thinking is qualitatively different from adults

C. Children have a lot of potential which includes taaka they can do with the others support

D. Children are bom unruly and society needs to teach them social behaviours

My Notes

Answer Key

1.	*(C)*	*11.*	*(B)*	*21.*	*(D)*
2.	*(D)*	*12.*	*(C)*	*22.*	*(A)*
3.	*(C)*	*13.*	*(C)*	*23.*	*(D)*
4.	*(C)*	*14.*	*(B)*	*24.*	*(B)*
5.	*(B)*	*15.*	*(D)*	*25.*	*(B)*
6.	*(A)*	*16.*	*(D)*	*26.*	*(D)*
7.	*(D)*	*17.*	*(B)*	*27.*	*(A)*
8.	*(D)*	*18.*	*(C)*	*28.*	*(D)*
9.	*(B)*	*19.*	*(B)*	*29.*	*(D)*
10.	*(A)*	*20.*	*(B)*	*30.*	*(C)*

CTET-2026

Held on: 8th February, 2026

Paper–1

1. **Misconceptions among students should be and intuitive guesses should be among students in primary grades.**
   A. dismissed; discouraged
   B. acknowledged; discouraged
   C. ignored; encouraged
   D. acknowledged; encouraged
2. **The ability of hand-eye coordination, balance and manual dexterity is affected in:**
   A. Dysphasia
   B. Dyspraxia
   C. Dyslexia
   D. Dyscalculia
3. **Development of children:**
   A. unfolds in a random manner which does not have any pattern.
   B. is multidimensional and multidirectional.
   C. is synonymous with growth.
   D. is a simple and unitary process.
4. **Principle of cephalocaudal development talks about of development.**
   A. multiple dimensions
   B. orderly sequence
   C. discontinuous nature
   D. linear nature
5. **Which of the following is an effective strategy for teaching children with autism?**
   A. Maintaining a predictable routine.
   B. Using strict discipline and punishment.
   C. Providing constant eye contact.
   D. Avoiding use of any audio-visual aids.
6. **Which of the following are examples of authentic learning tasks for students in primary grades?**
   A. Applying the concept to daily life.
   B. Memorising a set of definitions.
   C. Recalling factual information from textbook.
   D. Copying answers from a friends' notebook.
7. **Talking aloud to oneself with no intent to communicate with others is in childhood.**
   A. Abnormal but not uncommon
   B. Normal and common

C. Uncommon but normal

D. Uncommon and abnormal

8. Which of the following is an example of a question that requires students to generate creative solutions?

A. What are the various types of nouns ?

B. How would you rewrite the given text from the perspective of an object rather than a person ?

C. What is the definition of a noun ?

D. How do you identify the subject of a sentence ?

9. According to Vygotsky's theory, the zone of proximal development refers to:

A. The level of skill or knowledge a student is unlikely to ever achieve.

B. The level of skill or knowledge a student must master to pass a test or receive a grade.

C. The level of skill or knowledge a student has already mastered.

D. The level of skill or knowledge a student is capable of mastering with help.

10. Formative assessment assumes that:

A. qualitative parameters are biased and subjective.

B. learners should also be involved in the process of assessment.

C. competition is essential for learning.

D. only quantitative parameters give 'correct' feedback.

11. Assertion (A): sInvented spellings, free explorations of writings provide teachers with opportunities of authentic assessment of learner levels. Reason (R): Given the vast linguistic diversity in the classroom assessment in language should be dynamic. Choose the correct option:

A. (A) is true but (R) is false.

B. Both (A) and (R) are false.

C. Both (A) and (R) are true and (R) is the correct explanation of (A).

D. Both (A) and (R) are true but (R) is not the correct explanation of (A).

12. Which of the following skill is not actively practiced in the process of 'reciprocal teaching'?

A. Predicting
B. Questioning
C. Clarifying
D. Memorizing

13. Which of the following hinders the process of effective problem solving?

A. Brainstorming
B. Analogical thinking
C. Response set
D. Concept mapping

14. Assertion (A): Learning is always situated in a social context.

Reason (R): What is learned cannot be separated from how it is learned and used. Choose the correct option:

A. (A) is true but (R) is false.
B. Both (A) and (R) are false.
C. Both (A) and (R) are true and (R) is the correct explanation of (A).
D. Both (A) and (R) are true but (R) is not the correct explanation of (A).

15. Students with mastery goal orientation set :

A. low goals to avoid failure.
B. moderate goals motivated by fear and shame.
C. realistic learning goals.
D. high goals to impress others.

16. Attention Deficit Hyperactivity Disorder is characterised by:

A. Restricted and repetitive behavioural patterns.
B. Delayed motor and language skills.
C. High levels of depression and mood swings.
D. Ongoing pattern of impulsivity.

17. In inclusive classrooms the curriculum should be and instruction should be

A. flexible; uniform
B. standardized; differentiated
C. flexible; differentiated
D. standardized; uniform

18 . ...refers to the time of development when an individual is most ready to acquire a new skill or ability and it is difficult to compensate for the loss of this later on in life.

A. Sensitive Period

B. Zone of Proximal Development

C. Developmental Milestone

D. Developmental Task

19. Which principle of development is illustrated in the following statement? During infancy and early childhood, the limbs continue to grow faster than the hands and feet.

A. Principle of centration

B. Principle of integration

C. Proximodistal principle

D. Cephalocaudal principle

20. Which of the following is an effective way to reduce the influence of gender stereotypes amongst children prevalent in society?

A. Exposing children to diverse gender roles and encouraging them to pursue their interests.

B. Assuming that children will naturally incline towards gender-neutral activities and interests.

C. Encouraging children to conform to traditional gender roles.

D. Providing children with materials that are gender-specific.

21. Which of the following are important to ensure meaningful learning?

(i) Provisioning of emotional support.

(ii) An atmosphere of competition and rivalry.

(iii) Opportunities for doing and experimenting.

(iv) Standardised curriculum.

A. (iii), (iv) B. (i), (iii)

C. (i), (iii), (iv) D. (ii), (iii), (iv)

22. Assertion (A): Teachers should provide a lot of scaffolding to children in the forms of prompts and cues.

Reason (R): Jean Piaget emphasized that more knowledgeable others play a significant role in advancing children's cognitive skills through social interaction.

Choose the correct option:

A. (A) is true but (R) is false.

B. Both (A) and (R) are false.

C. Both (A) and (R) are true and (R) is the correct explanation of (A).

D. Both (A) and (R) are true but (R) is not the correct explanation of (A).

23. **Assertion (A) : An effective pedagogical strategy is to ask children to make linkages of new information with what they already know.**

    Reason (R): Identifying commonalities and differences can help children organize information which help them to think as well as remember better. Choose the correct option:

    A. (A) is true but (R) is false.

    B. Both (A) and (R) are false.

    C. Both (A) and (R) are true and (R) is the correct explanation of (A).

    D. Both (A) and (R) are true but (R) is not the correct explanation of (A).

24. **Extrinsic motivation comes from while intrinsic motivation is based on**

    A. avoidance of punishment; rewards such as prizes

    B. approval of others; personal satisfaction

    C. personal satisfaction; approval of others

    D. personal satisfaction; rewards such as prizes

25. **Assertion (A): Creativity needs to be nurtured by presenting practical problems and issues to children for contemplation and reflection.**

    Reason (R): Creative children have the ability to discover something that is novel and need intellectual stimulation. Choose the correct option:

    A. (A) is true but (R) is false.

    B. Both (A) and (R) are false.

    C. Both (A) and (R) are true and (R) is the correct explanation of (A).

    D. Both (A) and (R) are true but (R) is not the correct explanation of (A).

26. ccording to Piaget, which of the following is an example of assimilation ?

A. A child learns to ride a cycle with training wheels.

B. A child learns to tie their shoes for the first time.

C. A child learns a new word for a familiar object.

D. A child realizes that a dog and a cat are both animals.

27. In response to the question, "Is it alright to steal the chocolate from the freezer in absence of your parents?" 4-year-old Meera replied, "It will be wrong because doing so can cause punishment from the parent." Meera's moral reasoning depicts which stage of Lawrence Kohlberg's theory of moral development ?

A. Post-conventional
B. Pre-conventional
C. Conventional
D. Formal Conventional

28. As per Jean Piaget's theory of development, children develop by the end of sensorimotor stage.

A. Object permanence

B. Symbolic thinking

C. Conservation

D. Hypothetical logical reasoning

29. As per Lev Vygotsky, 'inner speech':

A. is a sign of cognitive immaturity among children.

B. occurs from birth until the age of three.

C. helps in reasoning and organizing thoughts.

D. hinders the cognitive development of children.

30. Critical thinking in students can be promoted by:

A. Discouraging collaborations

B. Encouraging students to do rote rehearsal

C. Encouraging questions such as what, why, how

D. Discouraging metacognition

My Notes

Answer Key

1.	*(D)*	*11.*	*(C)*	*21.*	*(B)*
2.	*(B)*	*12.*	*(D)*	*22.*	*(A)*
3.	*(B)*	*13.*	*(C)*	*23.*	*(C)*
4.	*(B)*	*14.*	*(C)*	*24.*	*(B)*
5.	*(A)*	*15.*	*(C)*	*25.*	*(C)*
6.	*(A)*	*16.*	*(D)*	*26.*	*(C, D)*
7.	*(B)*	*17.*	*(C)*	*27.*	*(B)*
8.	*(B)*	*18.*	*(A)*	*28.*	*(A)*
9.	*(D)*	*19.*	*(C)*	*29.*	*(C)*
10.	*(B)*	*20.*	*(A)*	*30.*	*(C)*

CTET-2026

Held on: 8th February, 2026

Paper-2

1. **Assertion (A) : If physical development of children is delayed then their social and emotional development gets affected.**

   Reason (R) : There is developmental continuity in the course of children's development.

   Choose the correct option :

   A. Both (A) and (R) are true and (R) is the correct explanation of (A).

   B. Both (A) and (R) are true but (R) is not the correct explanation of (A).

   C. (A) is true but (R) is false.

   D. Both (A) and (R) are false.

2. **According to Jean Piaget, cognitive development :**

   A. Is simple addition of new facts and ideas to the existing store of information.

   B. Is dependent upon the development of language capabilities.

   C. Is the process of acquiring the ability to use cultural tools.

   D. Is the process of adaption to the environment by changing one's schemas.

3. **Assertion (A): Teachers should avoid collaborations, group work and interactions among students.**

   Reason (R): Learning is a passive process and occurs most effectively through memorization and imitation.

   Choose the correct option :

   A. Both (A) and (R) are true and (R) is the correct explanation of (A).

   B. Both (A) and (R) are true but (R) is not the correct explanation of (A).

   C. (A) is true but (R) is false.

   D. Both (A) and (R) are false

4. **Rapid increase in height and weight during adolescence that usually precedes sexual maturity is referred to as :**

   A. Growth spurt B. Developmental trend

   C. Menstruation D. Pubescence

5. **Assertion (A) : When talking about differences, expressions that put the person ahead of the difference should be used such as using 'the student with disabilities' rather than 'the disabled student'.**

   Reason (R) : The language we use when talking about learners with differing needs shapes the perspective and attitudes.

   Choose the correct option :

   A. Both (A) and (R) are true and (R) is the correct explanation of (A).

   B. Both (A) and (R) are true but (R) is not the correct explanation of (A).

   C. (A) is true but (R) is false.

   D. Both (A) and (R) are false.

6. **Assertion (A) : Children in middle schools should be encouraged to write about their emotions on a daily/weekly basis and reflect upon them.**

   Reason (R) : Understanding one's emotions is a cognitive process that can lead to action.

   Choose the correct option :

   A. Both (A) and (R) are true and (R) is the correct explanation of (A).

   B. Both (A) and (R) are true but (R) is not the correct explanation of (A).

   C. (A) is true but (R) is false.

   D. Both (A) and (R) are false.

7. **Which of the following is not an effective strategy in problem-solving ?**

   A. Recognizing patterns and relationships

   B. Using logical reasoning to solve problems

   C. Overlooking relevant information

   D. Breaking down complex problems into simpler parts

8. **According to Piaget when children reach the point of being able to generalize and engage in mental trial and error by thinking up hypothesis and testing them in their heads they are in :**

   A. Sensorimotor stage

   B. Pre-operational stage

C. Concrete operational stage

D. Formal operational stage

9. Students learn efficiently and in meaningful ways when :

A. Content is presented to them in the form of incoherent pieces of information.

B. Focus is on avoiding failure instead of approaching mastery.

C. New concept is completely different from previously learned material.

D. Their responses and subjective experiences are attended and valued.

10. According to Lawrence Kohlberg around which ethics do very young children's moral reasoning revolve ?

A. Ethics of egocentricism

B. Ethics of care

C. Ethics of perspectives of others

D. Ethics of laws

11. Assertion (A) : Diversity and inclusion improve teaching and learning.

Reason (R) : Engaging in conversations across differences hinders children's ability to think critically and creatively.

Choose the correct option :

A. Both (A) and (R) are true and (R) is the correct explanation of (A).

B. Both (A) and (R) are true but (R) is not the correct explanation of (A).

C. (A) is true but (R) is false.

D. Both (A) and (R) are false.

12. Which of the following are effective teaching strategies to cater to diverse needs of learners in a classroom ?

(i) Differentiated Instruction

(ii) Standardized Curriculum

(iii) Individualized Education Plans

A. (i), (ii) B. (ii), (iii)

C. (i), (iii) D. (i), (ii), (iii)

13. According to constructivist theorists :

A. Children have a natural tendency to 'make sense' of the world.

B. Children learn only when extrinsically motivated.

C. Children learn best when information is presented to them in a final form.

D. Children have a tendency to behave in unruly ways that needs to be corrected.

14. Two commonly used strategies for effective problem-solving are:

A. Heuristics and algorithms

B. Heuristics and functional fixedness

C. Algorithms and response set

D. Heuristics and response set

15. A teacher is designing a lesson plan for a group of students with varying levels of understanding of a topic. According to Vygotsky's theory, which of the following should the teacher consider when designing the lesson ?

A. The teacher should ask each student to work individually on the specified problem.

B. The teacher should provide all students with the same level of challenge.

C. The teacher should consider each student's current level of understanding and provide appropriate support to help them to reach the next level.

D. The teacher should only focus on the students who are already at an advanced level of understanding and provide them with more challenging work.

16. Characteristics such as 'lacking reading fluency', 'reversion of words', 'tendency towards distraction' are typical identifying characteristics of :

A. Dyslexia

B. Autism Spectrum Disorder

C. Dementia

D. Attention Deficit Hyperactivity Disorder

17. Students feel more motivated to learn in an environment which ensures :

(i) Belongingness (ii) Fear

(iii) Rejection (iv) Safety

A. (i), (ii) B. (i), (iv)

C. (ii), (iii) D. (ii), (iv)

18. Moving from conservative education towards progressive education requires shift from ________.

A. Formative evaluation to diagnostic evaluation

B. Integrated curriculum to standardized curriculum

C. Performance-oriented goals to mastery-oriented goals

D. Teacher-centered pedagogy to exam-centered pedagogy

19. When learning new information, which of the following is a helpful strategy for children to use to ensure they understand the content material ?

(i) Rereading the information once

(ii) Asking questions and seeking clarification

(iii)Pretending to understand

(iv) Making up their own meanings for unfamiliar terms

A. (i), (ii) B. (i), (iii)

C. (iii), (iv) D. (i), (ii), (iii)

20. A teacher should create a classroom culture where students' motivation to learn is primarily focused to :

A. Avoid shame of appearing ignorant.

B. Compete with each other.

C. Understand and appreciate the process of learning.

D. Prove their worth to others.

21. Assertion (A) : Male characters in stories and books are often presented as strong and adventurous while female characters are shown as warm and sensitive.

Reason (R) : Schools and curriculum influence gender-role identity as they are powerful agents of secondary socialization.

Choose the correct option :

A. Both (A) and (R) are true and (R) is the correct explanation of (A).

B. Both (A) and (R) are true but (R) is not the correct explanation of (A).

C. (A) is true but (R) is false.

D. Both (A) and (R) are false.

22. Assertion (A) : Children who are struggling with dyslexia have trouble in phonological processing that makes it hard to decode words.

Reason (R) : All children benefit from being encouraged in their areas of interest and ability.

Choose the correct option :

A. Both (A) and (R) are true and (R) is the correct explanation of (A).

B. Both (A) and (R) are true but (R) is not the correct explanation of (A).

C. (A) is true but (R) is false.

D. Both (A) and (R) are false.

23. What is the role of peers in the socialization process ?

A. Peers have no major influence on socialization.

B. Peers have a minor influence on socialization compared to parents and other adults in all stages of development.

C. Peers are the primary agents of socialization for children.

D. Peers have a greater influence on socialization during adolescence than during early childhood.

24. Which of the following statements about learning is not correct?

A. Learners construct knowledge that makes sense to them.

B. New learning depends on current understanding.

C. Social interaction hinders learning.

D. The most meaningful learning occurs within real-world tasks.

25. As per constructivist approaches of learning, learning is facilitated when :

A. Activities are interactive and collaborative.

B. Content is disconnected and eccentric.

C. Pedagogy is teacher-centric and culturally indifferent.

D. Tasks are incoherent and disorderly.

26. Assertion (A) : Though height and body build are primarily inherited characteristics, good nutrition and exercise also make a difference.

Reason (R) : Heredity and environment interact in their effects on development.

Choose the correct option :

A. Both (A) and (R) are true and (R) is the correct explanation of (A).

B. Both (A) and (R) are true but (R) is not the correct explanation of (A).

C. (A) is true but (R) is false.

D. Both (A) and (R) are false.

27. Which of the following statements about intelligence is correct ?

A. Intelligence is a single, fixed trait that cannot be changed.

B. Intelligence is solely determined by genetic factors.

C. Intelligence is multifaceted and can be developed through learning and experiences.

D. Intelligence can only be measured through standardized IQ tests.

28. Which of the following is an example of intrinsic motivation ?

A. A student studies hard to get a reward from parents.

B. A student completes homework to avoid punishment.

C. A student reads books because they genuinely enjoy learning new things.

D. A student participates in class to receive praise from teacher.

29. In an inclusive classroom, a teacher should :

A. Treat all learners exactly the same irrespective of their needs.

B. Focus only on academically strong students.

C. Use flexible teaching methods according to learners' diverse needs.

D. Separate children with special needs from other learners.

30. According to Howard Gardner's theory of Multiple Intelligences, which intelligence is associated with sensitivity to rhythm, sound and music ?

A. Linguistic Intelligence

B. Logical-Mathematical Intelligence

C. Musical Intelligence

D. Bodily-Kinesthetic Intelligence

My Notes

Answer Key

1.	*(A)*	*11.*	*(C)*	*21.*	*(A)*
2.	*(D)*	*12.*	*(C)*	*22.*	*(B)*
3.	*(D)*	*13.*	*(A)*	*23.*	*(D)*
4.	*(A)*	*14.*	*(A)*	*24.*	*(C)*
5.	*(A)*	*15.*	*(C)*	*25.*	*(A)*
6.	*(A)*	*16.*	*(A)*	*26.*	*(A)*
7.	*(C)*	*17.*	*(B)*	*27.*	*(D)*
8.	*(D)*	*18.*	*(C)*	*28.*	*(B)*
9.	*(D)*	*19.*	*(A)*	*29.*	*(C)*
10.	*(A)*	*20.*	*(C)*	*30.*	*(D)*